RUN
RIGHT NOW

RUN
RIGHT NOW

WHAT A HALF-CENTURY ON THE RUN HAS TAUGHT

JOE HENDERSON

BARNES
&NOBLE
BOOKS

NEW YORK

A BARNES & NOBLE BOOK

ISBN 0-7607-5462-4

Printed and bound in U.S.A. by Jaguar Graphics

1 3 5 7 9 10 8 6 4 2

To the running writers who first taught me from afar how to go long:
Fred Wilt, Arthur Newton, Franz Stampfl, Ernst van Aaken,
and Arthur Lydiard

Contents

Part One: **Running Routines**

Part Two: *Running Races*

Part Three: *Running Long*

Foreword

Pioneers in various fields often miss the sweet smell of success that they deserve because their timing is just a bit off. They're ahead of their time, and therefore typically miss out on the fame and fortune bestowed upon those blessed with perfect timing and sterling placement.

Several historical figures in the two major North American gold rushes are cases in point. James Marshall, who discovered gold in the millrace at Coloma, California, in 1848, and Johann Sutter, the owner of the property on which the gold was discovered, never profited from their find, and in fact died destitute. Then in 1896 in the Canadian Yukon, amid circumstances bordering on Greek tragedy, two strikingly different men—tall, lean, hawkish Robert Henderson and laid-back, well-rounded George Washington Carmack—discovered gold in the Klondike, but neither man reaped the huge rewards their discovery precipitated.

This situation is similar in some ways to the best-selling running-book gold rush at the start of the running revolution in the mid-1970s. Several pioneers had long been standing knee-deep in the frigid waters, panning for gold in the stream of long-distance running. Hal Higdon, who worked in several streams (running, auto racing, and true crime), wrote a landmark book in 1971 entitled *On the Run From Dogs and People*. It's still in print today and deserves to stay in print forever, but is revered by only a few.

Joe Henderson, who became the editor of *Runner's World* in 1970 after a stint at *Track & Field News*, had written numerous running books: *Long Slow Distance: The Humane Way to Train* (1969), *Road Racers and Their Training* (1970), *Thoughts on the Run* (1970), and *Run Gently, Run Long* (1974). As an editor, he had shepherded a mass of George Sheehan's *Runner's World* columns into *Dr. Sheehan on Running* (1975). That's a lot of mining without hitting the mother lode.

But the whole landscape was to change, and all within the space of a year. Bantam Books bought *Dr. Sheehan on Running*, and in 1976 published it as a mass-market paperback—and it took off. In 1977, the reformed overweight smoker Jim Fixx, who had been "saved" by running and who had spent a year mining the ore pockets of long-distance running, published *The Complete Book of Running*. It immediately shot to the top of the best-seller lists and stayed there for nearly a year.

George Sheehan would follow up with *Running & Being*, which became a best-seller and a classic. But in all the excitement, Joe Henderson's *The Long Run Solution*, one of the best running books of its generation, was overwhelmed and overlooked. A handful of rickety codgers now lament the book's having been overshadowed by brighter lights, but the codgers also jealously hoard the memories of the book's flashes of gold.

The Long Run Solution was not a complicated book. It had no long, James Joyce–like run-on sentences, even though it was about running on, and on, and on. Joe Henderson doesn't write complicated sentences. He writes spare, insightful sentences, such as: "Goals are ends, destinations, stopping places. One of two things happens with them: either you reach them, or you don't. And either way you stop, from satisfaction or from frustration." Pretty simple and pretty profound at the same time.

Joe's little book wasn't filled with training advice. It didn't present the no-pain-no-gain philosophies. It quoted practitioners of running rather than philosophers who weren't really talking about running when they uttered their profundities. Joe's book was the simple manifesto of long-distance running for the common person at that very critical time.

It said, simply, that you don't have to run hard in organized competition until you puke. You can enrich your life (both physically and psychologically) by running gently for an hour a day, occasionally testing yourself against yourself by racing.

But, hey, if you don't feel like racing, that's okay too. Just run for an hour to fulfill your design as a human being, whose largest bones and muscles are in your legs—for good reason.

Joe's message was simple: just do it. His approach was simple: simple sentences, simple running habits.

There isn't a five-year period in which I don't pick up *The Long Run Solution* and read it again, both to bring back the energizing effect of validating long-distance running as an adult pursuit, as well as to rediscover the antidote to a too-pressured, too-stressed life. And over the years, I've done what little I could to persuade some publisher somewhere to commission Joe to produce an updated edition of *The Long Run Solution.*

While this hasn't happened (though the magazine I edit, *Marathon & Beyond*, did reprint the book in serial fashion during 2003 and 2004), fortunately Joe hasn't sat still since 1976. He has kept running and writing, discovering more nuggets of gold to pass along to his readers.

Which brings us to this, his latest book. I'm actually happy to say that it isn't a reprint of *The Long Run Solution*—it's so much more. *Run Right Now* is a delightful blend of old and new that retains Joe's original tone in a collection of observations and advice that has grown larger and richer over his good long run.

—RICH BENYO, EDITOR, *MARATHON & BEYOND* MAGAZINE;

CO-AUTHOR OF *THE RUNNING ENCYCLOPEDIA*

Introduction

I was born to run, as we all are. We come with long legs for a reason, and that's to cover ground on foot—sometimes short distances quickly, and sometimes great lengths slowly.

Running was required of everyone once. Now it's an option that only a small minority of us ever exercises after childhood.

I'm a product of two families that ran by choice. My father and two of his brothers were runners in high school and college. One of my mother's brothers ran in his youth and well into old age, and her other brother became an early coach of mine without either of us realizing it.

My parents were married the weekend of the largest track meet in the Midwest. The men talked more that day about the Drake Relays than about the wedding.

My dad took me to track meets before I was old enough to count the four laps of a mile. He never told me to take up the sport. But after I found it on my own, he made sure to see most of my big races for the rest of his too-short life.

I'm now older than Dad ever got to be. A half-century has sped past since I ran my first timed mile.

As a runner, I've gone from pre-teenager to elder... from the 1950s to the twenty-first century... from Iowa to Illinois, South Carolina, California, and Oregon... from student to farmhand, soldier, editor, writer, and teacher... from single to married to father... from single parent to remarried to grandfather.

Running has remained my one constant through all these changes. But my running hasn't always stayed the same.

I've gone from miler to ultramarathoner and everything in between... from track (outdoor and indoor) to cross-country to road... from sub-five-minute-mile racing to 10-minute-plus... from the back of the pack to the front and gradually back again...

from all-fast training to all-slow... from healthy to injured and back to healthy again (many times).

Running all these years in all these ways has taught me lots of lessons. Many were painful at the time, but the worst mistakes can teach the best lessons. Since I've made every possible mistake in running, I've compiled quite a catalog of lessons learned from them.

Running all these years in all these ways has taught me lots of lessons

Everyone does this. It's what living and learning are about. It's why the elders say, "If I'd known then what I know now, think how much better I would've done."

We can't go back and rewrite our past, but we do get a second chance. It comes when we pass on our lessons, pointing out how to avoid our early mistakes.

I'm able to do this in multiple ways: by teaching college students to run, by speaking to audiences of runners, and most of all by writing about running. The writing can reach the most runners for the longest time.

My writing was predestined just as much as my running was. I was born to write as surely as to run.

My parents were both journalists. Dad worked for magazines, Mom for newspapers. (The journalism gene remains strong in our family, with two of my siblings working in this field, along with a daughter and niece of mine.)

I began a written record of my running, in diary form, at age sixteen. A newspaper that employed my mother hired me to write about sports when I was seventeen.

Writing has stayed with me ever since. But again, as in running, consistency has blended with variety. I've written for a small hometown newspaper, a college paper, and a statewide daily... about news, sports, my favorite sport, and the distance-running branch of my sport...
for the magazines *Track & Field News, Distance Running News, Runner's World, Running,* and now *Marathon & Beyond*... in booklets and books, of my own and in concert with other authors... and almost every day in my private journal reaching from the 1950s to the present.

I've written personal, practical, technical, historical, statistical, biographical, physiological, psychological, and philosophical stories about running. My favorites among these are the writings that teach the reader how to avoid or correct a mistake.

This book is a memoir of lessons learned in a lifetime of running and writing about it. These chapters can't protect you from making mistakes of your own. But I hope that you'll make fewer mistakes than I did, that you'll learn these lessons faster, and that they'll take you even further than they've taken me.

Run Right Now is a collection of advice on running. It's about how to go out and enjoy running right now, and also how to run correctly, from your first step. But *Run Right Now* is also about running "long": my hope is that you will reap the benefits of running longer distances, and that you will enjoy, as I have, a long run of years in the sport.

—JOE HENDERSON
EUGENE, OREGON, 2004

Part One

Running
Routines

Y ou probably started running, or are about to start, the right way. Numerous magazines and books, coaches and advisers exist to support you.

You started or will start by running at a relaxed pace for short distances, or by running mixed with walking breaks, or by walking mixed with running breaks, or by just walking at first. You progressed slowly and steadily, or will do so. I did none of this. Instead, I started running in what you could now tell me was the wrong way.

Fifty years ago, there was only one reason to run: to compete in races. There was only one way to run: hard and fast. There was only one type of runner: young and male. And there were very few of us at that.

That described me then. Though I'd dabbled in running earlier, I date my true running start from my first official race—on April Fools' Day 1958. I hadn't really trained for that first mile, and had no idea how to train anyway.

Running books and magazines were rarities in those days, and hadn't yet reached small towns in Iowa. Coaches weren't well-schooled in training distance runners, so they simply raced us into shape as the season went along. If we weren't racing against other schools, we were competing against our teammates at home.

The "system" of that era was to jump into the competitive pond and swim or sink. Good luck let me survive this plunge.

I was lucky enough to start running at age fourteen, fitter overall than I'd ever be again. Before becoming a specialist runner I had played many sports—football in the fall, basketball in winter, baseball in spring, and swimming in summer.

Back then my body was flexible from being active in so many ways. Running would tighten me up. Back then I still had an upper body. Running would wear away twenty pounds, much of it muscle I'd built while working on a farm.

Most of our family's food came from local farms and gardens, not from supermarkets. My diet would never again be better than the one I had without thinking about it in the 1950s. Given the high level of general fitness I enjoyed as a youngster, I adapted quickly to racing. It took me much longer, however, to learn the basic rules of

healthful running. These I would pick up piecemeal for a long time to come.

You may not jump as early or deeply into running as I did. But you have a big advantage over me as a beginner. You came along in a more enlightened age.

You know there are better ways to start than my early way. Part One of this book looks into the lessons a runner must learn first if running is to last.

TEACHING
new runners to endure, excel, and enjoy

chapter
1

Coaching Lessons

Coaching was the topic of the pre-race program I was attending the day before the Royal Victoria Marathon several years ago. At my breakfast seminar, a woman identified herself as "self-coached" and wanted to know how to work better with her "team of one." At dinner, we speakers joined in a tribute to a pair of coaches who'd worked with hundreds of runners over four decades.

The honorees at the Royal Victoria Marathon that night were Doug and Diane Clement, Canadians who met at the 1956 Olympics, married, and founded a track club in the Vancouver area. Now they were easing into semi-retirement.

In my brief salute, I thanked the Clements as representatives of the early coaches who had helped me. And I apologized to them as stand-ins for the coaches I'd given grief.

Dealing with any group of runners is like trying to herd cats. We're headstrong by nature, drawn to an activity that encourages going our own way. Throughout high school and college I was one wild cat, determined to follow my own path even when it split from my coach's.

Dean Roe, Bob Karnes, and others sometimes rolled their eyes in frustration over my catlike meanderings. But they stood by me all the while, letting me make my own mistakes as I tried to find my way. I'll always remember these coaches for their tolerance and unconditional support. Dedicating my previous books to them seems too small a way to say thank you. They helped me more than they, or I, knew at the time.

During my second seminar in Victoria, I asked the runners, "How many of you are self-coached?" Hands went up all over the room.

Then I mentioned the woman who'd used that description of herself earlier in the day. She'd gone on to say that she took her leads from articles and books.

She might not have a coach she can look in the eye and ask for clarification, but neither is she self-coached. None of us truly acts alone. We all can point to people who have given us advice, encouragement, inspiration, and assistance, either in person or indirectly.

I used to pride myself on being self-coached. My training and racing plans from early high school onward were largely of my own design—or so I thought at the time. Now I know better. Every athlete I admired, every writer I read and speaker I heard, every running mate who served as a sounding board contributed to my running practices.

Without looking far, you can name coaches like these who may never know how they affected you. And you may not realize that you can be such a coach without recruiting a team, writing an article, or conducting a workshop.

You can be a coach simply by being a good runner. By "good" I don't necessarily mean fast. I mean being a good example of running's requirements and rewards. Then you might prompt someone to ask you that most flattering of questions: can you help me?

What we do well, others might want to emulate. If each of us can teach just one person to run, we have coached. If we coach just two people, we've helped the sport grow.

Class Acts

For all the trouble I once caused my coaches by questioning, defying, and ignoring them, I started college with the goal of becoming—what else?—a running coach. Life had other plans, and it detoured me into journalism.

Forty years after straying from my original college path, I finally became a coach of sorts by teaching running classes at the University of Oregon. These new runners now dispense to me delayed justice.

These frisky young cats dare me to try to herd them, as I once challenged my coaches to do. In doing so, they teach me at least as much as I do them.

My students are from running's forgotten age group. They're too old for kids' runs and have left high school competition behind. But they're too young for the fitness running and road racing that runners their age generally consider to be old-people's activities. Their parents and grandparents who run often think college kids are disinterested in following their lead, or are lazy.

I've learned otherwise. Most of my students are traditional college age, eighteen to twenty-two or so. They run for the same reasons we elders did at that age, or do now. They want to become fitter and faster. They delight in their improvements and despair of their setbacks.

These students care about their running, and, at the University of Oregon, more of them want to run than the classes can accommodate. They don't care who their teacher is, at least not at the start.

They come to my class their first day without knowing who I am. They come as they would to any class, wondering, "Will he teach me anything to make this hour worth my time?"

Some students think not. After one first-day talk a young man said, "Your program sounds too easy for me. I'm training for marathons and triathlons."

Yet sticking with me was a runner named Brian who'd already qualified for the Boston Marathon. Another, Liz, had run four years for the local university team and had served as an assistant coach.

Abilities range widely in these classes, as do body types. Matt, a student in my racing class, ran a 5K in well under twenty minutes— at 247 pounds. I'd never seen anyone so big run so fast.

I try not to play favorites based on ability. But I can't help feeling partial toward a woman who goes by the nickname Max.

She joined my basic running class one winter. She never finished anywhere but at the back of the pack in our test runs.

Her first run was an eleven-minute mile, but she progressed so well that she ended the term close to an eight-minute mile. She ran her first 5K race that winter, then a 10K in spring, a half-marathon in summer, and finally a full marathon in the fall—twenty-six miles at the same pace as her original single mile.

During their track sessions, my students mingle with hotshot young local athletes who finish their morning runs by striding the straightaways at speeds that brings gasps from my neophytes. The speedsters sometimes act amused by our pace and annoyed when my beginners don't move out of their way quickly enough.

I'd rather work with a Max than the speedsters who think she doesn't belong on the same track (or even in the same sport) with them. How many of them can improve their mile time by three seconds in three months, let alone the three minutes that Max did? How many still feel as excited as someone first finding out how much better her legs can move?

I encourage my students to gauge success not by their speed or finish position but by their improvement. Runners improve dramatically at college age, by minutes at a time in distances as short as a mile or 5K.

This progress is a joy for me to see, even while knowing that their times would have dropped no matter whose training they were doing. I'm flattered that they've chosen to try mine for a term.

My teachers and coaches were more successful than they ever knew. They taught me what I needed to know to manage without them.

The final exam for each of my students comes after the class ends. It's just a single question: will you continue running when attendance is no longer required? If the answer is yes, we've both succeeded.

Advice to Advisers

This first part of the book contains a collection of advice seemingly aimed at new runners. If you aren't a beginner yourself, you might wonder what this section has to do with you. It actually offers you more than you might think.

Once you've learned the basics of running, you become a potential teacher, coach, or adviser. You can then pass along what you were

taught—or what you wish you had been taught—to those just starting
out.

The ways to help are many. You can simply counsel and cheer
on a family member, friend, neighbor, or co-worker. You can lead a
marathon-training group, or work with Race for the Cure or Corporate
Cup runners. Or you can step in to coach a school or club team.

I received a letter from a runner in Minnesota who had
volunteered to organize a cross-country program at a high school
where none had existed before. She knew how to write training
schedules, but realized that building a team involves much more
than posting the week's runs.

"I'm becoming extremely excited to start what I hope will be a
very long-lasting tradition at this school," wrote the new coach.
"What would be on your top-ten list for a successful program?"

I've done no coaching of the type she was undertaking with a formal team. So I developed my ten tips on organization and motivation
based on what I'd want from any group running program involving
my child, a close friend, a student in my running classes—or myself.

My Top Ten Tips for Coaching Running Groups

1. **Let anyone and everyone run.** This includes runners who
don't look the part and don't appear to have much talent. You
never know which ones will catch fire, achieving surprising
results in the short term and making running their longtime love.

2. **Start slowly.** Assume that most of your runners have trained
little recently, or maybe never. Try not to discourage—or worse,
injure—them in their first weeks of training. Start with modest
distances and slow paces, and move up gradually from there.

3. **Reward improvement.** You can't praise or celebrate too
much your runners' progress in distance or pace. It's as big an
accomplishment for a beginning runner to drop from a ten-minute
to a nine-minute mile as it is for an experienced runner to drop
from the sixes into the fives. Let all your runners know that you
appreciate their efforts equally.

4. Emphasize PRs. A PR, or personal record, is an individual measure of success in races. Bettering a PR doesn't require beating anyone else, but if PRs keep dropping, higher placings will come automatically.

5. Preach pacing. New runners—especially the young—are notoriously impatient, typically starting their runs and races too fast and finishing too slowly. Show them that their best times will come from running at an even pace, or from finishing slightly faster than they started.

6. Require attendance. Improvement in running comes through repetition and consistency. Runners who keep showing up get better, and those who don't, don't. Make training so exciting and rewarding that they will never want to skip it.

7. Train beyond the season or the next big race. The foundation for success is laid outside the racing months. This is when persistent runners gain the edge on those with more natural talent who take long vacations. Even easy off-season training beats doing none at all.

8. Practice hard and easy. No runner can train hard every day. The harder days are essential to a racer, because racing is hard. But the easier recovery days are also important—maybe even more so because they're more numerous.

9. Watch for trouble. Look out for the early signs of injury or illness, which a committed runner might try to hide or choose to ignore. Cancel a run or stop it early to keep a minor problem from becoming major.

10. Teach by example. Show the runners your excitement for the sport. Work to improve your coaching, as they do their running. Don't ask them to do any training or racing that you wouldn't do (and haven't done) yourself.

One of the best lines I've ever heard about coaching didn't come from a coach of human runners but from a trainer of racehorses. He said, "A horse doesn't care how much you know until it knows how much you care." The same goes for two-legged runners and their coaches.

LEARNING quickly what runners need to know

chapter 2

Running 101

I teach running classes at the University of Oregon. But aside from the setting, my class is no typical college course, and in most ways it's radically different.

For their other courses, my students spend their days—and often many of their evenings—listening to lectures, joining discussions, studying assigned readings, writing papers, and taking written tests. So these students look to running as an escape from classrooms and textbooks.

We meet only twice a week, for fifty minutes per session. That time is best spent actually running (plus warming up and cooling down), rather than talking about it at length. If students do "homework," it should be additional runs, not long readings.

I've shrunk my instruction into mini-lessons that can be spoken in a minute or written in a paragraph. These nuggets deliver what I think new runners most need to take away from our time together. You might call this collection the "Cliffs Notes" for Running 101. I'll summarize the fifteen elements of running I consider most important here. Most of these are examined at length in later chapters.

Mile Trial. The mile time is the most important one in running (at least in the metric-challenged U.S.A.). Anyone who hears that you're a runner will ask, "What's your best mile time?" Soon you will be calculating your pace-per-mile on longer runs. Running a mile (four laps on a standard outdoor track) right away will tell you what your starting point is. Think of this run as a low-key test, not as a serious race. Run at a pace faster than easy but slower than a struggle, and count on improving your time in later mile tests as you improve your fitness.

F-I-T Formula. Early sessions should last an average of twenty to thirty minutes. This length of time is based on the research of Dr. Kenneth Cooper, a giant in the fitness field. Cooper's formula for improving as a runner is to run two to three miles, three to five days a week, at a comfortable pace. It's easier to remember as the F-I-T Formula: frequency (three to five runs a week), intensity (comfortable pace), time (about twenty to thirty minutes). Even with walking breaks you can cover two miles in a half hour, and many of you can comfortably run three miles (or more) in that time. Your effort should be moderate enough that you can repeat it at least every other day.

Your Pace. Pace has two meanings, one mathematical and the other physical. The first is a calculation of your minutes and seconds per mile—a key figure for any runner to know. Divide your total time by the distance (remembering to convert seconds to tenths of a minute; an 8:30 mile is 8.5 minutes). The second meaning is even more important: how you find your best pace. On most runs, this means pacing yourself comfortably—neither too fast nor too slow. There are several ways to arrive at that pace. The most technical is to wear a heart-rate monitor and to run between seventy and eighty percent of maximum pulse. Another is to identify your maximum speed for that distance, and then add one to two minutes per mile. The simplest is to listen to your breathing; if you aren't gasping for air and can talk while you run, your pace is not too fast. Your effort should stay constant throughout your run, but your pace-per-mile seldom does. Expect your pace to pick up as your body warms up.

Taking Time. What's your second most valuable piece of equipment after your shoes? (For much more on shoes, see Chapter 9.) No, it's not shorts or a T-shirt. It's a watch. Buy a digital model with a stopwatch feature, and make time your main way of keeping score. Time can make you an instant winner by revealing exactly how fast you ran a distance, and maybe how much you improved your PR. Another more subtle value of the watch is that it lets you run by time—by minutes instead of miles. This provides several benefits. It frees you from plotting and measuring courses, because minutes are the same length anywhere. It eases any pressure on you to run faster, because you'll finish at the assigned time limit you've set yourself no matter what your pace. And finally, running by time helps you to settle naturally into your comfort zone.

Walk Talk. "Walk" is not a dirty four-letter word. Pausing to walk during a run is not cheating; it's a common practice of experienced runners. It's actually a form of interval training, which breaks one big effort into many small pieces to make it more doable. You can mix running and walking for many purposes: to break into running for the first time; to regain fitness after a long layoff; to rebuild after a serious injury or illness; to warm up before a run and to cool down afterward; to make your fast runs faster (the classic use of intervals), your long runs longer, and your easy runs easier. Runners' walking breaks are most effective when they last at least one minute but not more than five minutes.

Going Places. The two basic raw materials of a running routine are time and place. And the two main excuses given for not running? "I don't have time for it," and " I don't have anywhere to do it." Let's dissect those excuses. You can run well in a half hour every other day. That's the time you might spend watching a sitcom rerun. As for places, anywhere that's safe for walking is also safe for running. Off-road is better than in traffic, soft surfaces are better than hard, but any choice is better than staying home. Your body doesn't care when or where you run, only that you do run.

Road Hazards. The biggest threat that a runner faces, by far, is the car. Traffic zips within an arm's length. A moment's lapse in attention by either you or the driver can bring disaster. The best way to avoid this risk is to avoid the roads. But this greatly limits your running options, especially in hours of darkness and in seasons of foul weather. When using the roads, follow the rules that your mother taught you: stay off the busiest streets, look both ways before crossing, face the traffic (by running on the left-hand side), and run when and where you can see and be seen. Run as if every car is a lethal weapon, which it can be.

Getting Hurt. Runners get hurt. We rarely hurt ourselves in the sudden, traumatic ways skiers and linebackers do, but our injury rates run high. Most of our injuries are self-inflicted—from running too far, too fast, too soon, or too often (and sometimes on surfaces or in shoes not right for us). Prevention is usually as simple as adjusting our routine. Immediate treatment seldom requires total rest, but only a change in activity. Use pain as your guide. If you can't run steadily without pain, mix walking and running. If you can't run-walk, simply walk. If you can't walk, bicycle. If you can't bike, swim. As you recover, climb back up this exercise ladder.

Getting Sick. Take symptoms of illness as seriously as those of injury. But instead of using pain as a guide, substitute the symptoms of fever and fatigue. The most common ailments are the flu and colds. Never, ever run with fever from a flu. And don't just rest while you are feverish. Take an additional day off for each day of illness, or you may risk serious complications. Colds are more mundane—and more easily handled. They usually pass in about a week. Rest during the "coming-on" stage (usually the first two to four days). Then run easily (slowly enough to avoid heavy coughing or throat and chest irritation) during the "coming-out" stage.

Choosing Shoes. This is your only major and recurring equipment expense. Spend wisely by buying well-made shoes made by a major brand. (The most available and reliable are, alphabetically,

Adidas, Asics, Brooks, New Balance, and Nike.) Search out a model that fits you properly and is right for your foot type, body build, running distance, pace, and surface. If in doubt about what your best shoe choice should be, shop at a running specialty store employing expert advisers. And recognize that even the best shoes have a limited life span. Plan to replace them after about 500 miles of wear.

Dressing Down. When discussing running clothing, we're really talking about the weather; that is, how to find protection from and comfort in the extremes of temperature and precipitation. Observe the "twenty degree" rule, which states that during a run, the temperature will feel twenty degrees warmer than it actually is. Dress for a warmer day than the temperature shows, or dress in layers that you can take off as you warm up. Choose fabrics that don't soak up sweat or rain. On truly cold days, cover your hands and ears, and you'll feel warmer all over. Wear a cap with a brim to protect you from sun and rain, or to keep auto headlights from blinding you.

Looking Good. Running form is as individual as a fingerprint, and is too inborn to change very much. But you can become a more efficient runner with practice and minor modifications to your form. Run upright, not with a pronounced forward lean. Look toward the horizon, not toward your feet. Run faster by increasing your stride turnover (the number of strides you take), not by overreaching with each stride. In uphill running, shorten and lower your stride, and drive more with your arms, while keeping your effort relatively constant instead of trying to hold a steady pace. In downhill running, let gravity work for you by leaning slightly forward, and bend more than usual at the knees to cushion them from shock.

Eating Well. Sports nutrition is an important subject whose surface we can barely scratch here. Start by realizing that runners' rules for good eating and drinking are about the same as for everyone else. Certain nutritional topics should especially interest you, however. Being overweight means that each extra pound you have to carry translates into greater effort and slower times. Overeating or eating the wrong foods too close to your running time can make your run difficult. Eat lightly, at least an hour before training and two hours before a race. Drinking too little before, during, and after runs can lead to chronic dehydration, which can slow any run and prove dangerous in hot weather.

Extra Exercises. Running is a specialized activity that exercises mainly your legs in straight-ahead movement. If you're seeking more complete fitness, you need to supplement your runs with other exercises. They can strengthen the muscles that running neglects, and stretch those that running tightens. Unless you take this corrective action, the older you are and the more years you've run, the greater your imbalance and tightness will become. Pay particular attention to strengthening your upper body and stretching your legs. Add a few minutes of these extra exercises after your run—that's when they'll do the most good and take away the least amount of energy from your main activity.

Supplemental Sports. You might not always be able to or want to run, or you might sometimes want to add other activities to your running. Alternatives abound. You can bicycle, swim, "run" in water (wearing a flotation belt), cross-country ski, snowshoe, or simply walk (one of the best but least appreciated options to running). In most of these sports, duplicate your running time to gain similar fitness benefits. If walking, double your usual running time.

STARTING a running program that will last

chapter

3

First Steps

My running is fun. Not ha-ha fun, but a quieter kind of contented fun. Not fun every minute of every day, but fun in its overall effect. But don't let me deceive you if you're about to begin running. Your first weeks, maybe even months, won't be much fun.

Starting out will be tiring and possibly even painful. Even the slowest shuffle for the shortest distance will be difficult because you're asking your body to do something it hasn't done in a long time, if ever.

You might dread your running because no one looks forward to discomfort. It might bore you because it's tiring, and boredom and fatigue are close relatives.

Bear up. Be strong and patient. Promise yourself you'll stick out this break-in period and I promise you much better days to come.

I've watched hundreds of people begin to run, and a minority has survived long enough to enjoy running and taste its benefits. The main reason beginners drop out is that they treat exercise like a vile-tasting medicine that they need to force down quickly.

They allow ten minutes or so for a run, and go the prescribed distance as fast as their untrained legs, lungs, and heart will carry

Promise yourself you'll stick out this break-in period and I promise you much better days to come

them. They try to run the distance faster today than yesterday, faster tomorrow than today. Their pace escalates until they hit a wall.

Legs break down and minds burn out from the strain of chronic racing. If you start running and get hurt or discouraged and quit after a few days or weeks, that's even worse than never having started. Now you're not only in no better shape than before, but you're convinced that the cure is worse than the ailment.

Right from the start, I want you to take an easier, safer, more positive, and, inevitably, longer lasting course. Start with a few simple guidelines (a word I prefer to "rules"):

✔ Make exercise an everyday habit—an essential part of each and every day, something you look forward to and miss if you don't have it.

✔ Set aside a full hour each day for yourself and your sport, even if you spend only a portion of that hour actually running. Include time to get ready and to shower afterward.

✔ Pace yourself for the long haul, in terms of years more than in terms of individual runs. Start with the idea that you won't ever stop.

✔ Don't rush the run too much or push the pace too hard. A habit can't take root in a mind that is always harried or a body that is always hurting.

Forming Good Habits

Running is marketed mainly for the physical benefits it confers: weight loss, muscle toning, heart-lung strengthening. But if you run long enough (in both senses of the word) you'll come to recognize that the psychological effects are more immediate and profound than anything that happens physically.

The kind of running commonly prescribed for beginners—a mile or two every other day—is enough to satisfy minimum fitness needs, but probably not enough to form a lasting habit. Those first ten to twenty minutes can be rather distasteful preliminaries, for seasoned runners as well as beginners. This is the warm-up, a time to slog through to reach the good part.

A friend of mine started to run ten to fifteen minutes a day, continuing this way for more than a year. "To tell you the truth," she said, "I despised it. I said to myself, 'What a horrible way to exercise.'

"I did it mostly from a sense of duty, to please my husband who's a marathoner. I honestly couldn't imagine what he saw in it."

Then her husband suggested she try running a little longer, maybe three miles instead of only one.

"That three miles, which took me about thirty minutes, must've put me past some invisible addiction point," she said." "Because from then on, I was hooked. I loved running." She has run several marathons since.

The sooner you make a habit of running well beyond ten to twenty minutes a day, the better you'll feel about running. I recommend a half hour of movement every day from your very first day, even if you have to walk some, most, or all of it at first.

Loosely fit that half hour of movement into the full hour that you've blocked out for yourself. Use the extra time leisurely, to dress for your run-walk, to stretch your muscles, to shower, and to simply sit down to think or talk afterward.

Devote half of your hour to activity and half to inactivity, and don't hurry through either one. Get away from your radio, stereo, TV, computer, newspaper, magazine, book, car, job, office, and house. Get away by yourself or with a small group of friends, and make this a relaxed and creative time.

Taking Walks

Nature's best runners—animals that must run to eat and avoid being eaten—never run at full speed for more than a few yards. They seldom run long distances without rest breaks. By loping along, walking, loping some more, sprinting for a short stretch to catch their prey, eating, and then sleeping off the effort and the meal, they can go all day without wearing down. This lesson has almost been lost to modern runners, whose gods are speed and continuous running—both of which are unnatural.

I used to time myself every day over measured courses and keep track of my records. As my times grew faster and I had to push harder to beat them, every day's run became a race.

Finally my feet broke down. Nature was telling me something, but I started listening only when I had no choice but to stop.

Later, after dropping the quest for "faster" in favor of "longer," I made it a point of pride never to stop moving during a run. If halted by a red light, I'd run laps around the light post. If my shoelaces came undone, I'd let them flap.

> *The sooner you make a habit of running beyond ten to twenty minutes a day, the better you'll feel about running*

Then my feet started failing me again. They couldn't take the unbroken distance any more than the unbroken speed. That's when Dr. Ernst van Aaken taught me how to walk.

The German physician-coach trained everyone from beginners to world record holders, using mostly comfortably paced running mixed with walking breaks. His advice: "Run as a child runs. Run playfully for five to ten kilometers a day, without pain or fatigue.

"The plan is the same for everyone from competing athletes to patients recovering from heart attacks. Only the pace and the amount of walking varies."

Five to ten kilometers—about three to six miles—sounds massive to a beginner, but the walking breaks bring it within reach. They allow children who wouldn't run a single mile continuously to cover several miles without tiring during a morning's play. And those walking breaks allow runners who don't train much to go far beyond their imagined limits.

One such runner was Kenneth Crutchlow. This English adventurer once ran from Los Angeles to San Francisco—almost 500 miles—in ten days. Interviewing Crutchlow afterward, I asked him about the kind of preparation he'd done.

"Oh, none at all," he said. "I wouldn't do any special training. That would take the sport out of it. The challenge to me was to do this totally unprepared, as any man on the street might."

"Yes, I see," I said. "But this is incredible. How could you run fifty miles a day for ten days straight? Few trained runners can even go that far in one day."

"You want to know my secret?" he asked. "I don't hurry, and I don't run very far at one time—only a mile or so—and then I walk for awhile. Then I run some more and walk again. It takes me the whole bloody day, but I get there."

I'm telling you to do the same, on a much-reduced scale. Take walks so that you'll run and keep yourself running.

Starting Season

Give yourself three months to establish the running habit. I chose three months because they equal one season of the year.

I also picked three months because they're part of the 3-3 rule, which I've seen work hundreds of times. New runners who last three months and reach three miles (or thirty minutes, whichever is longer) reach an addiction point and are likely to keep running.

Consider yourself honestly before you start. What's your fitness level? Do you use your legs regularly—by walking, bicycling, or playing running games? If not, you need some preliminary walking, and only walking, before trying any running.

Are you significantly overweight? Is your twentieth birthday a distant memory? Do you tire easily or gasp for air during moderate exercise? Do you smoke? Do old foot or leg injuries ever bother you? If you answer yes to any of these questions, start by walking rather than running.

Walk a steady half hour and monitor your response. Even thirty minutes might be too much now, so you might have to cut back.

You might never be able or want to go beyond half-hour daily walks. That's okay. Walking is enough to give you most of the same benefits as running, and it's a lot better than doing nothing.

If you can manage a steady half-hour's walk, you're ready to start running. At first, mix short runs into your walks, later swinging the balance toward runs mixed with short walks. Finally, work your way up to running steadily, walking only before and after.

Go at your own pace, which shouldn't leave you breathless. Run at a pace that lets you sing or whistle to yourself, or talk normally with a friend. Mix in whatever amount of walking you need to keep your effort relaxed and comfortable.

During your buildup period, plan to run three or four days a week. Run no more than two days in a row, and don't go without a run for more than two days in a row. On most of your non-running days, simply walk for a half hour instead.

Go anywhere and everywhere that's convenient—streets, park paths, or tracks. Anyplace you can walk, you can run.

Buy a substantial pair of running shoes if you don't already own one. It's an investment in safety and comfort, the only major money outlay in our sport. Other than the special shoes, any light, loose-fitting clothing will do for now.

Wear a digital watch to measure your running-walking. Don't check distances. At this point only time counts, not distance. Make friends with your watch by taking pride in running extra minutes, instead of trying to beat a time for a known distance.

Progress through the stages in the schedule below, with walking decreasing as running increases. Step up, skip ahead, or back down according to how you react to your current level. You should feel comfortable at each stage of running before you advance to the next.

Once you can run a half hour steadily, you're ready to graduate to running more days per week, to running longer (with or without walking breaks), and to running shorter but faster.

Starter Schedule

This program for the beginning runner allows you flexibility in choosing from a range of distances or times, and for deciding which day of the week to run. Prerequisites for entering the program are good general health and the ability to walk steadily and without distress for at least thirty minutes.

The program's ingredients are:

1. Run days, which mix periods of running with walking breaks for a total of a half hour. Walking occupies most of the time at first, but the balance steadily tips toward running.

2. Rest days, which don't require total rest. They can include cross-training activities (such as walking, bicycling, or swimming), as long as they leave you refreshed and ready for the next run.

Fit the running time below into a thirty-minute period. Run the scheduled time, and walk the remaining time. Either run steadily or divide the time into shorter segments. (For example, in the first week, run five minutes and walk twenty-five. Or run one minute, walk five, and repeat that cycle for a half hour.)

Week	Run Days	Duration of Run per 30-Minute Period	Rest Days
1	3 or 4	5 minutes	3 or 4
2	3 or 4	6–7 minutes	3 or 4
3	3 or 4	8–9 minutes	3 or 4
4	3 or 4	10–11 minutes	3 or 4
5	3 or 4	12–13 minutes	3 or 4
6	3 or 4	14–15 minutes	3 or 4
7	3 or 4	16–17 minutes	3 or 4
8	3 or 4	18–19 minutes	3 or 4
9	3 or 4	20–21 minutes	3 or 4
10	3 or 4	22–23 minutes	3 or 4
11	3 or 4	24–25 minutes	3 or 4
12	3 or 4	26–27 minutes	3 or 4
13	3 or 4	28–30 minutes	3 or 4

PROGRESSING
using the best running techniques

Running Better

My entry into a full-time running and writing job came in 1967, when the most explosive ingredients for the first running boom were beginning to combine. New Zealander Arthur Lydiard's revolutionary training methods had arrived in the United States, imported chiefly by coach Bill Bowerman who was testing these techniques on athletes in Oregon. Dr. Kenneth Cooper had tested his running-as-exercise training plan on Air Force personnel in Texas, and was finishing a soon-to-be-revolutionary book called *Aerobics*.

These separate forces of change were to meet on the street. The Lydiard system would take runners off the track and onto the road to train. They soon would want to race on the roads too, in a setting more relaxed than the track.

As athletes stepped down to road racing, average exercisers stepped up. Bowerman and Cooper started people running for fitness, and many of them didn't stop there. They graduated to road races, which didn't discriminate against sex, age, or ability.

In 1967, though, all of this was yet to happen. All but a few runners were men then, most were young and fast, and their training approaches and racing attitudes kept them from lasting a long time.

For the running revolution to succeed, it had to win on two fronts: first by recruiting more runners, then by finding better ways to keep them running.

Runners won the first phase early. Their numbers grew steadily through the late 1960s, then boomed in the 1970s.

Many of those early starters are still running all these years later. And the sport keeps winning new converts because of advances made on the second front.

Physiology-Based Advances

In the 1960s, runners accepted "no pain, no gain" as the only way to train. But more often, painful training gained them only injury and burnout. Likewise, in the 1960s runners knew little about fueling themselves for their sport. They ate meat before races and drank only water (if that) during them. Fortunately, over the second half of the twentieth century, a number of innovative doctors, physiologists, and athletes would change these ways of thinking. The improved running and training techniques they developed taught runners the difference between training and straining, and helped jump-start the running revolution.

This chapter offers an overview of some of the most successful training techniques developed since 1967:

"Aerobics." Dr. Kenneth Cooper plucked this obscure word from physiology jargon and made it an international phenomenon. His research concluded that low-intensity, prolonged exercise produced greater endurance-training benefits than did brief, explosive sessions. Training aerobically means choosing a pace that leaves enough breath to talk while running and keeps the heart rate at about three-quarters of maximum. The net effect is an easing of training effort.

"Train, don't strain." These three words formed a cornerstone of Arthur Lydiard's system, and provided an antidote to "pain equals gain." Effective training, said Lydiard, nudges the dividing line between hard enough and too hard. He put into practice the theories of Dr. Hans Selye, who found that repeated exposure to a mild stress (such as running training) stimulates adaptation, but that too much stress overwhelms the body's ability to cope.

"Overuse." Podiatrists—including, most prominently, John Pagliano, Richard Schuster, and Steven Subotnick—applied this term to the end result of straining. The foot doctors who treated runners in growing numbers noted that most of the injuries weren't accidental. They were self-inflicted. Runners who trained too far, too fast, or too frequently had found their breaking points. Once doctors identified controllable causes, they could suggest ways to prevent these injuries.

"Listen to the body." Dr. George Sheehan told runners they needn't follow complex training formulas or try to run at a certain fixed pace per mile. All that a runner needed to do in distance training, he said, was "set the inner dial to 'comfortable,' neither too hard nor too easy. The pace that feels right is right." He endorsed Dr. Gunnar Borg's scale of perceived exertion, which measured feelings instead of minutes per mile. Heart-rate monitors arrived later to do the same type of listening electronically.

"Specificity." This tongue-twisting term means that you reap in racing what you sow in training. Long, slow runs prepare you to race slowly, while short, fast runs only train you to race briefly. Marathoner Jeff Galloway recognized this rule of adaptation when his now-popular marathon training program made runs of marathon length a requirement. Dr. Jack Daniels introduced tempo runs at about 10K-race pace to lift slow trainers out of their rut.

"Carbo-loading." New menus came to the training table as runners began to shun meat in favor of low-fat proteins and high-energy carbohydrates. Swedish physiologists first tested the technique of carbo-loading before races, and British marathoner Ron Hill proved its value. Dr. David Costill's studies at his Ball State University physiology lab found that carbo-reloading after races and hard training was equally important. Runners recognized that a regular diet rich in complex carbs would aid their training and improve overall health.

"Drink up." Costill also pointed out the folly of not drinking enough water before, during, and after long runs. He showed that as the dehydrating body's temperature rose, performance declined and the risk of heat injury increased. Runners learned to drink more water. In addition to water, they began drinking sweetened and electrolyte-laden solutions. Florida researchers invented Gatorade. Bill Gookin formulated ERG (electrolyte replacement with glucose) to meet the needs of runners.

Training Techniques

In the 1960s, the racer's training pendulum was swinging from one form of overtraining to another: from too many track intervals to too much road mileage. Runners would learn that effective training balances the long with the short, the hard with the easy, and the fast with the slow.

Long runs. This concept was Lydiard's most enduring gift to training. Few runners still do his one-hundred-mile weeks. But almost everyone runs longer than his or her norm at least once a week. Track athletes do it as over-distance training. Marathoners do it to build toward their race. Hobbyist racers run long on weekends because that's when they can find the time and the training partners to make the run a social event.

"LSD" running. Long slow distance—a product of the 1960s and a pet theme of mine—was widely misunderstood and misused as an invitation to run too long and too slowly. A better name for LSD would have been "gentle running." As originally practiced, this wasn't so much a training method as a recovery system. It allowed runners to run easily between major efforts, and this remains its best use.

Marathon survival. A new breed of runner came to dominate marathons (at least numerically). This runner treated the event not as a race for time or place, but as a survival test to be passed just by finishing. These survivors began getting help from Dr. Jack Scaff's Honolulu Marathon Clinic in the 1970s. This program and its descendants trained runners to reach the starting line in good health (by de-emphasizing weekly mileage and speed training), and to finish (by emphasizing the long run).

Speed training. Runners once shunned speed training because it meant only endlessly circling the track in an exhausting race against time. Building speed once required enduring boredom and pain, but not anymore. Physiologist/coach Daniels provided more humane but still effective alternatives. He popularized two forms of speed training that met the specific needs of racers: "tempo runs" at a steady pace but lasting only about twenty minutes, and "cruise intervals" of modest number and pace.

Hill training. Hills, a staple of the Lydiard system, were overlooked early on in the rush to one-hundred-mile weeks. Lydiard's runners used hills two ways: as a regular part of their long runs on extremely hilly courses, and with hill repeats as a lead-in phase to speed training. We now know that hills are speed sessions in disguise. Uphill running builds the upper-leg muscles that produce speed, and downhill running forces you to go faster.

Races as training. Four-time Olympian George Young (later a successful college coach in Arizona) pointed out that the most effective speed training occurs where it's most exciting to do: in short-distance races. With races of all distances now available anywhere almost every weekend, many runners take their speed day this way. This fact helps explain why the 5K is the most popular race distance. Conversely, runners who want to train long with a group now fill out the fields for half-marathons on up.

Hard-easy. Bill Bowerman produced as many top runners as any college coach ever has. Tests on his young, strong athletes showed that none thrived on more than three hard training days in a row. Most did best by alternating a hard day with an easy one. Kenny Moore, a Bowerman-trained Olympic marathoner, trained hard one day and easily the next two. Costill's tests confirmed that most runners need forty-eight to seventy-two hours to recover fully from even a moderately hard effort.

Peaking. This concept is a longer version of the Bowerman hard-easy system, mixing harder and easier seasons or even years. Lydiard's runners, winners of five Olympic medals, were masters of peaking. (The all-time best peaker was four-time Olympic winner Lasse Viren, who came under Lydiard's influence.) Lydiard maintained that no one could race and train at the highest possible level year-round. He recommended scheduling alternate seasons of peaks and valleys.

Tapering. Runners training for marathons used to take their last long run—and often their longest one—just a week before their race. The smart ones now space these efforts two to three weeks apart, to ensure they can restore full life to their legs before competition. They take the advice of Costill, whose research emphasizes the need to taper down training for up to three weeks before a race. The amount of time depends on the degree of training, and the length and seriousness of the race.

Recovering. As the road-racing schedule grew to fill the year and to crowd each weekend, so too did the temptation to over-race. A variation of hard-easy that helped to remove this temptation was Jack Foster's valuable rule of thumb. The longtime world masters marathon record-holder followed his races with a recovery period totaling one day for each mile of racing. He didn't completely stop running during that period, but didn't race or train hard again until that much time had passed.

Cross-training

In the 1960s, runners trained simply by running. Rarely did anyone stretch or lift weights. Injured runners ran until they could run no more, then did nothing else until their injuries healed and let them run again. Soon they were to learn the value of mixing activities—and the value of running for its own sake, not just as training for racing.

Also known as "alternative" or "supplemental" training, the cross-training concept received its greatest boost from the triathlon boom that followed the running boom. Triathletes sent runners the message that total fitness requires more than running, and gave us the okay to switch activities on days when running a few more miles seemed unwise or unappealing. Many paths lead to the same destination of aerobic fitness. Swimming and bicycling are but two among dozens of ways to mix and match activities. I'll cite two of the most valuable separately.

Water training. "Running" in a pool while wearing a floatation vest or belt might be the single most valuable variation on land running. Injured runners can continue normal training efforts and stay running-fit without aggravating the problem that put them in deep water. Oft-injured Mary Slaney gave water running credence when she trained this way for six weeks following a mishap at the 1984 Olympic trials. A few days after returning to land, she broke the world 2000-meter record.

Walking. "Walk" used to be a dirty word to runners. They wouldn't think of stopping to walk during a run, and certainly not in a race. Tom Osler started changing this thinking. He'd successfully mixed walking breaks into his own ultra-marathons. He wrote that runners could greatly increase the length of their longest nonstop run by inserting brief walks at regular intervals. This trick became a favorite of marathoners whose only goal is to finish, of runners coming back from injuries or illnesses, of new runners building their distances, and of longtime runners looking to ease their efforts.

SCHEDULING
to make good use of limited time

Spare Time

A friend of mine once observed wryly, "To be a good runner, you must be single, unemployed, or both." He was newly divorced, working only a few days each month, and even though he was in his forties was racing better than ever.

Bill Rodgers would have agreed. During his years as America's top marathoner, running was his job, and he was between marriages for part of that time. He said he doubted that anyone who worked a forty-hour week could beat him.

Good running takes time. Those of us who never seem to have enough of it envy people like full-time runner Rodgers and my divorced friend who worked only part-time at his paying job. They enjoyed the luxury of scheduling their days around their runs, instead of squeezing their running into a crowded schedule.

Anyone with world- and national-class racing ambitions must treat running as a job, giving it his or her full time and attention. Professionals and would-be pros can and must take the time to do everything right in their running.

A pro runner of my acquaintance makes sure she gets enough sleep, waking at a civilized hour each morning. She lives on a hillside but worries about hill running causing injuries, so she drives down to the flats to train.

This full-time runner stretches carefully before and after each run. She supplements her twice-daily runs with gym work for strength.

Between training sessions she might visit her physician, chiropractor, physiologist, masseur, or sports psychologist. These activities might take up her whole day.

Such commitment to physical perfection is to be admired—but not to be imitated by people with more pressing commitments than running. The athletes we read about the most are those least like ourselves in terms of the time they can and will devote to running.

We don't need to be told to spend more time on running—we need to be shown how to use our limited time better

We don't need to be told to spend more time on our sport. We need to be shown how to use our limited time better.

Running coach Reg Harris wrote a book, *The Part-Time Runner*, with that purpose in mind. Harris now lives in Northern California, but in the early 1970s, he coached in Tunisia. He helped prepare three-time Olympic medalist Mohamed Gammoudi for the Munich Games.

The Tunisians, explains Harris, taught him one major lesson: "Train smarter, not harder. I became convinced that too many Americans have gone mileage-crazy. They have forgotten—or never learned—that excellent results can be achieved with relatively low mileage."

When Harris came home after his tour of duty as a national coach, he began training runners from the opposite end of the spectrum. He taught college running classes and coached high school and junior high teams.

Before starting to write his book, Harris asked potential readers what they wanted to know that they hadn't already learned from the dozens of running books and hundreds of magazine articles out there. The main thrust of their replies: tell us how to run better, not more.

A man who averaged sub-six-minute miles in his 10K races wrote, "I'd like to see more information on how to make the most of a twenty- to forty-mile training week for those who can't spare the time for more running."

Running is seldom your top priority in life

A woman marathoner who had qualified for Boston said, "There's too much stuff [written] for the serious marathoner. I wish writers would deal more with the real world, the runner who juggles job and running, and still has time for a family."

Such replies led Harris to adopt the phrase "part-time runner," develop a book with those words as its title, and self-publish it. "Perhaps the best definition of a part-time runner," he wrote, "is that he or she enjoys running and perhaps racing, but only as part of a busy life.

"While running does have a high priority, it is seldom the most important thing in his or her life. Most part-time runners must accomplish their goals in a limited amount of time and with a limited allotment of energy."

Our subject in this chapter is a continuation of Harris's theme: time management, making time to run, and using that time well.

Taking Time

Runners who are looking only for a quick bout of exercise aren't much troubled by time constraints. Anyone content to follow the Kenneth Cooper formula, devised by the doctor who has been spreading the gospel of aerobics since the 1960s, doesn't need much time to fulfill its requirements.

Dr. Cooper's wellness program calls for running two to three miles about every other day, or about a one- to two-hour time investment per week. Almost anyone can spare that small amount of time.

The problem arises when Cooper's quotas no longer satisfy you. When you run twice as far and twice as often as he suggests, the total mileage is still modest by the standards of full-time runners, but you've quadrupled the time requirement.

If you train for marathons and add total-fitness activities to your routine, the sport takes almost as much time as a second job. Even if that doesn't bother you, consider your family and boss. They probably aren't as tolerant of this time drain.

Running too much at the expense of higher priorities is one common pitfall facing a busy runner. Another comes from the opposite direction: running shorter distances too fast in order to substitute quality for quantity. Even if you're lucky enough to escape injury on the latter course, the run becomes an extension of the day's rat race instead of a break from it.

The solution to the time problem is one that applies to many other training and racing puzzles: strike the proper balance between enough and too much.

You might think mine is the ideal runner's life: writing, teaching, and speaking about running for a living. I wouldn't trade it for any other job, but this kind of work does have its unique time demands.

Strike the proper balance between enough and too much

I alternate between thinking I'm never working and wondering why I'm always working. Running writers/teachers/speakers share these mixed feelings with specialty-shop owners, school coaches, shoe-company representatives, and professional race directors. We're in the business of supporting other people's hobby. And since most people engage in this hobby after work and on weekends, we are kept busy working during those times. Ironically we "pros" might have less time to run than most hobbyists do.

My days and weeks fill up even without time spent running. Because I enjoy writing, I commit myself to too many projects and seem to face a deadline each day.

And since I love to talk with runners, I spend at least four days a week with my students, and at least one weekend a month traveling to speak at races. This schedule leaves little time for my own running, but I've learned to make time.

My current routine is decidedly ordinary in quantity and quality. It's worth noting only for its regularity: I run almost every day of every week of every year, despite dozens of trips and innumerable classes and deadlines. To proceed this steadily has required learning and applying the following lessons in time management.

Call time-out for an hour a day. Schedule one hour in every twenty-four that is yours alone, to do with what you wish. Use the full hour, but seldom take longer than that. Treat it as your island of stability and sanity in a turbulent day.

Taking time for yourself has great value even if you don't fill it with running. The busier you are, the more you need to take this break from the other duties of the day. This might be the only time all day when you can get away from phone calls and meetings at the office, and children and chores at home.

Why an hour? Because running at least half of that time-block is long enough for an adequate training session, and long enough that you won't be tempted to run too fast.

Schedule one hour in every twenty-four that is yours alone, to do with what you wish

Yet one hour is short enough for most people to fit into their daily schedules. You might make the time simply by waking up earlier in the morning or skipping one TV show at night.

Harris's book quoted several runners who took the first option. A banker reported starting before five a.m., saying, "That's the only time I don't have to steal from family or work."

Schedule your hour at the most convenient time, or the least inconvenient. Protect that hour from outside demands that would erode it. Think of the hour not as time lost but as an investment that pays dividends thereafter.

Run *with* the clock, not against it. Forget about how far you run, and think only of how much time you spend running.

Count minutes, not miles. Start your digital stopwatch at the beginning, shut it off at the finish, and record the time rather than the distance.

Why run by time? It offers several benefits. The practical advantage is freedom from the time-consuming job of designing and measuring running courses.

You no longer need to follow those routes step by step. You're free to alter old paths and explore new ones while filling the time quota. Minutes pass at the same rate wherever you run them, and an accurate measurement is right there on your wrist.

The greatest reward of time running is more subtle. Switching to the time standard relieves the pressure of running against time.

The natural urge when running a set distance is to finish it as quickly as possible, which often means pushing yourself too hard. You can't make a period of time pass any faster.

Count minutes, not miles

In fact, time seems to pass more slowly when you try to rush it. But when running by your watch, you'll tend to slip into a comfortable pace without worrying about how far you go.

Richard Watson wrote *The Philosopher's Diet*, which is as much a running book as a nutrition text. He recommended splitting the allotted hour this way: "Ten minutes to get ready, thirty on the road, twenty to shower and get dressed."

If you're a fast dresser, you can run more, but the advice remains the same: fit your run loosely into your daily hour. Run at least half an hour, and stop well short of an hour most days.

Keep the time of day and the time spent running fairly constant, but vary widely what you do within that time. When running by time, your pace self-adjusts to your feelings that day. Yet you still finish on schedule regardless of whether you spent your time running all-out or mostly walking.

Use the time efficiently by warming up for running by running slowly, not with stretching exercises that have little or no warming effect. Add faster running for its flexibility benefits and run hills as strength exercises.

The hour-long time period allows for some speed training, and a little is all you need. I repeat my earlier warning against trying to crowd limited time with too much fast running, but light interval training or tempo running is okay.

Fred Wilt, on whose technical writings I was weaned, once suggested a quick session for busy runners: a warm-up mile plus another mile alternating fast and slow, 110-yard (100m) intervals on a track.

I recommend a slight variation on Wilt's theme. Warm up for fifteen minutes, then alternate one minute fast and one minute slow for the final fifteen. Or simply follow the warm-up with a steady but faster run the rest of the hour.

Save the formal speed training, longer runs, and races for weekends and vacations. Limit these time-gobbling sessions to days when you have extra hours to spend driving to a special site, socializing with other runners, and recovering from the unusual effort.

A busy runner won't have many days like this. Treat them as luxury items, with the modest working-day runs as the necessities.

MOVING *efficiently, smoothly, quietly, and proudly*

Running Styles

How do you run? This isn't a question of how far or how fast, but how you move step by running step. How do you put your feet down and stride out? How do you look when you run?

You might not have thought much about it, and most of the time that's good. After all, you can't do much to change the form you've practiced since your second year of life, and concentrating too much on individual steps might disrupt the overall flow of your run.

Running is like breathing. It usually goes just fine without thinking about it all the time. It works most smoothly when it's done unconsciously.

The way you look while running doesn't matter much either. This isn't gymnastics or figure skating. Stylish running scores no points. If it did, the names Emil Zatopek and Bob Hayes would be unknown in our sport.

Zatopek thrashed his arms and grimaced like a crazed street fighter. Hayes was so pigeon-toed that he almost stepped on his own feet when he sprinted.

Yet these two were giants among Olympians. Their "faults" were no more than innocent personal quirks.

Take care when talking about running styles to distinguish between what's different and what's wrong. Running doesn't need to look pretty, but only has to feel right for the person doing it. "Right" covers a wide range of differences, and varies from person to person, speed to speed.

This chapter talks about the elements of running style that are adjustable. But before we move on to that, you should recognize that running form is:

▶ **Individually fitted.** A five-foot-two runner, for instance, can't use the stride of someone a foot taller, any more than they could wear the same pants.

▶ **Speed adapted.** Sprinters can't lean back on their heels without getting slow, while slower runners can't stay up on their toes without getting sore.

▶ **Mechanically efficient.** Humans have evolved into upright animals, and we run best with a straight back.

▶ **Relaxed.** Running with tension is like driving a car with its brakes on. You work harder to go slower.

Running is a complete, flowing action—not independent movements by your feet, legs, arms, and hands. But to improve your overall form, you need to take it apart like a broken machine and fix the faulty parts. Once they're reassembled, you can go back on automatic pilot and think of more important matters than how you take each step.

Noted technical writer Ken Doherty once advised, "Do what comes naturally, as long as 'naturally' is mechanically sound. If it isn't, do what is mechanically sound until it comes naturally."

Form Faults

Check yourself for the sights and sounds of your running form. Look at the trail of your footprints in fresh snow, on wet grass, or on a beach. Listen to your footfalls on the road.

Watch your shadow in front of you. Glance at your reflection in store windows. Have someone videotape your running for critiquing.

Focus on your form if you think it needs changing. Look for any of these symptoms and their probable causes:

▶ **Slapping.** Excessive noise as your feet meet the road or track means you're pounding the ground too hard. Make better use of your knees and feet as shock-absorbers.

▶ **Bouncing.** A pronounced rising and dipping with each step indicates that you're striding inefficiently. Avoid overreaching with your lead leg or pogo-sticking up and down instead of directing motion forward.

▶ **Leaning.** When your head and shoulders thrust forward, your butt sticks out in back. Straighten up, and tuck in your butt.

▶ **Flapping.** When hands and arms flap out of control or hang limply, they provide no power or balance. Keep your fists loosely clenched, wrists fixed, and elbows at a flexible angle.

▶ **Boxing.** Holding your hands and arms high, fists clenched tightly, and elbows locked, as if protecting your face from attack, produces tension and side-to-side sway. Lower your hands, relax your fists, unlock your elbows, and swing your arms lower.

▶ **Grimacing.** Holding your shoulders high, tightening your jaw, and wrinkling your forehead are key tension-producers. Let them all relax.

Focus on a mental picture of how to run. As you think, so shall you run. Think of running tall and straight, smoothly, softly, and silently.

Proudly, Quietly

Runners pass judgment on other passing runners. You evaluate them partly by how they dress, partly by their pace. But nothing establishes a stronger first impression than running form. Each runner moves in his or her distinctive style, which enables you to identify someone you know from a distance before seeing a face.

The ways people look while running fall into two main groupings. Those who run over the ground seem to use the earth as a springboard to keep them airborne. Those who run on the ground shuffle and tiptoe along the surface as though they might fly off into space if they break contact for too long.

One runner moves boldly, the other timidly. One runs as if the ground were a friend, the other as if it were an enemy on the attack.

Good running is quiet running

I began as the first type of runner. No one runs the track races I once did by being afraid to spring from the earth. But years of wear and tear made me more fragile and afraid. I finally woke up to that fact while running on Pre's Trail (named after Steve Prefontaine) in Eugene, Oregon, a runner-watching mecca.

As a pack of University of Oregon athletes bounded past, this thought struck me: I'm not one of you anymore. I'm one of them, meaning the timid who run on stiff legs and shuffling feet that barely clear the ground.

I slipped gradually into the shuffling style. Even while barely into my forties, I ran like an arthritic old man: stiff-legged, flat-footed, and short-strided. My feet felt like two clenched fists.

I ran this way thinking it would reduce pain, but I might have been adding to it. This style is jarring, jamming, and tightening to feet and legs. They act as ramrods instead of the shock absorbers they're meant to be.

After realizing all this, I began whispering remedial instructions to myself: lift your knees at push-off . . . flex your ankles . . . spring from your big toes . . . land with your knees slightly bent . . . lean a little farther forward on your feet. But the only time I ran correctly was when I was given no choice. This happened in races and on hills.

Once my speed picked up to racing rate, I was forced to land with my knees flexed . . . to spring from my ankles . . . to roll forward off my big toe. It wasn't by chance that I often felt my best—in my feet and lower legs, anyway—during and right after races.

Hill running also forces a more springy style. Uphills require more drive and lift from your knees and ankles, more involvement from your full feet. Downhill running requires flexed knees. Otherwise it can be a disastrous experience.

I had days when flat surfaces left me limping. Yet as soon as the ground tilted up or down, the pain eased.

The hills were trying to tell me something, just as the races were. They weren't saying that the hard effort of climbing or pushing the pace was inherently better for me than comfortable running. They were telling me that the running style required for harder, faster running might be the natural one for all terrains and efforts.

Prancing

Prance. If there's a single word that defines good running style, it's prancing. Not running like a drum major at halftime during a football game, but running as if you're proud of yourself.

For prancing, your body has three trigger points:

1. Foot. Make full use of it. A good style involves both heel running and toe running. Land at mid-foot, rock gently back onto your heel, roll forward onto your toes, and then push off from your big toe.

2. Ankle. Flex it. The more rigid your ankle is, the more jarring your contact with the ground. And vice versa, as a flexible ankle will provide better shock absorption and push-off. Think "flex" and "snap" as the ankle does its two jobs.

3. Knee. Lift it. As the knee goes, so goes the foot. If the knees ride low and rigid, the feet will too. Pick up your knee and bend it.

The result of improved form is taller, bolder running. That much is obvious. Yet the less obvious part might be more important. That's not what you see but what you hear—or rather, don't hear.

Good running is quiet running. The less you hear when your foot meets the ground, the less likely your footfall will hurt.

Uphill, Downhill

Shakespeare never ran a race, as far as we know. But runners agree with his lament that hills "draw out the miles and make them wearisome."

Uphill running obviously slows you down, but without giving you the usual ease of slowing. You might invest six-minute-mile effort while moving at nine-minute pace.

Downhill running is easier, but it isn't completely relaxing either. Gravity tugs you out of control. Your feet, calves, knees, and thighs take twice the beating that they do on flat ground.

Hill running has its own set of rules. The first word in running uphill is "conserve." The most important word in running downhill is "protect."

Conserving means not wasting so much energy going uphill that you have no energy left for resuming normal pace when the course flattens. Protecting means not letting the

Run downhill like a question mark

downhills pound you so hard that you can't run normally when the hill bottoms out. In both cases, try to get over the hills without getting hurt by them.

Efficient climbing has less to do with technique than with attitude. When you run up hills, neither fear nor fight them. Simply adjust to them.

If you were riding a bicycle uphill, you'd shift to a lower gear. Your pace would slow, but you'd pedal with about the same effort. Do this too when you run: maintain a constant effort while ascending, even as your pace naturally slackens.

Proper (read: protective) downhill running is more difficult than it might seem. An exchange at one of my talks illustrates this.

"I do okay on the uphills," said a man from the audience. "But coming back down gives me the most trouble. What can I do?"

I quoted Olympian Kenny Moore, a consummate downhill runner who once raced a sub-four-minute opening mile in a sloping 10K. Moore advised holding the body perpendicular to the surface and letting gravity take over.

"I know all that," said the questioner. "But have you ever tried running that way down a steep hill? It pounds you to death."

Another speaker on stage stepped in with an answer. Tom Miller holds a doctorate in exercise science, with an emphasis on how runners move. He also runs mountain races and coaches trail runners.

"Run like a question mark," said Miller. He began explaining this enigmatic advice by assuming the wrong pose.

"The natural tendency when running downhill is to reach out with the front leg, lock the knee, and slam down heel-first," he said while extending a leg. "You lean backward, arch the back, and possibly throw back the head.

"That's all wrong. You're braking and taking more shock than you should."

Then Miller demonstrated the question-mark style: "Instead of 'running tall,' as you would on the flat, you 'run short,' as if you're sneaking up behind someone. Keep your feet under you and the footfall as quiet as possible.

"Bend the knees more than normal. Hold your rear down and slightly protruding, looking at the ground in front of you." Slightly bent knees plus a slightly bowed head equals a question mark.

Practice perfects these techniques. And because hill running requires strength as well as technique, hill training builds the necessary muscle along with the skill.

EXERCISING with running supplements and substitutes

Strong and Loose

Like most runners with roots in the 1950s and '60s, I once thought extra exercises before or after running were a waste of time. Hurdlers might need to stretch for maximum flexibility, shot-putters might need to lift weights for explosive power, football players and military recruits might need calisthenics to build team unity. But distance runners' time was better spent running.

I thought I'd put extra exercises behind me when I stopped playing football at age sixteen, only to have them return during a few unpleasant months in the Army at age twenty-two. For almost ten years after that I didn't do a single push-up or toe-touch. Why bother?

Meanwhile, injuries began to nag me—little ones at first, not disabling me but nibbling away at my joy of moving freely. I ignored these little hurts, and they grew into bigger ones—the type that cost me a running day now and then, then several days, then whole weeks. Eventually I ran myself into foot surgery, and still hadn't figured out why.

George Sheehan told me why. Dr. Sheehan, the late medical columnist and philosopher-in-residence at *Runner's World*, casually tossed off lines that were the envy of anyone who wrote. His wisdom emerged in the form of short, simple statements that were easy to read and hard to forget.

The Sheehan proverb on the subject of runners' exercises concerned strength and flexibility. He said, "When you run, three things happen to you—and two of them are bad."

The good effect is that you become a faster and more enduring runner; you adapt to the type of exercise you do. But if running is your only exercise, bad effects can arise that in extreme cases may stop you from running.

The first of these is tightness, all the way from your heels to your lower back. If you're a longtime, long-distance runner and aren't doing corrective exercises, you probably can't bend from your waist with your knees straight and touch your fingertips to the ground.

The second bad effect is loss of muscle strength in your upper body, and the development of strength imbalances in your legs. A runner's arms, shoulders, chest, and abdominal muscles pretty much just go along for the ride; if neglected, they atrophy. The muscles on the front of your legs from your hips down get a good workout, the muscles on the back of your legs don't. This can account for strength imbalances.

At best, then, you aren't as fit as you'd like to believe, if you lack flexibility and balanced strength. At worst, you're an injury waiting to happen.

I suffered many injuries when I specialized too much in running. (This was particularly true while I was logging heavy mileage and neglecting speed training; faster running returns some of the strength and flexibility that long, slow distance takes away.) I know now that additional exercises are a good investment, providing hours of smooth running for a few minutes of supplemental activity. I invest in other exercises almost every day, stretching a bit and then hefting some weights, and now advise other runners to do the same.

Try this: first bend over and touch the ground (even if only with your fingertips). Then do ten honest push-ups and ten bent-leg sit-ups. If you can't pass these minimum tests of flexibility and strength, and especially if leg pains are eroding the fun of your running, you need to do more than run.

To Stretch or Not?

As editor of *Runner's World* in the mid-1970s, I jumped on a new body of information coming out at the time, and used the magazine to promote it. Stretching exercises were necessary and good for runners, the latest reports announced.

Much of the evidence came from a highly respected source: Dr. Herbert de Vries, a sports physiologist at the University of Southern California. He declared that runners were too tight and needed to add flexibility exercises to their routine.

De Vries said the best corrective stretches weren't the "ballistic" type—the quick, bouncy, repeated calisthenics we'd known from high school sports. He favored "static" stretches—stretch slowly until you reach a point of discomfort,

If running is your only exercise, bad effects can arise

and then hold for ten or twenty seconds. It is thought to be effective for increasing range of motion and lengthening the muscle fibers. Static stretching became the standard in running, and remains so today.

But now we're hearing reports that stretching can actually cause the very injuries it's supposed to prevent. What should we believe—that these exercises are a panacea or pain?

If you tend to stretch, keep toeing the party line and continue stretching. If you don't like to stretch, quote a contrary view to justify not stretching.

But what about those of us who stretch sometimes but don't truly believe in the benefits? I speak for us runners who can't quite make up our minds.

The following are my opinions as a semi-skeptical stretcher. I don't doubt the practice enough to drop it, yet don't do enough of it to reap the maximum benefits that its proponents promise.

▶ **Stretching is overrated.** Runners become tight-muscled because it's a normal and necessary adaptation to the activity. Otherwise why would running do this to us? Tightness is a training effect, producing a springy rather than floppy stride. Stretching too much negates that effect.

▶ **Stretching isn't for running.** What's good for running might not be right for overall fitness. Flexibility is one piece in the fitness puzzle. Anyone seeking balanced fitness needs to counteract the super-tightening of running with the loosening of other exercises.

▶ **Stretching doesn't eliminate injuries.** Done wrong—too aggressively and too many—stretches cause more problems than they prevent. Done right—gently and in small doses—stretches still don't guarantee pain-free running. The Big Three—too much running, too fast, and too often—cause most of our injuries.

▶ **Stretching isn't a warm-up.** It doesn't start you sweating or raise your heart rate. Done before running, it delays the true warm-up. You warm up by moving—first by running slowly or walking, then by easing into your full pace.

▶ **Stretching is for afterward.** Warm muscles respond best to these exercises. Run first, then stretch. Stretching after running has benefits beyond flexibility. It gives you a few extra minutes to cool down before you sit down. And it gives you the option of cutting out the stretches instead of cutting short the run when time is tight.

Good Words for Walks

In certain running circles, "walk" remains a nasty word. I think of walking as a valuable form of cross-training, perhaps the most valuable because it's so convenient and so closely related to running.

Yet some purist runners, reacting to the growing popularity of marathoners taking walking breaks, equate this practice with cheating. They claim that walking within a run is only for the untalented and undedicated.

To walk is to wimp out? Two good old friends of mine could argue that point, but let's let their efforts speak for them.

Their age averages over eighty at this writing. One had run all his life, achieved more than most of us could ever dream, then suddenly had to stop. The other friend waited until his mature years to start running, raced faster by his early seventies than most of us go at any age, then found he couldn't run as often as before.

When running changed or stopped for these two men, running's closest cousin started looking much more attractive. One became a full-time walker who covered enormous distances in his eighties. The other became a part-time walker who could still set marathon records in his mid-seventies.

Ted Corbitt had more to lose than any of us, because he ran more than almost anyone, when the great fear of runners came true for him. He found in the 1970s that his asthma made running intolerable.

This loss could have devastated Corbitt, an Olympic marathoner in his youth and later a renowned ultra-runner. He could have descended from high activity to none.

Instead he transitioned smoothly into walking. Not strolling through his New York City neighborhood, but a different way of traveling the many miles that he'd long covered.

At age eighty-one in 2001, he averaged almost fifty and a half miles per day in a six-day race named for him. He wrote to me then about his walking habit.

"Since I stopped running, I sometimes walk around Manhattan Island, which is thirty-one-plus miles by the route I take. I've probably run or walked this more than a hundred times."

Corbitt added, "Most of my walks are ten-milers." Running or walking, he remained a beacon for aging actively.

John Keston became, at sixty-nine-plus, the oldest marathoner to break three hours. At seventy-one, he ran the fastest time, three hours, fifty-eight seconds (3:00:58), for anyone past his seventieth birthday. Two months shy of his seventy-seventh birthday, he became the oldest runner to break three and a half hours.

The last of these races was a final test of the novel training method he'd adopted after turning seventy-five. For nearly half of his weekly training mileage, Keston walked. He didn't mix walking breaks into his running, but mixed walking and running days throughout the week.

"I predicated the concept of this kind of training that body-builders use," he said. "They base their approach on the premise of never working the same muscle more than every third day. I figured that I could save my running muscles by just walking two days in a row (usually five to six miles each day), and then running long (typically fourteen to seventeen miles) on the third day."

Keston added, "I'd like to see this system tried on some younger runners, since I believe that most youngsters over-train." We don't have to wait until our seventies to discover that "walk" is not a nasty word.

Warming Trends

The first mile of a run is the slowest, often the hardest—and the most important. Without it, of course, nothing can follow. But it also sets the tone for the rest of the run.

This opening mile is my warm-up and my test. And it's also my trick to get me up, out the door, and on my way. Once I've run this one short mile "just to see how I feel," I'm usually feeling good enough for more.

After reading these sentiments in one of my magazine columns, reader Kevin Casey from Australia recalled words from a college professor of his. When faced with students' grumbling about how tough the going would be on an assigned paper, the prof said, "Beginning is half done." The hardest part of any project is starting it, which is pretty much what my column said.

"It's so true," wrote Casey, "that the biggest battle is not the last two kilometers of a run but the first two meters just getting out of the door. How true of life as well.

"We look at our 'in' trays at work or at jobs that need doing around the home and find a reason not to do them. It requires more energy to get a ball rolling than it takes to keep it rolling."

I took too long to learn that the early rolling is best done very slowly. My longtime practice was to reach my day's full pace within my first hundred steps.

Then came yet another case of a bad break teaching a good lesson. I fell while running and hurt my hip. I kept up my normal runs, and the hip kept hurting.

The pain, not serious but nagging, didn't ease for almost a year. That's when I finally learned to start rolling more slowly than ever before.

I credit a Kenyan, Cosmas Ndeti, for inspiring the trial mile. The three-time Boston Marathon winner ran even less than a mile—just a kilometer—as his test of whether this was his day or not. He was willing to stop there and "climb back into bed," but usually found that his doubts and pains eased in those early minutes.

"Walk" is not a nasty word

In my travels, I often stay in the same hotels as Kenyan runners. I see them starting their morning runs at a shuffling nine-minute-mile pace.

I've never seen anyone so fast start so slowly. The Kenyans don't stay slow, though. They pick the pace up—way up—as they warm to the task.

Add multiple minutes to their pace to arrive at mine, but the pattern is the same. My second mile is typically a minute faster (or less slow) than the first, and the third another minute faster before my pace levels out. My laughably slow start usually allows my finish to be relatively brisk, which is a product of it being pain-free.

I've learned from the Kenyans. I've learned to shuffle out the door and keep shuffling for as long as it takes to ease out the kinks.

WEATHERING the imperfect conditions of running

Great Outdoors

This is not a perfect world. The weather is not always ideal for running. The path beneath you is seldom perfectly smooth, flat, dry, and unobstructed.

Rather than complain about these natural conditions—or worse, refuse to run when they're less than perfect—you must learn to adapt to them instead of expecting them to satisfy you. Only about one day a week is perfectly conducive to running, and that single day does not a runner make.

Take winter weather as a most dramatic example. I learned early on to accept that winters weren't going to warm up just for me. Eventually, I was able to appreciate the value of cold-weather running.

I came to view winter not as a period to suffer through, or as a season to be waited out indoors playing basketball, or as a time to give up this sport in favor of one more suited to snow and cold, like cross-country skiing. I looked forward to winter running as my time to sneak ahead of runners who were hibernating until spring.

My first winter runs came in Iowa, where athletes of that era (the 1950s) all stayed indoors between November and March, usually shooting baskets. I didn't leave the court voluntarily, but had to be shown the door out of the gym.

The saddest—and luckiest—day of my young life came when the basketball coach gently told me there would never be a place on his team for a nearsighted five-foot-five guard. Earlier that year I'd learned that football held no future for a timid 130-pound linebacker.

Our school had no baseball team. Track was my last chance to salvage any athletic success, and I'd found some the previous spring by reaching the state meet as a freshman runner.

I decided to jump the gun on the next track season by running all winter, starting indoors because I still believed that my lungs would turn to popsicles if I breathed too much icy air. "If it's okay with you," I said to the basketball coach, "I'll just run around the gym floor."

Imperfect days make a runner

He caught a loose ball, passed it back across the floor, and said, "It's okay as long as you don't get in the players' way. Just don't run here during our practices."

Those practices ended at six o'clock, and I couldn't wait that long to run. So I planned to squeeze in ten hard minutes before the players took over the court.

The first day, I worked the tight turns like a Grand Prix driver. The next day I limped into the gym on blistered feet and stiff ankles.

The coach spotted my pained walk. "What's wrong," he asked, "not in shape for running yet?"

Embarrassment and anger overrode my stiffness and pain. I went into the locker room, laced up my high-top canvas shoes, tied my baggy gray sweatpants just below my chest, pulled on a hooded sweatshirt that hung to my thighs, added a stocking cap and gloves, and went outside to stay.

Winter running made me the runner I was to become—successful in high school and still loving to run long after my best racing days were behind me. This course wasn't set by what happened on the mild, sunny days of spring and fall. Anyone can be a fair-weather runner. My attachment to the sport was tested and hardened on the bad days of winter, and equally on the worst days of summer heat and humidity.

The imperfect days make a runner because they are much more plentiful than ideal ones.

My advice about running in extremes of temperature applies to all environmental inconveniences: stay flexible. Accept what you can't change, and change what you can't accept.

Accept that you can't run as far or as fast as you'd like on some days. But get out when you can, where you can, and for however long you can run. Make the most of the conditions you're given.

More often than not, you can run something. More often than not, you'll feel better about it than if you'd run nothing. If you pass the tests of the bad days, you'll enjoy more of the good ones when they finally come.

Talking Dirty

Meeting on the run, we runners traditionally exchange a word or two, a wave or a nod. But sometimes the greeting only goes one way, with the other runner either casting a wary look or avoiding any eye contact.

Being snubbed this way annoys me. I want to turn and shout, "Don't worry, I'm not dangerous."

That's before realizing how I must appear. If you saw me running in early morning, you might mistake me for a homeless person: wild hair, tattered T-shirt from some ancient race, shoes stained the color of dirt.

I smell soap, shampoo, or perfume on some runners who pass by. I can only guess about the scents that must waft from me. An occasional runner gives me a dirty look for a reason. I look—and maybe smell—dirty. And that's okay. It's fun to start a run dirty and to finish dirtier.

I run alone by choice. My official excuse is that it's my time for thinking, which can't be a team sport. Running solo is also simpler. With no partner to offend, I don't need to clean up before going out.

I don't wash my hands or face, or brush my teeth. I don't comb my hair or shave my beard.

Alone, I spit and blow my nose without hitting anyone. I freely expel gas. I shamelessly relieve myself in places without plumbing.

I make a point of greeting passing runners, even those who refuse to respond in kind. But I don't give more than a monosyllabic grunt.

I run alone to get in touch with my inner barbarian. It's a rare treat in this civilized, sanitized, weatherized age.

My favorite quote master George Sheehan liked to quote one of his heroes, Emerson, who advised: "Be first a good animal."

I run alone to get in touch with my inner barbarian

Sheehan ran like a good animal, even when other runners were watching or listening. He confessed to urinating down his leg at times instead of sacrificing precious seconds to stop during a race. He belched and groaned for anyone to hear.

One of Sheehan's most talked-about and misunderstood columns sang the praises of sweat. He wrote that a runner's sweat doesn't stink.

This was widely misread as a statement against showering. Sheehan took showers and recommended them; he just said that you first must earn them.

"You can't take a shower anytime you want," he wrote. "The hot shower is the final act of a ritual. To take one without the proper preparation is as gross as eating when you're not hungry, or drinking when you're not thirsty."

Proper preparation means working up a good, honest, healthy sweat that you then shower off. You could say the same for other parts of the cleaning-up ritual: teeth-brushing, shaving, and putting on fresh clothes.

You don't know how good being clean feels until you've gotten dirty. Likewise you don't know how good being warm feels until you've chilled down; or how good being cool feels until you've warmed up; or how good rest feels until you've tired yourself out.

The same goes for hunger and thirst. Food and drink taste best after you've been running, ritually chasing down a meal and working up a thirst.

Only after proper preparation are you ready to feel and act reasonably civilized again. You can better appreciate the benefits and bounties of civilization after you've gone a little barbaric.

Fall Guys

Don Kardong, running's resident humorist, somehow manages to write funny lines about even the most somber events. This is evident in the title of one of the pieces he wrote for *Runner's World* online, "Running: It's a Fall Sport," about tumbling during a trail run.

I saw Kardong several weeks after that fall. He still wasn't able to run much, and by then could barely summon a smile about the mishap.

Accidents can be grim, such as the bad fall that former *RW* publisher George Hirsch took at the Chicago Marathon finish line. He went down on his face, and lost three teeth.

Kardong wrote that most runners have stories about falling. I have several. My first happened in high school when too many runners with too little experience started a mile race.

The rush around the first curve deposited me onto the track. There I rolled into a ball and shielded my face to ward off two dozen sets of spikes. Once the pack passed, I gave chase and passed everyone.

Looks of shock or disgust met me at the finish line. "What's wrong?" I asked. Someone pointed a finger at my left hip.

My shorts were ripped away, and blood trailed down into my shoe. The hip still carries a scar, with imbedded remnants of the cinder track, to remind me of that fall.

Four-legged runners have caused two of my worst tumbles. I can't blame strangers' dogs, as these were my own.

First to bring me down was my Lab pup named Goldie. During an early running lesson, she hadn't yet mastered the concept of moving in a straight line.

Goldie crossed in front of me, I tripped over the leash, and threw out my free hand to break the fall. My collision with the ground dislocated my shoulder. That hurt, but not half as much as the "relocation" of that shoulder in a doctor's office later.

My current dog Buzz is bred and trained for one purpose: to run. He does it ecstatically, almost blindly.

Late in one run, Buzz came at me like a defensive back. Approaching fast from my blind side, he struck at knee level. I flew sideways, horizontal to the ground, before landing hard on a mercifully soft surface.

Buzz received a bop on the head from me afterwards. For this he looked at me as if to ask, "What was that for?"

We like to blame someone else for mishaps like these. Most of my falls, though, have been my own fault.

The most damaging happened early one morning in Portland, Oregon. A breakfast meeting had pushed my wake-up run into the darkness.

I traveled a dimly lighted sidewalk beside the Willamette River, hugging the wall next to the water. I didn't see a ground-level cable until it had grabbed my foot and flung me onto the concrete like a base runner sliding into second.

After checking whether all my parts were still attached and working, I looked around to see if anyone had noticed. The shame of these falls is often worse than the pain.

"Are you okay?" a voice asked from the darkness. We runners always say we're okay, even if we aren't.

I'd lost skin from both knees and both palms. Worse trouble would appear later, when my banged-up hip would hurt for most of the next year.

Falls happen in this sport. A run is, after all, a controlled fall. You launch yourself upward and forward, trusting that each one-foot landing will keep you upright.

It doesn't take much to bring you down, so watch your step—but not so closely that you fear taking it. When you fall, take the advice of that well-known running expert, Frank Sinatra: pick yourself up and get back in the race.

Take Care

Runner's World magazine opens each month with the stuff of dreams—an oversized photo, usually featuring a long shot of dramatic scenery, titled a "Rave Run." You not only don't see cars in these shots, you rarely even see roads.

Our own running courses seldom measure up to these high standards. Yet we have routes that rate private raves. Definitions vary widely, but one trait links them—few or no cars.

An irony here is that we have to drive to places that let us run away from traffic. The finer the course, the longer the drive usually is.

I often have to take almost half as long driving to the course and back as I spend running it. One route travels in and around my local fairgrounds, where very few drivers go at my running hour.

One day, though, a fleet of rumbling, belching trucks invaded this spot for a loggers' convention. They disturbed my peace and offended my sense of place. I thought, how dare they take over my course!

But public roads are never ours, no matter what the laws say about shared access and rights-of-way. The roads belong to vehicles, if only because they're more than ten times our size and travel more than ten times our speed.

Most of us still run on roads because they're always right outside our door, they offer smooth, weatherproof surfaces, and (in town at least) they're lighted for early-morning and late-evening runs. We hit the roads for this convenience, and in doing so court their dangers.

Stories of collisions between cars and runners seldom end as happily as Laurie Corbin's. She ran in the 2000 Olympic Marathon Trials and was thrilled to be there—or to be anywhere—a month after being struck down by a car and seriously injured during a training run.

Many runners can recall near misses in chilling detail. One morning I shuffled into an intersection on a green light. From the left, through the red light on the otherwise empty street, came a taxicab at full throttle.

The cabbie saw me too late. His tires screeched and smoked as he slid past the spot marked with an invisible "X" where I would have been if my brakes hadn't worked. The driver looked at me with an embarrassed shrug, while I put a hand over my heart in relief.

This incident didn't result from the driver's intent to do harm, but from his inattention or impatience. That's the case with most of our encounters with cars. Our best defense as runners, then, is to stay hyper-attentive and extra-patient ourselves.

We see drivers much more clearly than they see us. We see them rubbing sleep from their eyes or checking their faces in the mirror.

We see drivers with the day's newspaper folded across the steering wheel. We see them eating, drinking, smoking—sometimes all at once—or holding a cell phone in one hand and gesturing to an unseen listener with the other.

Drivers speed as if the posted limits were the slowest pace they could legally travel. Drivers wander into biking lanes, which serve equally well as running lanes.

Drivers turn without signaling for us mere pedestrians, and drive at dawn or dusk without lights. Drivers gun through yellow lights and coast through stop signs, without looking to see who might be about to dash across their path.

If it helps you feel better, you may point a warning finger (no, not *that* finger) at an offending driver. But don't shake a fist or shout an obscenity—and please don't pound the side of a car, or run over its hood like a steeplechaser at the water jump. This is the runner's version of road rage, and it can have dire consequences when drivers hold a deadly weapon in their hands.

When you point a finger, remember that your other fingers point back at yourself. You drive more than you run, and probably make the same mistakes that infuriate you in other drivers.

Examine your own habits, both as a driver and as a runner. Then promise yourself and those who love you that you'll drive more courteously and run more defensively—and vice versa.

Run as if the drivers can't see you. Drive as if the lives of fellow runners are in your hands.

DRESSING
and shoeing comfortably and minimally

Function, Not Fashion

Running is not a style show. At least it doesn't need to be, though it sometimes appears that way in the era of $100-plus running shoes and designer "jogging suits."

What are the essentials? Good shoes and whatever else feels comfortable. Dress for function, not fashion; for comfort and according to weather conditions, not for attention; for protection, not for show.

One of the beauties of running as a sport is its low cost. It can be a very inexpensive activity. Don't deny yourself this advantage by outfitting yourself as if you were heading for the ski slopes.

Here are a few rules for dressing well to run:

▶ **Splurge on shoes**—running shoes, not those designed for other sports. Running shoes can be pricey, but they're your most important investment, not a luxury. Your welfare and performance depend on your feet, so protect them well. Plan to spend an average of $80 for a good pair of shoes, and to replace them at least once a year. This will be your major recurring equipment expenditure.

▶ **Keep the rest of your wardrobe simple and inexpensive.** Use what you have in your drawers and closets, improvising instead of running up a big clothing bill. Sure, the stylish clothing looks nice; by all means wear it if you already own it. But if your running-gear budget is limited, spend most of it on shoes. Any loose-fitting, non-chafing shirts, shorts, or pants will work almost as well as the high-fashion items.

▶ **Dress inconspicuously, except at dark.** This tip applies mainly to beginners, who already feel that all eyes are upon them. Beginning runners will feel better about running in public if their clothing doesn't draw special attention. Whenever you run at dawn, dusk, or in the dark in traffic, however, make sure to wear light colors and a reflective vest (or at least reflective tape).

▶ **Don't overdress.** Inexperienced runners tend to dress as if they're going to sit outside to watch a football game. They feel toasty warm at the start, but heat up as they run, and soon wish they'd left half their clothing at home. Leave excess clothing there, or dress in layers (for a cold day, a jacket over a sweatshirt over a T-shirt) that can be stripped off en route.

▶ **Don't over-sweat.** That is, don't intentionally overdress to over-sweat, imagining you'll lose weight that way. Your body temperature will soar and you will lose sweat, but you'll regain the "lost" water weight as soon as you rehydrate. Nothing will have happened to the rest of your body weight. Instead, lose weight the natural, safe way—with sensible exercise and diet— not by sweating yourself dry.

What to Wear, When

Weather tells you what to wear. Add or subtract layers of clothing depending on how hot, cold, or wet the day is.

This advice would be too obvious to mention if some runners didn't forget the twenty-degree rule. They dress comfortably for standing still, then grow uncomfortably—even intolerably—hot after the first mile of running.

Running causes the perceived temperature to jump by about twenty degrees. A nice seventy-degree Fahrenheit day suddenly feels like a steamy ninety; a chilly thirty becomes a pleasant fifty.

Dress with the twenty-degree rule in mind

Dress with this rule in mind. The right clothes for running will seem too skimpy while you're standing still, so build the twenty-degree factor into your rating of clothing needs.

You'll feel HOT when it's eighty degrees Fahrenheit or higher outdoors, and you're sitting or moving slowly. If you're running, you'll feel hot even when it's only about sixty outside. You'll feel WARM when the weather is in the sixties and seventies while you're at rest, but in the forties and fifties while running.

You'll feel COOL while lounging about in temperatures in the fifties, and when running at slightly above the freezing mark. When you're not running hard, any temperature below fifty degrees Fahrenheit will seem COLD. But when you're running, the cold-weather line might drop well below thirty degrees Fahrenheit and you'll still feel comfortable.

Dress for your running temperature. Start each run with a foundation of shoes, shorts, socks (if you use them; I don't), and underwear (if you need any besides what's built into running clothing). Then supplement this wardrobe as needed:

▶ **Hot day**—Add only the lightest top that modesty requires.

▶ **Warm day**—Add a T-shirt.

▶ **Cool day**—Add long pants and a long-sleeved shirt or light jacket.

▶ **Cold day**—Pull on a hat and gloves, and perhaps another pair of pants and a balaclava, for protection from extreme cold.

▶ **Rainy day**—Add a cap with a bill to keep your vision clear. Rain suits serve both to repel water and to keep out cold, without adding bulk or restricting movement. I definitely depend on a rain suit myself, especially since I live in the wet Pacific Northwest.

Remember, to a runner, there's no bad weather. There are only the wrong clothes for whatever weather the day might bring.

Going Barefoot

I'll always be a barefoot boy at heart, if not in practice or in age. As a kid, I hardly ever wore shoes unless I was in school or church. Later, I ran barefoot. This practice started during the Percy Cerutty craze of the late 1950s. Cerutty coached Herb Elliott, the greatest miler of his and perhaps any era.

Cerutty preached a back-to-nature approach. What could be more natural than running barefoot? Elliott trained barefoot but wore shoes in races. Another runner, Bruce Tulloh from Britain, went the next step and raced barefoot as well.

This looked good to me. I ran this way in training on a grass track, raced a few times shoeless in high school and college cross-country, ran unshod in beach races in California, even kicked off my irritating shoes and padded the last five miles of a marathon au naturel.

All of that happened more than 50,000 miles ago. My feet have weakened from mileage and abuse and, over the decades, have become so accustomed to shoes and orthotics that I can no longer run more than a few steps without protection.

The closest I now come to barefoot running is not letting socks come between me and my shoes. Truly naked feet are an ever-more-pleasant and ever-more-distant memory.

Rarely do I even hear now about anyone trying to run barefoot. In fact, the trend seems to be moving in the opposite direction, toward wearing shoes offering ever more cushioning and support.

So I was surprised to read a feature by Marc Bloom about Ian Dobson in *The Harrier* magazine. He's an Oregonian like I am, but I knew him only as one of the best high school cross-country runners in the nation, and then as a star at Stanford University.

Reading the article, I found him to be a boy after my own heart, a faster version of the me from forty years earlier.

Bloom wrote, "Whenever he can, like doing strides on the track or field, Dobson runs barefoot." Dobson said, "I try not to wear shoes. Barefoot, you strengthen your feet. I never have foot problems."

Dobson didn't manage to convince me to kick off my shoes again for the soft parts of my runs. However, he did suggest an alternative practice. If the best exercise for feet is barefoot running, the next best could be barefoot walking whenever possible the rest of the day.

Maybe I must wear shoes outside the house. But I can kick them off at the door, and pad around my house barefoot or wearing only socks during the cold season.

The Japanese have the right idea. They leave their shoes at the doorstep for ritualistic reasons, but this practice gives them some of the strongest feet in the world. On a visit to Japan, I eagerly went along with the local custom of leaving my shoes loosely tied, for easy slipping off and on.

A month before my Asian trip, I'd taken my longest run of the year, and an ankle injury had persisted ever since. But my pain eased on the trip, and soon disappeared after my bare feet touched home ground. Or at least home floors.

Running Lightly

I'll say up front that my views on shoes are not those that prevail in the running-shoe industry and in the magazines that survey this marketplace. The industry urges runners to provide their feet with the most protection that money can buy. The trend in shoemaking is more: more padding, more support, more stability, more heel lift.

However, you might be a runner who responds better to less, as I am. As allies, I have two New Zealanders who've made strong cases for wearing the lightest shoes that can be tolerated.

At age forty-one, Jack Foster ran a 2:11 (two-hour, eleven-minute) marathon, which stood for sixteen years as a world masters' record. Conventional thinking insists that an older body needs more protection, yet Foster preferred the most minimal of shoes.

"I was introduced to running over farmlands, where the under-foot conditions were soft and yielding, developing good foot strength and flexibility," he said. "I ran first in light tennis shoes because there were no suitable training flats in those days."

Foster believed that those shoes forced him to learn proper running style: "We ran in those flimsy, light shoes and developed a 'feel' for the ground. We learned to land properly or got sore legs, since we couldn't rely on the shoes to absorb any shock.

"We got into a light-footed gait that moved us over hill and dale very effectively. I'm certain this [style] helped me stay injury free."

Even after he set records and ran in the 1972 Olympic Marathon as a master, and shoe companies begged him to wear their latest high-tech training models, he stayed a minimalist. He ran daily "in shoes most people consider too light even for racing."

Perhaps Foster was one of the rare and lucky individuals born with perfect feet. This was not true for another New Zealander.

If any runner had reason to give her feet maximum protection, it was Anne Audain, an Olympic marathoner and onetime world recordholder at 5000 meters.

As a child, she could barely walk because of a deformity similar to clubfoot. Doctors corrected that condition when she reached her teens, and she started running as part of her therapy.

Audain's feet were never perfect, but she didn't baby them. Bob Wischnia, former shoe-review editor at *Runner's World*, once asked her if her feet still bothered her.

"Sometimes they can be very painful and feel like they did before I had them operated on," she responded. "When it's cold they have a tendency to throb a bit. However, they've never stopped me."

Did she wear special shoes? "Heavens, no. I race and train in the same pair of racing flats.

"You have to understand that when I first started running, my doctors weren't too keen on the idea. One of them told me—and I think he might have been trying to discourage me—'If you're going to do this running, run in the nearest thing to bare feet.' Since that time I've always raced and trained in the lightest shoes I can find."

Tips on Shoes

While I don't recommend racing shoes for everyone all the time, I do endorse several points made by these two Kiwis.

Here are my suggestions, as someone who has always responded best to the least of all shoes:

▶ Wear the lightest shoes you can tolerate, not the heaviest you can carry. If your current shoes feel clunky, step down to a lesser model and see if your running becomes smoother and quieter.

▶ Wear the same type of shoes (if not the same pair) for all purposes, rather than switching models from training to racing. Race day, the time of greatest stress on your feet and legs, is not the time to risk a shoe change that could introduce a new set of stresses.

▶ You're built to run unshod, though modern surfaces no longer allow that luxury. Stay as close as possible to barefoot, instead of distancing yourself as far as possible from the earth.

▶ Light shoes enhance good running form. Heavy ones let your shoes, instead of your feet and legs, act as shock absorbers, so your form can become sloppy.

▶ If your form improves in lighter shoes, but high mileage on hard surfaces still hurts, maybe the problem lies in your running routine and not in your shoes. Search your schedule for the trouble spot.

▶ The biggest drawback of racing shoes isn't your risk of injury, but their cost. You usually must pay more for less material and less durability.

▶ The biggest drawback of lightweight, cushiony, and flexible training shoes is that they're hard to find. Today's models increasingly veer away from those traits.

But I'll leave the final statement about shoes to someone who knows running shoe–making intimately, from the inside. Jeff Johnson was in charge of research and development at Nike in the company's early years, designing its top-of-the-line models.

He wouldn't fully agree or necessarily disagree with my conclusions above. He insists that the choice of shoes must depend on an individual's feet. Johnson said after leaving the company, "It is the responsibility of serious runners to learn their particular needs. This isn't an easy task, given the proliferation of products. But the rewards of finding the shoe that ranks number one in your personal survey is well worth the effort."

Shoe Abuse

Is this any way to treat a new pair of shoes, which I claim to embrace as an object of affection? Fresh out of the box, before I'd even run a step in them, I gutted the original insoles that had been glued inside.

These shoes escaped with less abuse than my typical pair. Usually I follow the gutting with razor-cutting the seams that bind my forefeet too tightly. But this was a rare pair offering enough room for my duck-like quadruple-Es.

Abusing shoes is a longstanding practice of mine. I don't recall any model ever going onto my feet without needing alterations. I know without running in it where the shoe will cause me trouble, and take corrective action before it does.

The surgery is less severe than it once was. I've been known to slice across the width of the sole to increase forefoot flexibility, to put heels to a grinder to decrease their flare, to take a hole puncher to the toe box to increase ventilation.

I've never cut away the upper front of a shoe, exposing my toes to the breeze as ultra-runners do. This was the only way that Paul Reese (author of three books on multi-day running) could make room for his swelling feet while running across the United States. I'd probably do the same if I ever ran great lengths.

As is, the surgery I perform is rather minor compared to past practices. But it's still necessary if my feet are to stay happy in direct contact with my shoes, without any socks intervening.

I've given up looking for the elusive Perfect Shoe, but I keep searching for a better one. Each new pair props up my hopes, then more often than not dashes them.

This happened recently with a model that's best left unnamed here. It started life on the road—after my customary alterations—with great promise. But it soon caused me a groin and hip problem that eased only after I retired the shoes.

This left me one pair short in my usual two-shoe rotation. So I went shopping at my favorite discount sports store, which specializes in closeout and unpopular models. There I found an Asics model. It met all of my requirements except two.

These shoes were cushy enough, flexible, and fairly light. So I paid more than my normal maximum, then a few days later groaned when it went on sale for half its original price.

But paying too much wasn't the reason I soon abused the shoe. The fact is, even the most promising shoes need some whipping into shape.

This pair avoided the too-tight strapping design of the forefoot, which is now nearly standard in running shoes. But these Asics carried two other features that have also become standard: round laces that don't stay tied as well as the flat kind, and glued-down insoles that are again winning out over the removable type.

The first change was easy. I yanked out the round laces and replaced them with a grungy old flat pair.

Surgery on the insoles was more difficult. I first attacked them with pliers, then followed with a screwdriver to gouge out the left-over rubber so my orthotics would lie flat. Finally I slipped a used insole over the orthotics.

My first run in these shoes wasn't perfect. But they would've abused me much more if I hadn't worked them over first. And their fit improved on subsequent runs.

FUELING
by eating and drinking in moderation

Pro-Protein

Warning: what you're about to read here could confuse you, if it contradicts what you've been taught about nutrition. Or it could anger you, because it questions your fondly held beliefs.

The advice in this chapter defies conventional wisdom about what a runner should and shouldn't eat. Most experts will tell you that carbohydrates are good, fats are bad, and proteins are questionable because they often come in packages with few carbs and loads of fat.

Until the late 1990s, I ate the usual high-carb, low-fat, and therefore low-protein runner's diet. But I began to change my regimen when spells of dizziness suddenly hit me and continued rather dramatically for a year.

Lowering my intake of refined carbohydrates (especially sugar, to which I was addicted) and eating more protein helped me more than any other therapy. Eating meat acted as quickly and dramatically as a prescription drug to bring my head back to level.

I've suffered from no apparent penalties. My visible fat, as body weight, hasn't increased. Nor has my invisible fat, as cholesterol readings, gone up.

Lower-carb diets have grown to faddish proportions these days. But a runner introduced me to the idea before Dr. Atkins and his fellow authors had the chance.

A testimonial to protein-power eating came from one of my oldest friends. Jeff Kroot was the first runner I met after moving to California in 1967. He was an architecture student at UC Berkeley and moonlighted as a photographer for *Track & Field News* (where I'd come west to work). I already knew his name when we met at a race in Sacramento.

My first impression of Kroot was how big he was for a guy who ran so well. He wasn't fat; he was just solid. Our abilities were similar, and I was pretty good then. He outweighed me by fifty pounds, then forty, and finally thirty as his mileage went up.

Kroot quit running races in the 1980s. Though he kept running, he cut back his mileage—and his weight inched up over the years to an all-time high. Traditional dieting had little effect. Extra running injured his overburdened legs.

Then he found an adviser who told Kroot exactly what he needed to hear: "You're one of those people who's sensitive to carbohydrates. Cut way back, especially on sugar and flour, increase your protein, and see what happens."

Kroot did as he was told. He ate all the meat, poultry, seafood, dairy products, and legumes he wanted, but studiously limited the carbs.

"I've lost thirty pounds," he told me soon after changing his food balance. His mileage had gone up as his poundage had come down. "I've run several ten- to fifteen-milers recently," he said.

Kroot didn't diet, at least not in terms of cutting back total calories. He just said no to constant carbo-loading.

I asked him whether his change in diet had affected his energy. The party line among runners states that carbs are our fuel of choice. What happens if they run low?

"My energy stays steady all day," said Kroot. "Before I felt highs and lows, because I was in effect hypoglycemic." In other words, his body had trouble regulating blood sugar, but his low-carb diet stabilized it.

A diet that offers weight loss and energy gain is tempting. Unfortunately, a stronger everyday temptation, the urge to carbo-load, stands in the way of carbo-lowering.

Keep a sense of balance in your eating

I'm not warning you to never again eat a slice of bread; I'm just recommending not to eat half a loaf in one sitting. I'm not inviting you to eat a daily pound of steak—just not to skip meat completely. This is a plea to keep a sense of balance in your eating—and to consider tilting that balance slightly differently than runners usually do.

Big Drinkers

I'm not a big drinker. I've never carried or worn a water bottle or a camel's-hump pack. I find it's easier to carry cash to buy drinks at machines or stores, or to stop at water fountains or hoses. Yet I seldom feel the need for these impromptu aid stations. And I've never run into serious trouble from drinking too little.

A few times, though, I've suffered from taking in too much water. My usual symptom has been late-race or post-race nausea, quickly eased by downing a salty snack such as pretzels or chips or a salty drink such as broth.

Seeing runners with bottles bouncing and sloshing against their butts during their easiest cool-weather runs seems amusing to me. But I can't judge them wrong, and myself right. No one else can be sure how much and how often you as a runner need to drink.

On a trip in May 2002, I happened to pick up a copy of the *Wall Street Journal.* It isn't on my usual reading list, but was the only free newspaper offered at the airport gate. In it I read an article entitled, "Why You're Drinking Too Much Water." It debunked the "eight-by-eight" plan, the supposed need to drink eight, eight-ounce glasses of water each day.

Betsy McKay wrote, "Bottled-water makers heavily market their products based on this theory. But a growing number of health experts say the advice might not hold water. Researchers who have tried to pinpoint the origin of the eight-by-eight rule have come up dry."

McKay then quoted several medical authorities. The consensus is that the drinking "rule" is nothing but an averaging of extremes. Some of us need much more, while some of us can get by on far less.

Wanting a fixed formula grows out of a more-is-better mindset common to runners. We're tempted to think that if a certain amount is good, then doubling it must be twice as good. This happens with mileage and speed, so why not with fluids?

Thirst has evolved over the eons as a health and safety signal

Many runners force fluids. They worry about finding or carrying enough to drink during their runs. "Enough" can at times be too much.

"For most people the consequences of drinking too much are simply extra trips to the bathroom," wrote McKay in her *Wall Street Journal* piece. "But for a few, excessive amounts can be harmful, even fatal."

I don't want to alarm you, but only to inform you of the rare condition of hyponatremia, also known as "water intoxication." Drinking too much water can dilute your body's sodium to the point of serious consequences. (The nausea I've experienced a few times might be a mild form of this ailment, since salt relieves it.)

Within the last few years, a Chicago doctor sued San Diego's Rock 'n' Roll Marathon because he suffered a post-race seizure that left him permanently impaired. He charged race officials with negligence for not supplying enough drinks. Yet his own medical experts testified that he'd fallen victim to hyponatremia because he'd drunk too much.

I'm not suggesting that running and drinking don't mix. It's dumb, if not dangerous, to drink too little. This can cause you to overheat, which can drain you of strength and endurance—and even raise the risks of heat exhaustion and heatstroke. But this debate brings up that tricky question: how can we know our true needs?

McKay wrote at the end of her article, "After much thought, nutritionists have come up with an almost-too-obvious-to-mention guideline for determining hydration needs: drink enough so you don't get thirsty."

Runners have been taught that thirst is an unreliable indicator of dehydration. But is it?

Thirst has evolved over the eons as a health and safety signal. It hasn't suddenly failed us.

As one soft-drink ad admonishes, "Obey your thirst." Tune in to it; trust it to tell you when to drink and how much.

Golden Rules

We're able to make life-enhancing and life-extending choices every day. In the 1970s, a team of California researchers concluded that people who regularly practiced seven Golden Rules of health could add seven to eleven years to their lives. Of these seven rules, five deal with what we put in our stomachs and lungs, the fifth with rest, and the seventh with exercise.

1. **Don't smoke.**

2. **Maintain normal weight.**

3. **Eat regularly, and not between meals.**

4. **Eat breakfast.**

5. **Sleep eight hours a night.**

6. **Drink (alcohol) only moderately.**

7. **Exercise regularly.**

Dr. Lester Breslow of the UCLA School of Public Health said, "The daily habits of people have a great deal more to do with what makes them sick and when they die than all the influences of medicine. A man of fifty-five who follows all seven good health habits has the same physical status as a person twenty-five to thirty years younger who follows less than two of the health practices."

Exercise is at the bottom of the list, but that doesn't imply that it's the least important. Dr. Nedra Belloc of the California Health Department, who worked with Breslow, said, "In our study the men who reported that they engaged in active sports had the lowest mortality—just half that experienced by men who reported they only sometimes exercised."

Running wasn't mentioned by name, but certainly would be included among the "active sports." And running usually, though indirectly, promotes most of the other good health habits on Dr. Breslow's list.

Runners almost never smoke, for example, because the potential damage from lung pollution seems too obvious. Dr. Peter Wood, who in the 1970s began a long-term study of runner's health habits at Stanford University, said, "Our sample of forty-five older runners contained not a single smoker, although the average number of smokers of similar age is 38 percent [at the time of his study]. However, several of them had smoked at one time when not running."

Become better at listening to what your body needs

Runner's World magazine surveyed its readers on that same topic in the mid-1970s, and found similar results. Only one runner in 500 was a smoker, though 20 percent had smoked regularly before taking up the sport.

The non-smoking habit, said Dr. Wood, immediately gives runners "an enormous health advantage, since the evidence linking smoking to cancer, heart disease and emphysema is now overwhelming."

Evidence is equally strong that obesity is a drag on health. Adult runners typically carry at least 10 percent less fat than inactive people their age.

"Everyone knows that exercise burns fat," said Dr. Wood. "But it takes up to fifty miles of running to burn one pound. Less well known is the fact that vigorous exercise regulates the appetite.

"This is probably the runners' secret. They manage to adjust caloric intake very nicely so that they neither waste away nor become overweight."

Alcohol is, in Wood's words, "an interesting subject." A high percentage of runners drink it, he said, "but I know of no runners who drink it obsessively." That is, runners seem better able to judge their limits. They become better at listening to what their bodies need, and what they can and can't tolerate.

Great Weight Watch

Weight can sneak up on you. Just one pound per year multiplies into twenty pounds over two decades. This happened to me while I wasn't paying attention.

I had quit weighing myself in the 1980s. I knew I'd gained some pounds, but didn't know how many and didn't care enough to do anything about it.

I'd never dieted. Oh, I'd kept watch on some foods in my diet and the timing of meals versus runs, but I'd never tried to control the total amount I ate.

Take care of your running, I thought, and your weight will take care of itself. Problem was, though, that my running had dropped by half since my weight was at its twenty-year low.

Then I visited my doctor. Usually only a stubborn illness would send me to his office, and at those times my weight would've dropped due to sickness.

This time I went for routine tests. At weigh-in I recorded my highest reading ever. The doctor lectured me about my unattractive BMI (body-mass index), and the weight's effects on my blood-pressure readings. I thought more about my weight's direct effects on running.

I'm beyond worrying about race results; I've run my best times. Current concerns are more physiological than statistical. Each added pound adds at least three extra pounds of force to your feet and legs. Running heavy feels tighter and less fluid. It's also less efficient aerobically, since the aerobic-capacity (VO2-max) formula features weight as one of its components.

Plus it can be embarrassing when I can't fasten the top button of my pants without turning it into a tourniquet.

The solution, of course, would be to run more and eat less. Run more? At this point, I probably can't run enough extra miles to make much of a difference in weight control. Instead, I need to pay more attention to the other side of the weight-control equation.

Eat less? That's so easy to write, but so hard to do for this runner, whose appetite hasn't changed much from his teenage years. Losing weight without running more requires adopting the second most important exercise habit: the table push-back.

Weighting Games

Being super-skinny doesn't always make a runner better; I'm not promoting eating disorders or obsessions here. But most adult runners could profit from losing some pounds.

If you have some weight to lose, as I did (and maybe still do), determine what your ideal weight should be; recognize how much better you could run at that weight; and compare yourself to other runners, pound-for-pound.

What should you weigh? Please don't look at the tiny 120-pound front-runners (and those are the men!) in big-time races and think you're too fat. You haven't looked like they do since puberty. And please don't listen to your mother or other well-meaning kinfolk who say, "You're too thin." If you look healthy by the standards of people who don't run, you're almost surely overweight for a runner.

Don't trust the standard charts, which fail to account for differences in frame size and muscle mass. Body-fat readings are better, but inconvenient to check regularly.

Your scale can give you a daily figure, but only for what you actually weigh and not what you should weigh.

For longtime runners, the best guideline to use is the weight at which you ran your best. For newer runners, that might be your weight when you stopped growing taller. Or it could simply be the highest weight you'll accept before vowing, "The rest must go."

Most adult runners could profit from losing some pounds

What difference does weight make? One of my all-time favorite teachers is Tom Osler, who in his *Serious Runner's Handbook* wrote, "Every pound of unneeded weight has a measurable effect on a runner's final time. From my own experience I estimate that I lose two seconds per mile for each excess pound of body fat."

This is only Osler's experience, but he's one of the wisest and most analytical runners I've ever known. His formula means that a ten-pound gain would slow a runner's times by twenty seconds per mile, which would become a full minute in a 5K or four-plus minutes in a half-marathon.

How fast can you carry your weight? Size matters in our sport. The best athletes are small and light.

Very few runners ever "beat their weight" in a marathon. That is, they rarely run fewer minutes than their weight in pounds—which would require a 130-pounder to break 2:10 and a 200-pounder to run sub-3:20.

Very few runners ever "beat their weight" in a marathon

This formula discriminates against women, the best of whom seldom run within thirty minutes of their poundage. The fastest woman for her size appears to have been Marian Sutton of Britain, who weighed about 140 pounds when she ran 2:28 (a weight-to-time factor of plus eight).

The fastest man, pound for pound, probably was Derek Clayton. The Australian set a world record of 2:08:34 (about 129 minutes) while weighing about 160 pounds—an amazing minus-thirty-one factor. Much more typical is Bill Rodgers, who PR'ed at 129 minutes (2:09) and 128 pounds.

How close have you come to running your weight? My best was plus-twenty-two, and that was a long time and many pounds ago. I'm less of a runner now in terms of my distance and time, and I'm happy to say also in terms of my weight. I determined what would be an acceptable weight (midway between my old low and recent high), ran a little more, ate a little less, and reached my ideal.

Running far more and eating much less probably would mean I'd shed more weight, but I enjoy both activities too much to make grim work of them.

HEALING
and preventing injuries and illnesses

Getting Hurt

I'm not a doctor, but I often play one in my working life. Questions about running medicine come my way almost every day. I decline to guess at specific diagnoses or to suggest medical treatments, despite having soaked up some knowledge from editing the books of four different doctors.

But I do talk in general terms about getting hurt and getting well. In that area I'm an expert, having done both so often myself.

This I can tell you about injuries: everyone gets hurt eventually. You might argue that you've never been injured. You've read all the right books and taken all the proper precautions.

But there are other ways to hurt yourself. While you may be smart enough not to make running mistakes, you probably aren't lucky enough to avoid all the accidents that can interrupt your running.

I've repeatedly made all the dumb Big Three Mistakes—running too far, too fast, too soon. These injuries were self-inflicted and therefore largely preventable.

But accidents happen to the smartest runners: trip over a dog and crack a rib (yours, not his)...stumble over a sidewalk and smash a knee...step off a curb and sprain an ankle.

Don't let the dire tone of the preceding paragraphs scare you. This too I can tell you about injuries:

▶ **Most are minor.** Seldom do these injuries interfere with normal life, or require a doctor's help, or extensive and expensive care.

▶ **Most are temporary.** Usually they respond quickly to simple adjustments in training type, distance, and pace.

▶ **Most allow other activities.** If you can't continue to run for a while, you can still choose an agreeable alternative.

Let's say an injury has knocked you off your feet. A doctor can diagnose why you're hurting and suggest what to do about it. But only you are responsible for your own rehab.

Your best friend now isn't a medical professional. It's your own pain, which tells you what you can and can't do while recovering. Whatever the specifics of the injury that ails you, you can find a path back to health that enables you to heal while staying active, fit, and sane.

First Aid for Injuries

Too many runners get hurt. This year, as in any year, at least one of every two of you reading this page will be hurt badly enough to cut back on running, stop completely, see a doctor, or all of the above.

Too many injured runners react to their problems the way mechanical incompetents do when their cars break down. They're helpless against any gadget more complex than a can opener, so breakdowns confuse and scare them.

Unfortunate drivers react in one of three ways: (1) they take their ailing car to an expensive expert, (2) they try to keep it limping along, or (3) they quit using it and hope it recovers by itself.

Injured runners are likewise frustrated and frightened by their own breakdowns and by the technical articles they read about them. So they turn their problems over to a specialist, keep running through pain, or quit.

Actually, the running body is so predictable in its operation that you can do most of its routine maintenance yourself, if you know a few basic rules. Engage it in the type of activity it wants, in the amount and at the intensity it can handle, and it keeps running well. If you abuse it instead, it breaks down.

To treat your own injuries, first banish the notion that you can do nothing to help yourself

To treat your own injuries, first banish the notion that you can do nothing to help yourself. You don't need to be a doctor, or know the names of your bones and connective tissues, or know the physiological principles behind your injury to practice effective first aid and then to prevent the same breakdown from happening again.

The following self-help plan tells you how to assess the seriousness of an injury, how to help your body recover from an injury, and how you can prevent injuries from happening. These are things you can do without going to a doctor, spending a lot of money, or losing too much running time.

Injury Self-Help Plan

How Serious Is the Injury?

When you first hurt, assess how serious the pain is by testing what you can and can't do. Pain comes in degrees, defined by how much it limits your running distance and pace. Fourth degree is the worst level of pain and decreases to first degree pain.

▶ **Fourth degree pain:** It is impossible to run without sharp pain, a pronounced limp, or both.

▶ **Third degree pain:** Walking is relatively pain-free, and some running is possible, but your pain increases as your distance and pace go up.

▶ **Second degree pain:** Walking is easy, but running still hurts. Races, speed training, long runs, and hills are the usual suspects. Uneven surfaces can sharpen some pains.

▶ **First degree pain:** Your low-grade pain is evident at the start of training, decreases as your run progresses, then reappears after you stop.

How to Recover

Throw away your old training schedule for now, and maybe forever, because it might have put you in the bad shape you're in. Avoid your usual training partners, because you'll either feel depressed about not being able to keep up with them, or you'll forget your injury, attempt to keep up, and do further damage.

Choose your activity and its intensity according to the severity of your symptoms. Tune in to your pain, then carefully follow these steps through rehab to recovery until you can train comfortably at the first-degree level.

▶ **Fourth-degree injury:** Substitute a related activity such as swimming, bicycling, or walking that causes no pain and allows you to keep training. Do this activity during your usual running times. These activities take nearly all pressure off most injuries, while still allowing steady effort.

▶ **Third-degree injury:** Start running cautiously, and call off the day's run if your discomfort causes a limp or favoring of your injured limb. Continue walking as long as you can move ahead without limping or increasing the pain. Observe these two conditions at all stages of recovery.

▶ **Second-degree injury:** While walking, add intervals of slow running, as few as one minute in five at first. Eliminate the types of runs that cause distress. Gradually build up your amount of running until you reach the next stage of recovery.

▶ **First-degree injury:** Tip your training balance in favor of running mixed with walk breaks when you can't yet tolerate steady pressure. Many injuries respond better to intermittent rather than constant running. Stay alert to signs of slow or sudden decline into second- or third-degree pain.

Once you've worked your way to first-degree training, all pain and tenderness should be blessedly gone. Run steadily again, but gently for a while as you regain lost fitness. Run a little slower than usual, resisting any long or fast efforts until you can handle the short, slow runs comfortably.

This same sequence of advice applies to stretching and strengthening exercises during your recovery period. Again, let pain be your guide. The right exercises in the right amounts will promote your healing. But if you exercise too violently, you can set back your recovery.

When you start to hurt, stop! Cutting short any painful activity during rehab isn't a sign of weakness but of wisdom.

How to Prevent Injuries

Nearly all running injuries are self-inflicted. They usually don't happen by accident, but result from going too long, too fast, too often, or some combination of these mistakes.

Nothing grabs your attention so much as a serious injury. Consider the following injury-prevention (or at least injury-reducing) lessons I've learned the hard way—by ignoring them and thus suffering injury.

▶ **Warm up slowly.** You never quite know in advance how a run will go, so withhold judgment until you've run very easily for ten minutes, or about a mile. This time of testing will either loosen you up or wake up latent pains, so wait until you're warmed up before making the day's decision to push on or pull out.

▶ **Set speed limits.** Run fast—in a race, or in speed training at race pace or slightly faster—no more than 10 percent of your miles. Some speed is essential to a racer, but a little goes a long way, and too much leads nowhere.

▶ **Do less than your best most of the time.** Run about nine miles in every ten at a relaxed pace—at least one minute per mile slower than you could race that same distance. For a twenty-two–minute 5K runner, and a forty-five–minute 10K runner, this means averaging about eight-and-a-half–minute (8:30) miles on runs of similar length.

▶ **Progress slowly.** Add no more than 10 percent to the length of any run from week to week. For a marathon trainer starting long runs at ten miles, this means increasing mileage only to eleven a week later.

▶ **Rest after races.** Take off at least one day of running for each hour of racing (and one day regardless of how short that race was). Resting is the quickest way to shake off racing soreness. If you run a four-hour marathon, take off at least four days before running again.

▶ **Recover carefully.** Follow the Jack Foster Rule, named for the legendary New Zealander who ran a 2:11 marathon as a master. Allow at least one day of recovery (meaning easy running) for each mile of the race you ran, before you train long or hard or race again. If you run a 10K, run only easily for the next week.

Sneezin' Season

It comes every November, as surely as the falling leaves and falling temperatures. November is my traditional month for a cold, and one such month brought a double whammy.

That November started with the sneezes and sniffles of a common cold. I blamed it on watching a cross-country race in the rain, then sitting too long afterward in soggy clothes.

Then that month ended with a new cold. I blamed that one on too much travel and too little sleep.

Colds usually come for good reasons. You don't "catch" them; you earn them. Rather than berate myself over the mistakes I've made, I'll tell you what I do once a cold settles in. In a single word: nothing.

Sheehan introduced me to the simplest, and possibly best, medical wisdom for treating a cold. The advice wasn't originally his, but he passed it on to me.

"If you do everything you can to combat the cold—rest, fluids, vitamins, medicines, chicken soup—the cold goes away in about a week," Sheehan said. "If you do nothing to treat the symptoms, the cold lasts about seven days."

My own timetable is a little longer. I figure the cold will take three days coming on, three days hanging heavy, and three days clearing up.

During those nine days, I pretty much just wait out the symptoms. At most I drink more, and suck lozenges to cool my initial sore throat.

To run or not to run? I've gone both ways, resting and running easily. Neither seems to have much affect on the cold's timetable, so I run... but within limits.

I don't allow myself any long or fast runs, and definitely no races. Sheehan said, "The cold is a signal that you're already overworked." Continuing to run too hard can turn the cold into something more serious, such as the persistent bronchitis I once suffered for six months.

For a straightforward cold (no fever, no internal upset or loss of appetite, no serious cough, no exhaustion), easy runs most likely won't hurt. Science suggests they could even improve cold symptoms.

Runner's World happened to print an article on this subject that November of my twin colds. Marlene Cimons, a medical reporter, wrote "Cold Truths." The part that most interested me was the subtitled section "To Run or Not to Run?"

The writer cited David Nieman, an exercise scientist at Appalachian State University. He said that modest activity during colds probably won't hurt, but that you should avoid running if you have flu-like symptoms.

"I have a friend who ran a marathon with a fever," said Nieman, "and he suffered from chronic fatigue syndrome for the next two years. He could barely run a mile."

Cimons added, "If you only have a cold, easy running probably won't do any harm—and in fact might even help. Exercise releases adrenaline, also called 'epinephrine,' a natural decongestant, which might explain why so many runners with colds find that a run seems to clear their nasal passages."

Sounds good to me. But I still have to sneak past my well-meaning wife during the cold season to run my few head-clearing miles. Barbara thinks the best way to treat a cold is the one "nothing" that I resist, which is no running at all for the duration.

Predictable Flu

Someone using my name spoke at a race in Reno. This guy was sweating, shaking, and stammering. He acted terminally nervous, stumbling around in search of a theme. Finding none, he cut his remarks short and let the program move on to interviews with the invited runners.

Okay, that actually was a pale version of myself on stage. But I was trying to speak through a deepening case of the flu. By this point in the weekend I could barely remember my children's names, let alone give a coherent talk.

Wait, wait, and wait some more before running hard again after a marathon

The story behind this illness would have been a good one to tell in Reno if the words had been there with me. I could have confessed my mistakes and drawn widely applicable lessons. Now it goes into writing instead.

First let me say that flu is a rare visitor in this body. This case, the worst in memory, started at the Vancouver Marathon. The symptoms didn't appear then, but that's when I put this illness on the next month's calendar.

Marathon recovery is slow. The body can absorb that one blow but doesn't want to take another sizable one for a long time afterward. I've written of runners needing one easy day for each mile of the race before running anything hard again. That's nearly four weeks.

Now I know it's not long enough for me. In fact, pro-marathon experience tells me that the four-week mark is my most risky time. Recovery isn't complete, yet I'm itching for some normal running after all those shortened days. Getting back to normal for me means climbing again to runs of an hour or more. Normal can still be too much at a time like this.

The next race came exactly four weeks after the Vancouver Marathon. The running would take little more than an hour, and I wouldn't race the distance; this was how I rationalized starting. The going was still tough, and the flu symptoms arrived the next day.

This flu wasn't an unlucky break. It was a predictable event, caused by the old mistake of not respecting the recovery time that a marathon demands.

While suffering, I checked old diaries to see when my last flu had been. It had started four weeks and one day after a marathon, or precisely the timing of the latest case.

Coincidence? No, I'd call it a direct correlation.

Lessons? Just the old one that I have to keep relearning. Wait, wait, and wait some more before running hard again after a marathon. A month's wait clearly isn't long enough for me, and I'm still learning what's right.

Easy runs aren't often thrilling. But they're much better than the nothing at all that I ran for fourteen days out of fifteen (the one try ended after a mile) because of the flu.

Part Two

Running Races

Once you start racing, you can expect to improve for a long time. But you can't keep beating your times and increasing your mileage indefinitely.

The improvement clock typically runs for five to ten years. This is how long it usually takes to adapt to the demands of racing and to learn the game.

You can look forward to increasing your pace and distance no matter when you start. Start at age fifteen, and you can count on improving into your twenties. Begin at age fifty-five, and you can improve into your sixties.

Some lucky runners put more than a decade between their first and best races. But their history usually reveals a prolonged stoppage of their clock (usually for injury), a big jump in effort in their later years, or a major shift in emphasis (such as from short track races to long road runs).

Long before I realized it, I was operating according to this classic runner's timetable. I continued to improve my racing performance for seven-and-a-half years (exactly halfway between five and ten years). And in fact, I improved on this timetable twice.

I began my first season of racing as a fourteen-year-old. From then through age twenty-one, I was mainly a miler, running that distance hundreds of times. My personal best dropped by ninety-three seconds during those years, a fairly typical improvement.

Then my progress stalled, for two reasons. I suffered from persistent pain in my Achilles tendon from too much speed training. And I graduated from college and lost the opportunity to race on the track.

I floundered for almost a year, serving on active duty with the Army Reserve, looking for a job, and then settling into work—wondering all the while what to do with my running, if anything. The answer came to me at age twenty-two.

If I couldn't run fast anymore, then why not go long? Road races were sprouting up all across the country at that time, even in my state of Iowa.

I reset my improvement clock, starting over at long distances. A whole new set of PRs came to me in the next seven-plus years, in races ranging from 10K to 50K.

When I reached age twenty-nine, however, my second cycle ended with my most serious injury, one that required foot surgery. Only then did I quit pushing to improve as a racer—but not before I'd put in fifteen years, when training to race was my overriding reason to run.

Both of my improvement cycles ended with injuries. But what happened to me is not what you have to expect when your improvement clock winds down.

Your feet and legs don't have to fail you. Typically, runners' racing performances don't suddenly drop; instead, they gradually level, and then slowly trail off.

This is when you see that you've finally gone as far as you care to push. But this doesn't have to be the end of your running. Instead, it can become the beginning of a new phase, when you can find gentler ways to run.

So when you're in your racing stage, enjoy the fast ride I map out in Part Two. Just realize that this phase will end, and that you can continue to move on afterward.

WINNING without having to outrun anyone

Winners Never Quit

A key lesson to learn early about running is how to win at it. Without this lesson, you'll never learn the others. People who think of themselves as losers don't last long as runners.

I was lucky to last beyond the second minute of my first race day. Everything I do now in this sport is a thank-you to my first high school coach, Dean Roe, who spoke just the right words at the critical moment.

Running my first one-mile race, I thought the only way to win was to stick with the leaders. Their pace chewed me up and spat me off the track after little more than a single lap.

My coach rushed up to ask what was wrong, and I told him with a pained look that distance running wasn't for me. He patted me on the back and said, "You owe me one."

He didn't rub my nose in the locker-room slogan of that era—"Quitters never win, and winners never quit." He just made me promise to run another mile.

The way to finish, my coach said, was to run my own pace instead of someone else's. I managed to run my whole second race, reaching the first level of winning simply by finishing.

Improving is a higher level of winning

Then I aimed to run the distance faster. I couldn't control who else ran the race or how they ran it, but I could find ways to improve my own performance. Improving is a higher level of winning.

Ironically, even while I wasn't trying to finish first, I moved steadily in that direction. While I kept my eyes on my watch, my better placings took care of themselves. I became a state-meet qualifier as a freshman, and then in succeeding years became a placer, winner, and record-setter.

Time improvement stopped in my twenties, but my winning never has. That's because I've refused to let my old times, my permanent PRs, haunt me.

Instead I've adopted a line spoken by the grandest old man of our sport, John A. Kelley, who in the 1930s and '40s was a two-time Boston Marathon winner and three-time Olympian. "I don't judge my success by what I once did," he said much later, "but by what I keep doing."

Kelley continued to run into his nineties. He achieved the highest level of winning, which is continuing long after the fastest times are run and the biggest prizes won. That kind of winning is the best because it lasts the longest.

"Winners never quit" is more than just a locker-room slogan. Runners who feel like they're still winning don't ever want to stop.

I spent my earlier years of running learning and practicing to win in this way. And I'm spending my later years teaching and preaching the idea that winning has little to do with your position in the pack. Some of the biggest winners finish nearer the back than the front.

This message has never been more important to hear. Today's runners find themselves caught between two extreme views of winning. Each is equally misleading.

Words and images from sports media bombard us with the idea that, "There's only one winner, and second place is the first loser."

We see silver medalists sobbing in despair. But if all but one of us is doomed to "lose," why bother even trying against such impossible odds?

The opposite opinion, the one we hear at mass-running events, is that, "Everyone's a winner." If this were true, however, all we'd have to do is show up. If winning were guaranteed to all of us, all the time, how could we enjoy the feeling of triumph?

The truth is, winning is never automatic. Everyone can win, but not without making the effort, and risking defeat, to earn the victory.

We all lose sometimes, and this is necessary and good. Overcoming our occasional losses sweetens our victories.

Most of the student runners I now see each day are new to the sport. I try to play the same role with them as my first coach, Dean Roe, did with me. I strive to not let them drop out in defeat when they're just getting started.

Competition at Its Best

More than forty track seasons have raced past since I first hit my stride as a runner. Stumbling onto the right combination of speed, distance, and consistency led in the spring of 1961 to my first state high school title in the mile. But that season brought me another prize far more lasting—my first lesson in what competition can be at its best.

My story's prologue took place in Chicago, where I'd spent the previous summer working on a farm. During my off hours I ran races with the elders of the sport, grizzled vets in their twenties and thirties.

Until then I'd viewed competition as me-against-the-world. I didn't hate my competitors, but I did fear them for what they tried to take from me. And I didn't care to cozy up to them between races.

Hal Higdon would find later fame as a writer, but at that time he was an Olympic hopeful. Gar Williams would later serve as the president of the Road Runners Club of America, but then, he was a runner almost as talented as Higdon.

The two of them warmed up together for their races. Imagine that: competitors acting like friends.

Arne Richards was an early prototype for today's road racer, compensating with enthusiasm for what he lacked in talent. He offered to pace me in my first track race longer than a mile. Imagine that: competitors cooperating.

I took their lessons back to my high school. In my senior year, I intended to race against the stopwatch, as all my serious competitors from the past season had graduated. I didn't count on creating a rival.

Don Prichard, a half-miler from another school, said, "I'm thinking of stepping up to the mile. Would you be willing to give me some training advice?"

Because this is the nicest question one runner can ask another, I happily handed over some tips. Prichard would repay that favor by locking us in a season-long contest. Thankfully, however, it was between runners who liked and respected each other. We worked together in training, without giving an inch to the other in competition.

Prichard trained through the winter like I did. Almost no one else in Iowa did at that time, so we shared a big head start.

He followed my usual regimen of mixing modest distances with regular speed training. But I tried something new—the longer, slower, base-building approach suddenly in vogue since Arthur Lydiard's New Zealanders won two Olympic races in Rome.

Runners who feel like they're still winning don't ever want to stop

Prichard's training worked better than mine, at least at first. He won the first mile he ever raced, while I lagged ten seconds behind. We raced three more times leading up to the state meet. Prichard won twice, and we tied once.

In a panic to recoup lost speed, I raced mostly half-miles that season. My time at that distance led the state.

I could've dodged Prichard by skipping the mile in favor of the shorter race, but that would've cheapened both of our victories. We'd come this far together, and needed to finish our high school careers in tandem.

As the fastest qualifier at states, Prichard took the pole position. I started to his right as second-quickest.

He offered a clammy hand, and I took it, with mine equally wet with worry. "I hope we both get it," he said with a pained smile. He

didn't have to explain what "it" was—a time at least under 4:21.6
(four minutes, 21.6 seconds) for the state record, and at best a
sub-4:20 mile.

"Good luck," I said with a grin that was almost a grimace. I really
did wish him well, because his luck would help determine mine.

The day didn't go quite as well as either of us had hoped. I
won the race, but missed the state record by a measly six-tenths
of a second.

Bent over at the finish line, hands on knees, we gulped back the
oxygen we'd spent in the past several minutes. "Good ... job,"
Prichard said, his chest heaving as he exhaled.

"Sorry ... it wasn't ... closer," I gasped. I wished we could have
tied ... well, I admit, maybe inches apart but with equal time.

As it turned out, Drake University recruited both of us. We
faced our next race as teammates that fall. In a way we already were.
Team effort had carried us higher than either of us could have
climbed alone.

Ban the Bandit

A running dictionary might carry this definition: "Bandit: One who
runs a race without paying an entry fee or wearing a number. Also
known as a 'turkey'."

Banditry is one of the least-proud traditions of the venerable
Boston Marathon, where these turkeys swell the field by more than
10 percent. The lure of the old race is so strong, and entry standards
so high, that party-crashing here is a spring sport among local
collegians. But the practice also extends to runners old enough to
know better.

I confess I did run as a bandit a few times, before I was old enough
to know better. But I didn't go near the finish chutes or drink from the
water stations.

But I now realize that running numberless was still wrong. I'm
ashamed to have violated one of the two basic rules of racing, and
apologize to those race directors.

The first rule of racing is to enter properly. You register, and you pay the fee. The second most fundamental rule is that you run—or run-walk if that's what it takes to finish—every step of the way. Anyone who does less than that and still claims to have "finished" is a cheater.

The first rule of racing is to enter properly

Cheaters and bandits aren't partners in crime. In many ways they're opposites.

Cheaters pay to commit their crime by entering the race. They run only part of the way but claim all the credit. When caught, they're universally reviled because they bring shame on us all.

Bandits pay nothing. They go the full distance but seek no credit. They're tolerated, even celebrated in some circles as running Robin Hoods who take from the rich races that can afford it.

Cheating is a major crime against the self-policing nature of our sport. Cheating is an attempt to steal honor from those who've earned it. If cash is involved, the thief deserves a lawsuit.

In comparison, banditry is a misdemeanor. Courses are designed to handle a certain number of runners, and race or city officials often limit that number. Bandits throw off the count and are guilty of trespassing.

Races supply their water stations based on the number of registered entrants. Each time a bandit grabs a cup, a legitimate runner might miss a drink. This is a violation akin to shoplifting.

When bandits cross the finish line, they mess up the scoring of entered runners. Think of this as malicious mischief or vandalism.

Cheating is a more serious crime. But banditry is a bigger problem, because bandits far outnumber cheaters.

The freeloaders defend themselves by saying, "It's a public roadway. I pay my taxes, so I have a right to be here." This argument is like insisting it's okay to drive on the road without a license, paying no heed to speed limits or stop signs.

Runners complain about bicyclists, inline skaters, skateboarders, and parents pushing strollers on the course and many races ban them.

Bandits are an equal nuisance, and race directors say their numbers are growing.

Some bandits consider their act a protest against high entry fees. They fail to recognize the hidden costs of conducting a safe and efficient race. Permits, police protection, and insurance are required and necessitate those fees.

Runners who disapprove of the entrance fee should protest by skipping the party, not crashing it. Run on that road the other 364 days of the year when it's open to all, not on race day when other runners have paid to control its traffic.

Cheaters Never Win

If one particular cheater intended to expose himself to maximum ridicule, he couldn't have picked a better place to do it. New York City is the world's leading media center, so the marathon there ranks among the world's most heavily publicized.

The New York City Marathon also utilizes computerized timing chips, which runners must wear attached to their shoes. This computerized scoring system makes cheating almost impossible to hide. Yet in 2001, one runner from Washington State (who I won't even honor by naming) still tried to cheat in this historic race.

After "finishing" nineteenth overall, and thus ranking fifth in the concurrent U.S. Championships, he was quickly exposed as a fraud. He hadn't "chipped in" at any scoring mat except the last one, and hadn't been spotted at any visual checkpoint.

What the cheater did was even worse than stupid; it may have been criminal. By pretending to be a legitimate marathon finisher, he tried to steal the $4,500 that rightfully belonged to true fifth-place U.S. finisher Keith Dowling, who would've won no prize money if the cheater hadn't been caught. The cheater also tried to bilk the Olympic Trials out of expense money as a phony qualifier.

This cheater's lasting punishment will be having to live with the personal and public knowledge of his sin. How could he ever show his face at any race again?

There are lesser ways to cheat, though, ways without such obvious victims or consequences. Regrettably, I've sinned in most of these ways, and maybe you have too:

▶ Running while wearing someone else's number (and chip).

▶ Starting ahead of the starting line, or before the official starting time, or farther forward in the starting crowd than your ability warrants, to "avoid the congestion."

▶ Shortening the course by crossing lawns or cutting through gas stations at corners, thereby running less than the measured distance.

▶ Jumping into mid-race to pace someone, or recruiting such a pacer, or entering a race "for a workout" without intending to go all the way.

Confessing to these and other transgressions can help us to recognize our wrongs and sin no more. All are attacks on the fundamental honesty of the sport, and all are insults to the vast majority of runners who follow running's honor code.

That code is to be true to yourself and the runners around you. True winners never cheat, and cheaters never win.

RACING tips for newcomers to racing

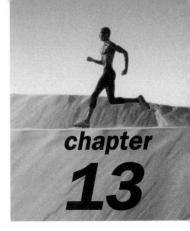

Racing 101

"Teacher" is an honorable title, one that I wear proudly even if it doesn't quite fit. In my running classes at the University of Oregon, I basically tell my students what distance and where to run. I'm less a teacher than a run-planner, route-plotter, way-pointer, clothes adviser, cheerleader, and record-keeper.

I deliver my lessons to students by e-mail, not lectures. Each lesson is brief, about a hundred words, and reading it is optional.

In Chapter 2 of this book, I furnished my mini-lessons for beginning runners. I've designed the following lessons for students graduating into 5K and 10K racing. These are the lessons that I believe all runners must take away from my class, even if they've heard or read nothing else.

Why Race?

Running in races is not a requirement for calling yourself a runner. Running is easier and safer without this added effort.

Racing is hard and moderately risky—but also exciting, challenging, and motivating as it pushes you farther and faster than you could go alone. A race puts you on the line—not just the starting line, but the borderline of your abilities, where you can push no harder without breaking. Racing puts your training and resolve to their final test. But you don't take this test alone; instead, you're in the company of dozens, hundreds, or even thousands of runners like yourself. You aren't competing with them; you're competing against the distance, course, conditions, and voice inside your own head that pleads with you to ease off. Everyone else in the race is tested in the same ways. You actually cooperate together, as you push, pull, and pace one another to the finish line.

Winning Ways

One of the beauties of running is that it gives everyone a chance to win. Winning isn't automatic; you still have to work for success, and risk failure. But unlike other sports, running doesn't require you to beat an arbitrary standard (such as "par" or an opponent's score). You measure yourself against your personal records.

To the runner, a "PR" doesn't stand for public relations or an island in the Caribbean. It means "personal record," a concept which might represent the greatest advance in the history of our sport. The invention of the digital stopwatch worn on the wrist turned everyone into a potential winner. Here was a personal and yet objective way to measure success and progress. Achievement didn't depend on beating anyone else; it only depended on beating the fastest time you had recorded on your watch.

Race Distances

Nearly all road races now run by the metric system, so if you grew up with the mile system, you must learn to interpret these distances. See the conversion chart for popular race distances on page 316.

Big Days

Most runs need to be easy. This is true whether you're a beginning racer or an elite athlete. (Of course, the definition of "easy" varies hugely for these groups; easy for the elite would be impossible for the beginner.)

Training for the distance and pace of races, and actually running these events, should be by careful prescription, best taken in proper, well-spaced doses. New racers are wise to limit themselves to one tough day a week. On this day, run longer than usual (as long as your longest race distance, but at a slower pace); run faster than usual (as fast as your fastest race pace, but for a shorter distance); or run an actual race (combining full distance at full pace). Experienced racers can work a long run and a fast run into the same week, but don't include both of these plus a race all in one week.

Most runs need to be easy

Going Longer

Distance, unlike speed, is almost limitless. No matter what your level of talent, no matter how many years you've run, no matter how old your personal records are, the possibility of covering longer distances still exists.

This helps to explain the appeal of the marathon. First-year runners can take pride in finishing a marathon in twice the time the leaders take, and longtime runners can feel good about going the distance an hour slower than their PRs. Not all runners can go faster, but just about anyone can go longer. It isn't a matter of talent, but of pacing, patience, and persistence. But don't try to increase your distance all at once. The safe limit for progress is about 10 percent per week, so add no more than one mile to a weekly ten-mile run.

Going Faster

A little bit of speed training goes a long way. In fact, a little bit is all you should do, because too much can injure you.

Most runners can tolerate fast training for a total of only about 10 percent of their weekly mileage. You can choose three ways to speed train.

One major way is to run "intervals," which are series of short, fast runs with recovery breaks in between. Another major way is to use "tempo runs," running at race pace or faster for a shorter distance. A third, minor, way to gain and maintain speed is with "strides"—

ending your warm-up by striding out for a hundred yards or so, one to five times, at the fastest speed you'd ever race. Strides can also prove valuable at the end of relaxed runs, when you need a reminder to push at the end of a race.

Going Easier

You shouldn't save pacing just for certain runs. You should practice pacing from day to day throughout the week.

Some of your runs must be hard if you're training to race, but most of your runs should be easy to compensate for that effort. In other words, you run less than your best much of the time, neither too long nor too fast.

When your run ends, resist the urge to stop suddenly

You can calculate your ideal pace for easy runs in several ways. You can figure at least one minute per mile slower than you could race the same distance; you can aim for about 75 percent of your maximum heart rate; or you can simply decide whatever pace feels comfortable. The last of these guidelines is the simplest to use; what feels right usually is right.

Warming Up

Don't confuse stretching with warming up. Stretching exercises don't start you sweating or raise your heart rate. You warm up by moving—first by walking or running slowly, then by easing into your full pace after a mile or so. I recommend walking for five minutes or about a quarter-mile (not counting this time or distance in your total), before starting to run.

Treat the first mile of running as your warm-up, making it the slowest mile of the day. The faster you plan to run that day, the more you need to warm up.

For relaxed runs, start slower and blend this warm-up period into the rest of your run. Before speed training or racing, warm up separately by running a mile to several miles, and then add some "strides" at the day's maximum pace. Strides will prepare your legs and lungs for what you're about to do.

Cooling Down

When your run ends, resist the urge to stop suddenly. Instead, walk to cool down more gradually.

Just as a warm-up helps to shift your gears from resting to hard running, a cool-down period serves as a necessary transition from racing to resting. Continued mild activity gradually slows down your revved-up metabolism, and also acts as a massage to gently work out any soreness or fatigue generated by your earlier effort.

You set the pattern and pace of your own recovery during these first few minutes after you stop running. Some experts may advise you to run easily during your cool-down, but walking gives you the same benefits with much less effort. You've already run hard enough. After walking is the best time for stretching, which loosens the muscles that running has tightened.

5K Training

You probably routinely run 5K and beyond in training. The quickest way to improve your race time, then, is by upping your pace one day a week for a distance well short of 5K.

Try one to two fast miles total, excluding your warm-up, cool-down, and recovery intervals. Run at your projected 5K race pace or slightly faster, so you can become familiar with that speed. Then extend the length of one weekly run beyond the 5K race distance, perhaps to four or five miles. Run at least one minute per mile slower than race pace, to make your upcoming 5K race seem shorter. Your three to four easy runs each week should average about a half-hour each, at a relaxed pace.

10K Training

The 10K program resembles the one for 5K above, but the distances naturally increase for a race twice as long.

Again, mix over-and-unders: do fast runs at shorter than the 10K distance (totaling two to three fast miles, not counting warm-up, cooldown, and recovery intervals, running the fast portion at 10K race pace or slightly faster), and long runs farther than 10K distance (seven to eight miles, at least one minute per mile slower than race pace). For each of your three or four easy runs per week, average about a half-hour, at a relaxed pace. By slightly modifying this plan, you can run races at two other popular distances—8K (or five miles) and 12K (about seven and a half miles).

Predicting Times

You can predict fairly accurately what speed you'll run a certain distance without having run it recently. You can base your prediction on races you've run at different distances.

Pace obviously slows as racing distance grows, and speeds quicken as distance shrinks. But how much of a slowdown or speedup is normal? A good rule of thumb is a 5-percent slowdown as the distance doubles, or a 5-percent speedup as the distance drops by half. Multiply or divide by 2.1 to predict your time for double or half the distance. For instance, a twenty-two minute (22:00) 5K would equal about a forty-six minute (46:00) 10K.

Race Pace

Even if you've done everything right in training, you can cancel all that good with just one wrong move on race day. The most common and worst mistake is to cross the starting line too quickly.

Crowd hysteria and your own nerves conspire to send you into the race as if fired from a cannon. Try to work against the forces of the crowd and your natural impulses. Keep your head while runners around you are losing theirs. Pull back on your reins even when the voice inside you is shouting, "Faster!"

Be cautious in your early pacing, erring on the side of being too slow rather than too fast. Hold some power in reserve for the race's later kilometers. This is where you can reward yourself for your early caution, by passing other runners instead of being passed by them.

Even Pacing

Talking about even-pace running is much easier than running it—or calculating it. The problem is that races in the U.S. combine two measurement systems. While most events are run at metric distances, such as 5K and 10K, intermediate times referred to as "splits" are often given at mile points and pace is usually computed per mile. So you need to calculate metric-to-mile, and vice versa.

Even-pace running is most efficient. The two halves of a race are best run in about equal time, within a range of a few seconds (plus or minus) per mile. In a forty-five-minute 10K race, for instance, plan to run each half within a few seconds faster or slower than twenty-two-minutes, thirty seconds (22:30). Slightly "negative" splits (running the second half of a race faster than the first) are preferable to "positive" ones.

Race Recovery

One of the most important phases of a training program is also one of the most overlooked. This is the recovery phase, or what you should do after a race.

Your effort shouldn't end at the finish line, because your continued running will depend on what you do, or don't do, in the immediate and extended period afterward. How long your recovery takes will depend on the length of your last race.

The longer the race was, the longer your rebuilding period should be. One popular rule of thumb is to allow at least one easy day for every mile of the race (or about a week of easy runs after a 10K). One day per kilometer (or ten days post-10K) might work even better if your race was especially tough. During this recovery period, avoid long runs, fast runs, and races. Run easily.

JOINING the crowd at the starting line

chapter
14

Race Start

You've probably already taken the hardest step a runner ever takes. That was the first one out the door on your first run.

A runner's second-hardest step is the one you might be thinking of taking. That would place you on the starting line of your first race.

The thought of racing may alternately intrigue and intimidate you. Say you've been running for a year, and you've graduated from those first painful trudges around the block to comfortable two- and three-mile runs. You're looking for new challenges. You watched the big local race last year, and now you think, "Maybe this time I could run it."

Then the dream gives way to doubts: What if I finish last, or can't finish at all? What if I make a fool of myself in front of my family, friends, and neighbors?

Should you race? Only if you're convinced that racing will make you a more complete runner. If you enjoy running for the solitude it offers, and if you feel no urge to increase your distances or improve your times, then racing has little to offer you.

However, if you yearn to mix with other runners both as companions and competitors, and if you're hungry to test your distance and

The thought of racing may alternately intrigue and intimidate you

speed limits, you're ready to go public as a runner. Fill out that entry form.

Perhaps all race forms should carry a warning label: "Caution—this event could be hazardous to your health." That would tell you what you're getting into.

Racing can be hard, and that effort has the potential to hurt you. It will contribute little or nothing to your health and fitness, and can sometimes produce the opposite effect.

So why race? While the racing itself could at times be counterproductive to fitness, the thrill of racing does offer an incentive to stick with the everyday runs that do keep you fit. For this reason, Tom Osler, author of *The Serious Runner's Handbook*, praises racing for its "indirect benefits."

"I can't imagine one of my almost 2,000 races that did my health any good," Osler told me. "Racing is simply too hard to be placed in the healthful-exercise category.

"Yet if it were not for my interest in racing, I probably would have abandoned my training runs long ago. These runs have been an enormous boon to my general well-being, both physical and mental."

When you begin racing, running becomes less an exercise and more a sport. Distance racing, like all sports, involves taking a few risks before earning its rewards. But this sport, more than any other, hands out its rewards to anyone and everyone who can pass its demanding tests.

When you enter a road race, be prepared to win. You win not by crossing the finish line first, but by meeting or beating your own expectations. That might simply mean completing the course for the first time, or later running it faster than before.

The odds of winning in this way are heavily in your favor, since this type of winner far outnumbers losers at most road races.

Winning is fun; failing isn't. The following tips for the first-time racer are intended to maximize your chances for success and to minimize your risks of failure. As you approach your first starting line, plan to:

✔ **Select your event carefully.** Find a race that won't embarrass or discourage you, at a distance you're capable of finishing.

✔ **Be prepared.** Assume you're ready if you've run the full race distance at least once in training, and your other runs average about half the race's length.

✔ **Pace yourself.** Keep your goals, your emotions, and your competitive urges in check at the start, so they can work well for you at the finish.

Choosing a Race

Road racing revolutionized the sport of running. Before road races developed, only young, fast men did much racing, and this was limited to track and cross-country.

That all changed in the 1970s. Road racing grew from a small twig of the sport into a dominant branch. While track and cross-country running still involve mainly elite athletes—now women as well as men—the roads have grown increasingly crowded with runners of every description.

The Bay to Breakers race in San Francisco draws as many as 100,000 entrants a year. The Bloomsday run in Spokane, Washington, and the Peachtree event in Atlanta attract more than 50,000 each. Dozens of other races, including marathons, throughout the country boast casts of thousands and even tens of thousands.

Racing can be hard, and that effort has the potential to hurt you

Several factors explain this popularity. The main one is that these races offer the most democratic arena in the sports world. Runners of every age, ability, and ambition come together at common starting lines.

There are races to fit any bill: big ones and small, short and long, flat and hilly. As a new racer, you'll fit most comfortably into a short road race. Your best entry-level distance is five kilometers, which

When you begin racing, running becomes less an exercise and more a sport

translates to 3.1 miles. 5K's are numerous and crowds there are often large.

Avoid track or cross-country races. These are small and serious, and the shock of jumping into such competition might turn you away from racing immediately and forever.

Choose a big event. One numbering in the thousands would be better than one in the hundreds, and hundreds better than dozens. That way you'll have the company of many first-timers like yourself. The contagious excitement of that crowd should carry you along faster than you could travel alone.

Race Training

Your goal as a first-time racer is to reach the finish line with a proud smile on your face. You might be surprised to learn that you can do that with little, if any, special training. When registering, ask yourself these questions:

▶ Is this a 5K race?

▶ Do you regularly run at least two miles?

▶ Have you taken any runs three miles or longer?

If you answer yes to all three, you're already ready to enter. If you meet the first two requirements but not the third, you need to make only one minor revision in your normal program—and for only for a few weeks. Simply make one run each week a longer one.

Say your longest current distance is about two miles. On consecutive weekends extend that to two-and-a-half, three, and three-and-a-half miles (the last to give yourself extra confidence about handling the race distance).

Consider these longer-than-normal runs to be tests, or dress rehearsals for the conditions you'll experience in the race itself. Rehearse at the same time of day that the race is scheduled. Run on that course or one of similar terrain.

Wear the shoes and clothes that you'll use on race day. Eat and drink (or don't eat and drink) as you plan to before the race. Leave none of these factors untested before your race. The only surprises you want that day are pleasant ones.

Once you have passed the three-mile-plus test, you can safely enter the race, confident of finishing. Only if you want to race farther than 5K, or considerably faster than everyday pace, does your training program require further modifications, and these need only be slight.

Training for improving in races is no great mystery. The two essential ingredients are:

▶ Some runs of full racing distance or longer, but at a slower pace.

▶ Some runs of full racing pace or faster, but at a shorter distance.

These "tests" in training grow longer and faster as the demands of racing do. You only combine elements one and two—full distance at full pace—in actual races.

Two- to three-mile runs are long enough to maintain your fitness while still entering 5K races, yet short enough to let you relax between the harder efforts. A rest day or two each week is not only allowed but encouraged. You're asking more of yourself while preparing to race, so you need these recovery breaks more than before.

First-Race Survival Tactics

Survival. That's the only tactic you need to think much about as a novice in this game. Preparation and restraint result in survival.

Runners talk in hushed tones about the prospects of "hitting the wall" in a race. They act as if this feeling of suddenly dragging anchors or carrying pianos on their backs, finishing slowly and painfully or not at all, is an inevitable part of racing.

It's not. Hitting the wall is a mistake of either inadequate training or improper pacing. We've talked about training requirements. Based on your background there, finishing should only be a matter of keeping your wits about you. That advice, of course, is more easily given than followed.

Resist the urge to start too fast in the first half of the race. Then resist the opposite urge to slow too much in the second half. Try to run the halves in nearly equal times, or the latter part slightly faster.

Check your watch at the finish, and expect the time to please you. It probably will be significantly faster than you ever ran by yourself. The adrenaline stirred up by racing produces that effect.

Your halfway time is second in importance only to your final time. Compare your first- and second-half splits.

If the first was considerably faster, plan to start more conservatively next time. But if the second half was vastly superior, feel free to go faster earlier next time.

Here are some other tips for first-race survival:

✔ **Go to the race with a more experienced adviser.** This sport is all new and a little frightening at first, and someone who has raced at least once before can steady you.

✔ **Set no specific pace or place goal.** Remember that your only objective this first time should be to complete the distance. You'll win simply by finishing.

✔ **Start in the middle of the pack or farther back.** The serious folks line up in front and race away from the line very quickly, threatening to trample anyone who gets in their way.

✔ **Time yourself.** "Official" times at big races are notoriously inaccurate. Start your watch as you cross the starting line, not when the gun sounds. Stop it when you come to a halt at the end, which may not be at the official finish line if runners are backed up there.

✔ **Examine your experience.** Do you want to race again? If so, look at ways to improve: by training longer or faster, by choosing a smaller (and thus more competitive) event, by racing harder, or by pacing better.

TRAINING for faster pace and longer distance

Ageless Advice

I learned my most important running lessons by age twenty, and continue to live them as well as teach them. I tell them to the students in my running classes, who average age twenty, because these lessons aren't ancient history recalled by an aging writer with fading memory.

My lessons and memories have remained clear, because I've refreshed them repeatedly for more than forty years. Approaches and attitudes that work don't go out of date; they apply at all ages and stages of a runner's life.

The following lessons began to work for me very early, starting on my first race day and extending almost to my last.

> **Lesson 1: Run your own race.** The other runners are there to help you run better than you could alone. You compete against the distance, course, conditions, and your previous times.
>
> In my first mile race, I tried to beat everyone who ran that day—and only managed to defeat myself. I started with the leaders and dropped out exhausted after only one lap—out of the race and, for all I cared, out of the sport. Thankfully, my coach wouldn't let me quit, and made me promise to start slower next time and finish what I'd started—even if it meant finishing last.

Lesson 2: Race for PRs. These records are your truest standard of success. They give you a chance (but no guarantee) to win every time, no matter how you place.

Once I posted my mile time, it became the one to beat. My personal record fell again and again, by a full minute within the first year. While I took care of the times, ever-higher placings took care of themselves.

Lesson 3: Pace yourself evenly. This means working against your natural urge to surge when you're fresh and to slow when you're tired. Hold back early, and hold on later.

Early experience taught me that times improved quickest when I spread my effort evenly over the full distance. I adopted a style that went against the grain of high school racing: resist the starting stampede, and then begin pushing the pace as other runners slow theirs.

Lesson 4: Use races as training. You get better at racing by racing. No form of speed training is more effective than racing, so race often—and sometimes longer or shorter than your usual distance.

We did little else but race at my high school. When not running actual meets my first season, my schoolmates and I raced half-miles among ourselves. All this racing improved my half-mile time by twenty-five seconds, and landed me in the state meet as a freshman.

Lesson 5: Run overs-and-unders. Train for your race distance by going a little longer but at a slower pace. Train for your race speed by going a little faster but at a shorter distance.

Half-mile racing became "under-distance training" for the mile in my second season, when I placed in the mile event at the state meet. The mile was the longest race for high school runners back then, but my time trials of two and three miles served the "over-distance" purpose.

Lesson 6: Train hard-easy. Some hard days are a must, because racing is tough, but you can't run hard all the time. More days of the week must be easy than hard.

Our school took the hard-easy system to the extreme, as we either raced or rested. My written records don't reach back to the first year, but I'm guessing that the resting days outnumbered the racing days in my first track season.

Lesson 7: Run regularly. You get back from this sport almost exactly what you put into it. If you run most days each week (even easily much of the time), and you run most weeks each year, you get better at it. If you don't, you don't.

Seeing no future as a five-foot-five basketball player, I quit that sport in midseason of my sophomore year to become a year-round runner. That first winter's training didn't amount to much, but anything was better than the nothing I would've done while riding the basketball bench.

Racing as Training

I credit my best season to frequent and fast racing, with an assist from the relaxed recovery runs in between.

My first high school coach, Dean Roe, admitted that he didn't know the finer points of running training. But he knew very well the mind-set of young runners, who run to compete.

He trained us for racing by racing. He raced us often and always all-out, if not in true meets then against teammates in simulated races. Roe had moved on to another school by my senior year. But he'd left his lessons with me.

My only addition to his simple racing-as-training plan was to fill the gaps between races with slower and longer runs, for recovery and endurance-building. That senior track season I raced myself from bad to great shape quicker than ever before or after.

An illness and then an injury (from a mid-race fall) cost me most of the first month of the season. My season didn't really start until late April, leaving just a month before high school track would end for me.

In my first post-tumble race, the state's best miler, Don Prichard, beat me by a full straightaway. Shocked by my sluggishness, I took a crash course in speed.

I credit my best season to frequent and fast racing, with an assist from the relaxed recovery runs in between

I started that same night at that same meet, "doubling," or running a second event, in the half-mile. Over the next three weeks I raced nine more times, usually at the shorter half-mile distance.

Results: eighteen seconds of improvement in the mile and a ten-second PR in just a month, a win at the state meet over Prichard, who'd beaten me by a hundred yards a few weeks before, a bonus state title in the half-mile, and the next week my "5K" (we actually ran three miles back then) PR that would last my lifetime.

I credit this best of all track seasons to frequent and fast racing, with an assist from the relaxed recovery runs in between. Later I ran farther, faster, and harder on more complicated training programs— but never raced better until I relearned those simpler methods. Again the formula came down to the two basics: "race often and hard and run longer and easier."

Recently I've been dismayed by the trend in training to avoid races. Some runners and their coaches treat racing as risky business, limiting it in high season and shunning it in others.

High school runners run some races with little effort, to "save" themselves for bigger ones. College runners skip the smaller meets to peak for a few big ones. Marathoners stop racing for months while training for a single event.

Runners who go raceless miss what can most motivate them to run at all. They also miss the wonderful training effects of racing. You can't match the excitement, or the effort, any other way. The racing atmosphere brings out your best in each race, and again in those that follow.

Please don't read this as an argument to over-race. Racing four times a week surely is too much. But racing only four times a season is too little, especially for the young who run to race.

When I ask the college students in my basic class what they want to accomplish, three-fourths of them give a racing goal: to run a faster mile or enter a 5K race.

I began one class with a simulated 5K race. Then, once a week, my students ran another thinly disguised race—a shorter one to improve speed. They ran longer and easier runs in between.

By the end of the term, they actually looked forward to taking the final exam, because they'd done their homework and success was all but guaranteed. And seventeen of my eighteen students dropped their 5K times by an average of eighty seconds.

Going Long, Fast

I'd run hundreds of high-school and college races by 1963, but none on the roads. That July, I became a road racer—instantly.

My previous day's journal entry described an easy run while "trying to get myself ready for a fast mile tomorrow." I woke up the next morning still thinking "mile."

I planned to run my mile workout after watching a morning road race. Luckily I showed up early at Fremont High School in Sunnyvale, California, to watch friends start the National 30K.

I noted in my daily journal: "Today I really went out of my mind. Seeing all those distance runners got me excited, and I jumped into the 30-kilometer run. That's three-fourths of a marathon!

"I wasn't excited or nervous about it at all. Just wanted to plod the course and finish in around two hours."

My "plodding" began at about six-minute-mile pace. This felt slow, as my racing miles usually had been far below five minutes and my training miles weren't much slower. But I certainly hadn't trained at even one-fourth of that day's race distance.

"It was really easy at first—almost hard to hold back," I wrote in my journal. "But it got tougher, and tougher, and tougher still."

This became my first experience with walking breaks. They weren't planned, but they were required. My first walk, I confessed then, was on the "mountain" at about eleven miles. From then on I didn't go much more than a mile without walking twenty to thirty seconds at a time.

"I passed guys all the way. I was barely moving, but they were barely moving slower."

"Barely moving," I averaged 6:08 miles even with the walks. My 30K time would stand as my PR for another five years.

Payment for not training for this race came due the next day. I could barely walk. But without knowing it yet, I was already on a new course that would serve me well in all the years to come.

Runners who go raceless miss what can most motivate them to run at all

The next year was my best ever in cross-country and track, thanks to a new piece in the training puzzle: long runs on the road. After the 30K, I was ready to come under the indirect influence of Arthur Lydiard. A California high school coach named Forrest Jamieson had just returned from studying at Lydiard's feet in New Zealand, and we took some runs together.

I'd read Lydiard's book, *Run to the Top*, but hadn't yet adopted any of his ideas. Jamieson convinced me to try them, though I took only one bite from his whole program. This piece was the long run.

When I tried to nudge up Jamieson's super-slow pace, he asked, "What's your hurry? The idea here is to cover the distance, not to race it. Save the racing for the days when someone is keeping score."

I carried these almost-weekly long runs back to college with me, and continued them through the next spring. But they weren't slow. My pace averaged close to six minutes per mile, on runs that stretched as far as twenty miles.

My final month of long, fast distance was March 1964. The last long training run was a half-marathon—faster by almost four minutes than my race PR would ever be at that distance. This run came in the final weeks before my outdoor track season opened with a mile PR. Another came a week later.

I thought then, if I'm excelling like this with an endurance base, imagine how fast I'll go when my real speed training starts. As it turned out, I didn't run any faster. When I cut out my long runs, my race times leveled off.

And when I began long training runs again, they became more like races, as I tried to set training-course records each time. Between these long runs I worked in heavy doses of short and fast training.

Regrettably, all of this distance and speed training took a toll on my legs, then injured one of them more seriously than ever before. That Achilles tendon injury effectively ended my college running career, before my final track season had even begun.

Another year of struggling on dead legs led to the most dramatic change in my running life. If I'm going to be slow, I thought in 1966, I might as well enjoy it. I turned to the all-long, all-slow running that came to be known as "LSD."

I had been slow to learn, but now understood what Forrest Jamieson had tried to teach me in the summer of 1963: what's the hurry? Don't confuse long runs with races.

My racing didn't end with this slowdown. In fact, one of my most satisfying PRs came with a better 30K than the one that had started my road racing.

PACING by the minute, the heartbeat, and the feeling

chapter **16**

Running by Heart

The only time I shared a stage with John Parker, he was a show-stealer. When he came out dressed as Gadget Man and poked fun at the tools that we runners think we need, we other speakers were forgotten.

Yet Parker is an old-time runner, slow to fall into step with current trends. So when he sang the praises of heart monitors, I listened.

Parker is an author and publisher whose own books include *Heart Monitor Training for the Compleat Idiot.* He recommends only what has passed his own running tests.

"I am an old-time curmudgeon when it comes to gimmicks and shortcuts with regard to fitness," he wrote to me. "But a few years ago, I became convinced that a heart monitor could be an amazingly effective tool to help a coachless runner train the way Jack Bacheler taught me, Frank Shorter, and so many others to train in the old days in Gainesville [Florida]."

Parker ran in the glory days of the Florida Track Club. He recalled that Olympian Bacheler's training involved hard tempo and track workouts buffered with very easy mileage.

"Runners who joined our group were astonished at how slow those easy runs were. That's how we were able to run one-hundred-plus miles per week, increase the intensity of our intervals over the season, and gradually become stronger and faster without getting injured. Doing it any other way would either lead to breakdown from intensity or to mediocre fitness from easy miles and nothing else."

A heart monitor can be an invaluable tool for keeping easy runs easy enough

But it seemed impossible to explain proper pace to runners who weren't in Gainesville running it. "You could tell people about it," said Parker, "but until they actually joined in and ran with us, they didn't really get it."

Years later when Parker discovered the heart monitor, he found it an invaluable tool for keeping easy runs easy enough.

"You could use it to determine precisely the heart rate a runner should stay below in order to get aerobic benefits, burn less glycogen (and more fat), and thus get good recovery and good training," he said. "That number, by the way, is 70 percent of max HR [maximum heart rate], which I call your easy-day ceiling."

Parker was gratified by the response to his "Compleat" book, not so much because of its strong sales but for the feedback it produced from readers.

"The book has helped hundreds of other runners accomplish PRs they'd long since given up on," he told me. "And they've done so while enjoying their running more and staying healthier.

"Nearly all of them discovered initially that they'd been doing most of their running too fast. Except when they were doing tempo runs and intervals, in which case they were so tired they were going too slow."

Parker trained with a monitor himself before the 1996 Boston Marathon. "Though I'm no marathoner," he said, "I'm gratified to report that my time at age 49 had slipped only 26 minutes from my PR at 23."

That's what can come from listening more to your heart, whether closely monitored or not, and looking less at your watch.

On Pace

George Beinhorn and I teamed up for several years on the *Runner's World* staff. He left the magazine in the mid-1970s and didn't return to full-time sports journalism. But he never stopped running, and never lost his fascination with the sport's practical-technical side.

"I'm refining my understanding of training," he wrote. "If it ever becomes my fate to train hard again, I'll run high mileage, mostly at aerobic training pace.

"I'll train for endurance-endurance-endurance, and I'll race short distances frequently. I'll never run faster than tempo pace in training."

Beinhorn explained what he meant by "tempo" pace: "Dr. Jack Daniels defines it as five miles at half-marathon race pace. I don't think most runners, even young runners, could get away with doing that every day."

I never heard the term "tempo run" until the 1990s, and always thought it was a vague term. Don't all runs have a tempo, or in other words pace or speed?

My definition of comfort-zone "LSD" pace, from the time I first wrote about long slow distance in 1969, has been a pace one or more minutes per mile slower than your race pace for the same distance. Refining that now, I'd say that adding one minute brings you down to the dividing line between a moderate and a hard pace. And adding two minutes takes you down to the line between moderate and easy.

Ideal everyday pace probably lies between plus-one and plus-two minutes. Students in my college running class support this estimate.

I tell them to run comfortably, not too fast or too slow. Don't worry about time, but just let what happens happen. Their pace naturally settles at about one-and-a-half minutes per mile slower than their top speeds.

I'd guess that was my everyday pace during the years when I raced

Ideal everyday pace lies one to two minutes per mile slower than race pace for the same distance

often and hard, but that's only a guess. I quit checking my pace in the late 1960s, and just let it find itself naturally most of the time.

I can identify only one definite statistic distinguishing my usual pace from my race pace. It comes from my first marathon, Boston 1967.

My longest run before that race was twenty miles. I ran on a measured course in Des Moines, Iowa, and averaged exactly eight-minute miles.

Not knowing what awaited me in the unexplored black hole beyond twenty miles, I just hoped to hold that eight-minute pace for the extra distance. But I didn't even come close.

My marathon pace was a shocking 6:29 per mile—or almost precisely one-and-a-half minutes faster than I'd trained. This was an early lesson to me on how much the excitement of a race day could improve my pace.

Time on Your Side

It's a simple question: "How far did you run today?" Runners ask it of each other, and non-runners sometimes feign interest by asking about our distances.

People who ask want to know how many miles, so I never have a quick answer. Mine begins with, "Uh ... hmm ... let's see," as I work some mental math that's never more than a wild guess. If they'd ask me instead, "For how long did you run?" I'd tell them instantly and accurately. You see, I'm not a distance runner but a time runner.

Time means a great deal to every runner. It means everything to me, because on most days, miles don't count, only minutes do. Once a stern taskmaster of mine, time has since become a good friend. It used to taunt me with impossible records to beat, but now offers satisfying quotas to meet.

I used to fear the ruling of my watch, for it would decree whether I'd lost my race against time that day, or would lose it soon by making my own record even harder to break.

Thank goodness Arthur Lydiard offered me an escape route. The coach from New Zealand told me in a 1970 interview that his runners, once known for their hundred-mile weeks, largely ignored mileage.

They trained mostly by time periods, checking their pace for known distances only on certain occasions.

I stopped mile counting back then and never resumed. Admittedly, I started running by time for a mostly practical reason: to keep score without having to measure a course and follow it as calibrated. I've continued to run by my watch for better reasons: to ease down and make friends with time. Time can't be hurried, so I relax and let it tick away at its own rate.

On most days, miles don't count, only minutes do

Almost any digital watch will work. All you really need is one that freezes your time at the end of your run. That time is important. It gives you a comforting illusion of permanence not found in running by miles.

The hours, minutes, and seconds stand as visible reminders that your own effort put them all there. Preserve them until your next workout, to congratulate yourself on your last run and motivate you on your next one.

If today's inexpensive digital watches had existed when I set my best PR (most watches still had hands and ticked, and digitals cost more than a trip to Boston), I might have retired my digital instead of erasing my time. My result would have shone on the watch face until the batteries died. But trying to make time stand still in this way would've been a mistake. It's just as important to eventually erase times as it is to save them at first.

Savor time for a while, yes, but also pay attention when you clear your watch. Hold down the button that wipes out that hard-earned time and see it replaced with a line of zeroes.

This act will demonstrate graphically a turning away from your past, and a forging ahead into your future. You now can refresh your time in a friendly way, by running with it instead of against it or away from it.

Good Pains

A student reporter from the University of Missouri once asked me about pain: what a pain running can be, how much a runner can and should tolerate, and how to train to immunize oneself against it.

"I'm writing a story about the pain runners go through both in really hard workouts and in races," said James Carlson. "I'm trying to delve into why runners ignore the body's most basic cautionary response, pain, and the ways they go about doing it."

He wanted to know my thoughts on the "pain barrier." What allows some runners to punch through it better than others?

Good pain is what we typically feel after some tough runs

I began by distinguishing between bad pains and good ones. The bad pains are serious aches and injuries that block continued progress and enjoyment in running. Good pain is what we typically feel after some tough runs. It's the discomfort of fatigue or mild soreness that follows a race or hard training session.

These feelings are temporary and not entirely unpleasant. This type of pain reminds us that we've done as well as we could, and that we're entitled to feel a little bit heroic.

The pain barrier exists, but I see it less as a wall to break through than as a line to push. It tells us how hard we can safely run. If we break through that barrier too far or too often, bad pain is sure to follow.

I don't think runners truly break through the pain barrier—not for long, anyway. We simply learn how to deal with it.

The first way to work with pain is to recognize what auto racers call a "redline pace." In our hard training and racing, this line separates good pain from bad, discomfort from destruction. Ambitious and successful runners learn to nudge that line without crossing over.

The second way to deal with the pain barrier is to move it. It's not like a steeplechase hurdle, remaining in the same place for all runners, all the time.

Training pushes the redline farther away. What might have been a destructive effort early in training becomes a mere discomfort later on, and what was once uncomfortable becomes easy.

I see all types of runners, from the fastest to the slowest. I don't see the top ones, as a group, enduring a great deal more pain than the rest of us. The front-runners distinguish themselves more by their talent and training.

The marathoner Kenny Moore, who ran in both the 1968 and 1972 Olympics, was only beginning to earn his living as a writer when he penned an article about runners and pain. More than thirty years later, his essay still makes more sense than anything else I've read on the subject.

"Good distance runners are reputed to possess either great resistance or little sensitivity to pain," Moore wrote. "I have heard coaches state flatly that if an athlete doesn't have a high 'pain threshold' he might as well forget about running well. Yet I doubt whether runners as a group are any braver when it comes to sitting in dentist chairs or receiving tetanus boosters than the general populace."

He recounted his participation in a study measuring the effects of altitude training. This involved running to exhaustion and then giving blood samples.

Moore noted, "It seemed strange to our doctors that while we showed no reluctance to run ourselves into unconsciousness at the end of a hard workout (quite easy to do at 7,500 feet), the mention of another session with the needles set us all to whining like tormented alley cats. The explanation, of course, is that we were used to our kind of pain.

"Over the years we had developed a familiarity with our bodies that let us know how much of the discomfort of extreme fatigue we could stand. Part of a runner's training consists of pushing back the limits of his mind. But the needle pain was relatively new and exposed our 'innate toughness' for what it was—a learned specialty."

PREVIEWING and reviewing your race day efforts

Scary Thoughts

There, I've started and I feel better already. I was afraid to start, even though I've done this hundreds of times before. It should get easier to face this test, but it never does. Each time I start, it's as if I'm a rookie.

All the familiar signs appeared today: the doubt, the confusion, the wish to be anywhere but here, doing anything but this. But I started. I took the first step. I'm better now.

I'm writing here about writing—about how I felt when facing this chapter. As always, I balked at putting the first word on a blank computer screen.

Yet I know the fear I feel is important—not pleasant, but normal and necessary to ready me for writing. Fear makes me work better.

This is the mind's way of preparing the body for any kind of emergency: entering an argument, facing a boss, delivering a speech, or running a race. Fear gets the juices flowing. They in turn fuel larger, stronger, more concentrated efforts than we could make otherwise.

Athletes call this "psyching up." It works like magic. There's no other word to explain how it's so effective. In my prime racing years, I rarely ran even a half-marathon at eight-minute-mile pace in training, but raced the marathon at sub-sevens. Magic.

The great marathoner Frank Shorter said he couldn't possibly force himself to run even fifteen miles at less than five-minute pace in training, yet in races he could run this way for twenty-six miles. He credited "the excitement of the race" for making the difference.

> *I can't tell you how to dispel fear, all I can do is help you recognize it as a friend in disguise*

We tend to think of excitement only in its thrilling sense. But fear is another side of it.

Anticipation and dread work together to put us on the alert. Anticipation is pleasant; dread isn't.

I can't tell you how to dispel fear, and I can't make you like it. All I can do is help you understand how it feels and why, and help you recognize it as a friend in disguise. Know the normal behavior patterns and how to react to them.

Anticipation typically gives way to dread the day or so before a race, when you have time to sit, wait, and think about what you're asking yourself to do.

The last hours drag along, and a troubled mind fills them with a month's worth of worrying. You tend to obsess about every thought and action:

"Should I eat this? It might upset my stomach."

"Oh no. My shorts are rubbing. How will my crotch feel after a couple of miles?"

"I have to get some sleep. How can I run if I'm tired?"

"My left shoe has a rough spot. Will my foot hold up during the race?"

"I feel nauseated! Could it be the start of the flu?"

"Uh-oh, there's a twinge in my calf!"

"I have diarrhea. What if I have to stop in mid-race—or can't stop in time?"

The race scares you with both its knowns and unknowns. You know it holds surprises, but you're left to guess whether they'll be good or bad, and where they'll appear. It's like knowing that a mugger lurks in the shadows, but not knowing exactly when and how aggressively he'll strike.

Most of the time, waiting for the first problem to pop up feels worse than any problems that do occur, probably because pre-race fear later acts as an anesthetic. Your mind and body get ready for racing with reactions that scientists call "fight-or-flight responses." These act as psychological and biological warm-up exercises for stressful encounters.

You know your stress mechanism is working when you feel any of the following thirteen symptoms identified by Scottish sports doctor A.M.D. MacIntyre:

▶ Dryness of mouth, often called "cotton-mouth."

▶ Stomach distress: an unsettled feeling often accompanied by decreased appetite, and in some cases vomiting.

▶ Heavy perspiration.

▶ Frequent urination and mild diarrhea.

▶ Deeper, more rapid breathing.

▶ Faster, stronger heartbeat.

▶ Tense, tight muscles, particularly in the neck and shoulders.

▶ Overall feeling of weakness and lethargy.

▶ Pale complexion.

▶ Fingernail biting and other unconscious hand-occupying actions.

▶ Irritability and restlessness, along with difficulty falling to sleep and staying asleep.

▶ Withdrawal from social contacts.

▶ Desire to escape the event at hand, and to establish excuses in advance for failing to perform up to expectations.

Expect these symptoms and accept them. A little fear is nothing to be afraid of.

Useful Fears

After setting a Boston Marathon record in 1970, Ron Hill commented, "I was worrying like hell all the way. But this is a good thing to develop—this fear. It keeps you moving."

Hill had long before come to grips with fear, recognizing it as a component of competition that he could channel to work for him. But Hill had learned from tough experience. He recalled how fear had overwhelmed him during the 1964 Olympics.

"When I was in Tokyo," he said, "I was the second-fastest man in the world at 10,000 meters. But the night before the 10,000 I was thinking, 'Tomorrow's the day!' There I was, lying in bed, turning the race over in my mind.

"And the first thing I thought about when I woke up was, 'Today's the day!' My stomach turned over. I didn't want to get out of bed, but finally I dragged myself out.

"During the warm-up my legs felt like lead, and I was just dragging them around the track during the race. There was no desire to get into the competition.

"In fact, the only desire was to get away from it. If somehow I could have gotten out of it, I wouldn't have run at all. I finished a disgusting eighteenth."

Hill subsequently set about finding ways to cope with his pre-race anxiety. And he succeeded, winning marathons at Boston, the Commonwealth Games, and the European Championships. He became the second man in history to break 2:10 in the marathon.

Fear can be a positive force—it keeps you moving

The fear remained, said Hill. But he learned to make it work for him instead of against him.

"The fear of running a long race can come from the fact that you know it's going to be physically painful," he said. "And unless you're a masochist, nobody likes pain. I certainly don't like it.

"I developed some ways of turning off thoughts of the race, some ways I could step outside myself. I could even talk about the race in terms of what it was going to involve physically, and where the pain was going to come, and what it was going to be like, and how distressing it was going to be—without actually thinking that the guy who was speaking was going to be in that position so many hours hence."

By knowing fear's signs and symptoms, and accepting them as normal, Hill became better able to control his anxiety and put it to work on his behalf.

Past the Finish Line

You've trained for weeks or months for this moment. Now you're at the finish line ... but not yet finished. Just as this race didn't begin at the starting line but rather when you began training for it, it doesn't end at the finish line but rather when you finish recovering from it.

Your recovery phase starts at the finish line and will take days or weeks to complete. You must approach this post-race repair as systematically as you did your pre-race training. Know that letdowns—both physical and emotional—can occur as a normal after-effect of racing.

Race day works magic. The crowd of runners pulls you to a pace a minute or more faster than you could run alone, or carries you twice as far as you could go solo.

You can't start training for another race until you forget how hard the last one felt

But realize also that this magical effort comes at a price. You start paying it immediately after finishing, and keep paying it for a while afterward.

The hardest most of us ever run is in a marathon. A newly minted marathoner e-mailed me two weeks after his race, worrying about recovering too slowly.

"My aches and pains have left," he wrote, "but I don't seem to have my energy back, in spite of staying well hydrated and carbo-reloading. What has surprised me the most is that I don't feel motivated to run like I did before the race."

This runner's post-marathon reactions were a textbook case: leg soreness, low energy, lost interest in running. These symptoms all pass in time, but it takes longer than you might think.

Recovery comes in stages, each longer-lasting and more subtle than the one before. Here's what you can expect to feel at each stage, how to deal with it, and for how long:

▶ **Immediate recovery.** Besides feeling happy, you feel hot, tired, and maybe woozy from fatigue. Resist the urge to sit down; keep walking until your body cools down.

After drinking and eating, take another walk later in the day to assure yourself that some energy has returned and your legs still work.

▶ **Muscle recovery.** Soreness will settle in the day after the race, and you'll feel even more stiff the second day after racing. Rest completely or cross-train gently (walking, biking, or swimming) on these days.

Don't try to "run out" the soreness, which can delay healing and risk injury. Wait out the pain, which will seldom linger longer than a week, even after the toughest races.

Once soreness disappears, or if you skipped it entirely, you may begin to feel lazy from your rest days and fear losing your fitness. You may be tempted to resume full training quickly.

But don't! You haven't fully recovered at this point, and have two more stages to go.

▶ **Full-body recovery.** Probably no part of your body will hurt after a week, but you still may not feel quite right. Fatigue can linger, especially in legs that seem deadened and heavy.

Start running briefly and easily. Give your body what it wants—usually more food, fluids, and sleep. Don't force your body to do what it doesn't want to do, such as a hard run. Keep your runs short and slow, until your legs liven and lighten up again.

▶ **Psychological recovery.** Even when your body is able to run long and fast again, your mind might resist it. Running may not excite you now. Don't fight these post-race blues, but accept them as normal—and temporary. This reluctant spell is your mind's way of protecting your body from doing too much, too soon.

You can't start training for another race until you forget how hard the last one felt. How long this will take depends on the length of your race and the degree of your effort.

Your shortest races can be repeated within days. Your longest ones might require weeks or even months of recovery. Take whatever time you need.

You earned a good race with your training beforehand and your effort on race day. You also earned a break afterward. Use this chance to recover, yes, and also to savor all you've just accomplished.

Race Spacing

Too many runners limp into doctors' offices a week or two after a hard race, complaining, "I had no problems in the event itself, then this happened in yesterday's long run. What bad luck!"

Luck had nothing to do with it. Heaping abuse upon an already battered body yielded this predictable result. The prepared body can absorb one hard blow, but often not another while still weak from the last.

Distance racing can be as destructive as it is exciting. Relish the excitement, but take extreme care in rebuilding after the destruction. Recover from the race as if it were an injury that takes time to heal.

Exciting as racing is, it's also the most common cause of injuries and poor performances. More precisely, over-racing is to blame—racing too often without enough recovery and rebuilding time in between.

Two innovative coaches from different sides of the world, Arthur Lydiard of New Zealand and Ernst van Aaken of Germany, taught how often—or seldom—to race.

Lydiard said that speed in all forms should amount to no more than ten percent of an individual's running. Van Aaken lowered the bar even more, limiting racing and speed training to five percent of the total.

Using these formulas, a runner should limit him- or herself to one mile of racing in every ten to twenty of running. If you train regularly for speed, then keep your racing limit even lower. The formula automatically lets you race more often at shorter, less-taxing distances, and less frequently at longer, tougher ones.

One year I stumbled into the ideal race-spacing range, and collected its rewards. Not realizing what that range was, I proceeded to stumble out again, and a few years later suffered the consequences.

My best year of long-distance racing was 1968. Almost every race produced a PR, and I stayed injury- and illness-free.

My worst racing year was 1972. No performance was memorable, but my main injury, among many, left a permanent scar.

I later determined that the only striking difference between those two years was how much I raced. I trained the same total mileage both years, at the same relaxed everyday pace. I ran fast only in races, so the frequency of races was the key variable.

In my good year, 1968, my racing had averaged 8 percent of my total running. By my bad year of 1972, my average had jumped to 21 percent.

Comparing these figures with my results, both positive and negative, led me to an unmistakable conclusion: I raced best when I observed the Lydiard/van Aaken limit of 5 to 10 percent racing.

If I exceeded that limit, my racing ability became the first casualty. If I ventured far above it, my general health suffered.

Only after running 500-plus races did I realize that pacing between races is as important as pacing during them.

MILING at the most basic and famous distance

chapter
18

Memorable Miles

Running started for me with a single mile. That mile now holds my oldest memories as a runner.

Throughout 2004, our sport honored the great miler Roger Bannister for the gift he gave running fifty years earlier. And I personally saluted him for what he gave me in May 1954, inspiring my first timed mile.

News of Bannister's race hooked me permanently into the magic of the mile. I was only ten years old then, and most of my other memories of that time are lost in the haze of too many birthdays.

This was long before I developed the habit of recording every scrap of my own running memorabilia. Yet my memory of Bannister's achievement is indelible. I'd heard for years from my track-fan dad of the struggle to break the four-minute mile. And I heard his joyful whoop when he learned that Bannister, a medical student from England, had just run 3:59.4.

The excitement of that event prompted me to imitate the barrier-breaker. I set out to run half his speed, which put my target at eight minutes. That wasn't too slow for a short-legged ten-year-old with no training as a runner.

Our little Iowa town didn't have a proper track, but we kids still held impromptu track meets each spring. We'd hurdle over window screens propped up with bricks, pole vault with a metal water pipe, throw javelin with a bamboo fishing pole. By counting steps, we measured our home block at about a quarter-mile, with an uphill and a downhill on two sides. My block became my course.

Four pals paced me, running a lap apiece. Without asking permission, I'd borrowed my dad's precious stopwatch for timing.

My first result: a 7:23 mile. The later result: extreme soreness from my waist down, including sharp pains in my lower legs that I later learned were shinsplints.

This painful race shelved my mile ambitions for several years, but didn't cure my fascination with the event. I came of age as a miler in the golden age of the mile.

Don Bowden ran the first sub-four mile by an American during my first year as a high-school miler. And Herb Elliott completed his unbeaten career in the mile during my last year of high school. Jim Beatty ran the first sub-four mile indoors during my first year of college. Jim Ryun broke the high-school four-minute barrier the year I broke 4:20.

Four minutes or faster wasn't in these legs and lungs of mine. But improvement had come steadily and added up nicely in the ten years between my first mile and my final PR.

PRs eventually become permanent, but times keep changing.

Fifty years after my first timed mile, I completed an almost perfect circle. My mile time had gradually slowed down to where it had started. What better way to celebrate my half-century of running, then, than by running another timed mile?

Jeff Galloway had given me this idea. At eighteen, Galloway had run his first marathon, a 2:56 in his hometown of Atlanta. Forty years later, he tried to match his original time in that same Thanksgiving Day race.

The 2:56 escaped him, but the race was no failure. Not many runners can say they're still running forty years after their debut at any distance.

I celebrated at a much shorter distance than my friend Galloway. My dream run would have taken me back to Coin, Iowa, to circle my childhood block as I had in 1954. Instead, I had to settle for my current hometown of Eugene, Oregon. And not at famously fast Hayward Field, but on a gravel road, with ninety-degree turns and some slight ups and downs.

I didn't train for mile speed, because I hadn't had training before that first run. I didn't take a formal warm-up, either, for the same reason.

My target was a 7:23 mile. It seemed faster to me than in any other year since 1954, and it managed to escape me this time, a half-century later. But the numbers on my watch meant much less to me than the years on the calendar. Running that mile let me glimpse again for about eight minutes the little boy who first ran around the block fifty years earlier.

Young Milers

A few years ago, I received two phone calls within hours of each other from two sportswriters. One came from my current home state of Oregon, and the other from my early home of Iowa.

Both asked the same question: "What's wrong with today's high-school runners?" The reporters referred to the boys who run metric versions of the old mile and two-mile, now 1600 meters and 3200 meters, in times that compare poorly with those that led the nation twenty to thirty years ago.

This isn't the lament of an old-timer who complains that, "They don't make athletes like they used to when I was a lad." Unfortunately it's a reality in most states and nationwide. The times don't lie.

Jim Ryun held the national high-school mile record for thirty-five years before Alan Webb finally broke it in 2001. Jeff Nelson's two-mile mark has stood since 1979. Webb's and Nelson's times also stand as records for the slightly shorter 1600 and 3200 meters.

The girls' marks at those distances have been around awhile too. Kim Mortenson set the girls' 3200 mark (which is far superior to the best two-mile) in 1996. Polly Plumer's mile/1600 record (4:35.24) has stood since 1982.

Girls have a shorter history in high-school track than boys do, and tend to be overlooked in such discussions. The sportswriters, both male, who called for my comments asked only about the boys in

Oregon and Iowa. Not only were the records old in those states, but few of today's runners could even crack the all-time top ten.

The reporters wanted to know what was wrong with young runners today. Was it that they don't train hard enough?

My answer wasn't that simple, because there's no single answer. I meandered through a half-hour of possible explanations for the reporters. My best guesses were these five:

1. Training. This might be called the "fun-run factor." A generation of runners and their coaches has grown up exposed to the attitude that running can be a low-key, long-term activity that doesn't have to hurt. They see this at road races and read about it in magazines, and so might take this approach to the track.

Moderation is the way to enjoy lifelong running. But it isn't the way to run a sub-4:10 mile or a sub-9:00 two-mile race. By its intense nature, that type of racing hurts, and so must some of the training for it. The fun should come afterward.

2. Talent. Today's young runners are in most cases doing their own best training and racing. Take care not to criticize them as individuals when commenting on how today's best runners aren't as good as yesteryear's.

I believe the problem isn't so much in these runners as it is in the lack of other athletes on the track with them. Kids who once might have run track now play soccer. That booming sport, little known in high schools a generation ago, now dips into the same talent pool as running.

3. Over-racing. The race seasons have stretched so much that they blend together. Cross-country now leads to indoor track, outdoor track, summer road races, and back, in a year-round cycle.

The current tendency to "double," or run two races in the same meet, creates problems as well. (Runners often race in both the 1600 and 3200, and sometimes even in an additional 800 or relay leg.) Teams encourage their best runners to compete the most so they'll score extra points. But they can't run their best times when they have to spread out their efforts in this way.

4. Heroes. Young runners need someone like them to idolize. In the golden age of high-school running, during the mid- to late 1960s, they had Gerry Lindgren, Jim Ryun, Marty Liquori, Steve Prefontaine, and Rick Riley to inspire them. These runners had all competed internationally in their teens. With the recent exception of Alan Webb, this doesn't happen anymore. Today's youth don't relate as well to the country's top runners, who are usually ten or more years older than they are.

A runner's heroes can also come from among his competitors. Runners need other fast runners in their own races. A high schooler who can win in 4:20 lacks the incentive to run 4:10, unless someone pulls or pushes him there.

5. Patience. The better coaches encourage their runners to look ahead, instead of racing themselves into exhaustion in search of high-school glory. I consider this a plus, not a minus, for the current U.S. system.

We hear that only one American high-school miler has broken four minutes since 1967. But we don't hear how many milers have broken through that barrier just a year or two after graduation. They waited a bit, and their times came.

Mile and 1500m/1600m Training Schedules

This track training program for the mile, and its metric equivalents of 1500 and 1600 meters, spans thirteen weeks, which is three months or one full season of the year. The plan allows you to be flexible in choosing from a range of distances and times, and in deciding which days of the week to run. I recommend that you don't run hard two days in a row, nor rest for more than two straight days.

Prerequisites for entering this program are recent runs of at least 5K (about three miles), racing experience at any distance, and an acquaintance with anaerobic (out-of-breath) running. Greater experience might allow you to start at a higher level than week one, and to skip some weeks later on. However, if a week seems especially tough to you, repeat it or even back down a level before progressing again.

The program's ingredients are:

▶ **Longer runs,** to make the race distance seem shorter. These total one-and-a-half to three miles, at near-maximum pace for that distance.

▶ **Fast runs,** to make the pace seem manageable. These include either a race, or a training session at race pace (or slightly faster) and a shorter distance. Training either can be a straight run of up to a half-mile, or shorter intervals totaling no more than a mile.

▶ **Easy runs,** which are unchallenging in both length and pace. These are best done in a modest time period (about a half hour), and are meant for recovery.

▶ **Rest days,** which don't require total rest. They can include cross-training activity, as long as it leaves you refreshed and ready for your next run.

Week	Longer Runs	Fast Runs	Easy Runs	Rest Days
1	1.5–2 miles	Up to 1 mile	30 minutes	1 or 2
2	2–3 miles	Up to 1 mile	30 minutes	1 or 2
3	1.5–2 miles	Half-mile race	30 minutes	1 or 2
4	2–3 miles	Up to 1 mile	30 minutes	1 or 2
5	1.5–2 miles	Mile race	30 minutes	1 or 2
6	2–3 miles	Up to 1 mile	30 minutes	1 or 2
7	1.5–2 miles	Half-mile race	30 minutes	1 or 2
8	2–3 miles	Up to 1 mile	30 minutes	1 or 2
9	1.5–2 miles	Mile race	30 minutes	1 or 2
10	2–3 miles	Up to 1 mile	30 minutes	1 or 2
11	1.5–2 miles	Half-mile race	30 minutes	1 or 2
12	1.5–2 miles	Up to 1 mile	30 minutes	1 or 2
13	None	Mile race	30 minutes	2 or 3

5K-ING *on the track, the road, or cross-country*

Faster Five

My mail from advice-seekers typically comes from opposite directions. I hear from marathon trainers panicking because their races are a month away, and their long runs haven't gone as their schedules say they should. And I hear even more often from 5K racers who want to run faster. Three of them recently wrote me in as many days.

Tim wasn't experienced enough to know how good he already was. "I've been running for four months," he said, "and I'm up to fifteen miles a week, with no speed work except for races. My 5K time has come down from 21 minutes to 18:25."

He wanted to improve, and was willing to double his mileage and add speed training, he wrote, "as soon as I get over my iliotibial-band injury." (This is a common injury to connective tissue on the outside of the knee.) He asked, "Is there any way to know how fast I'll be able to run in the future or how long it'll take me to peak?"

I told him he should be thrilled with his progress. Sub-six-minute mile pace with little experience and limited training was most impressive.

Doubling his training mileage wouldn't necessarily make him faster. It might help, but adding faster sessions would help much more.

You run cross-country for the purest of reasons: it tests your love of running for its own sake

I suggested adding at least one speed run a week (and no more than two), in which he ran at 5K race pace or faster. This run could take several forms: intervals, a single mile at race pace, or a race or time trial shorter than 5K.

It was impossible to say how much Tim could improve and for how long. His age, thirty-five, and his light training told me he had lots of time yet to beat his own times—if he could keep the injury bug from biting.

Steve wanted to again break twenty minutes for 5K. He'd done it before, but had been stuck lately at a slower pace. Like Tim, Steve ran fifteen miles a week, with no interval training. Steve's pace was eight to nine minutes a mile.

I assured him that if he broke twenty once, he could do it again. The single quickest way to up his speed, I told him, was to race one and two miles, or 1500 and 3000 meters. These races are the best training for the 5K, but can be hard to find.

Steve wrote back: "The only mile or two-mile runs in my area are fun runs before 5Ks and 10Ks, and these are usually run only by children. Would running time trials on a local track, with a friend who's faster than I am, also work to improve my speed?"

It's much better to run with your friend than to go solo, I said. In addition, I recommended that Steve add a fast mile to one of his runs each week. This would not be a time trial or race, but a paced effort.

I instructed Steve to warm up, and then run the mile a little faster (no more than ten seconds faster) than his current 5K race pace. It should seem quick but not all-out or exhausting.

Lee was a 21:30 5K runner who hoped to break 20. With that in mind, he'd added speed training to his workout, but it troubled him.

"I have experienced a lot of chest/lung pain," he wrote. "Is this from trying to go too fast, too soon, or am I doing something wrong?"

He added, "It is very frustrating to me to see all the world-class runners running 400s in the 40s, while I'm stuck in the 80s and 90s. What is a realistic timeline to run a sub-70-second 400?"

I urged him to forget what the world-class sprinters do. Their efforts had nothing to do with his.

Lee was almost surely pushing for paces faster than he needed to go, or might ever go in a 5K. His current 21:30 worked out to 104 seconds per 400, and his twenty-minute goal pace would mean 96 seconds per lap. Little would be gained by aiming to run faster than about 90 seconds.

Pure Sport

You don't run cross-country for flat, fast courses accurate to the inch. You don't run cross-country to have every step watched, as in a track stadium, or to mix with the masses, as on the roads. You don't run cross-country for the glory, since in American schools it shares the fall season with King Football.

You run cross-country for the purest of reasons. You run to test yourself against other runners on whatever surface and terrain nature provides—on a course where no car can go, and where your family and fans can't catch glimpses of you unless they run from one point to another. You run with teammates, and everyone's result helps or hurts your team's score.

Cross-country tests your love of running and racing for their own sake, not for PRs you might set or attention you might grab. Once you've fallen for it, you never stop loving it.

Decades have passed since I last ran a full cross-country season. My final race for Drake University was my worst, as I trailed most of the finishers in that snowbound NCAA meet.

The pain of that race, of failing my team and dismally ending my college career, soon eased. The fond memories of those seasons remain, and I eagerly refresh them each fall at my favorite annual running event. It isn't a big-city marathon, or a championship track meet in my hometown. Instead it's the Oregon State High School Cross-Country Championships.

Running writer Marc Bloom wrote in his magazine, *The Harrier*, after an overcharged 2000 Summer Olympics, "At least we've got the warm and cuddly cross-country season to make us feel better."

Bloom's first love is mine as well. The best day of the year to be a running fan in my home state is the first Saturday in November. That's when high schools of all sizes run their state meet in six races on the same cross-country course.

This is a gathering of kids who often are ignored or misunderstood at their schools where football rules, where the competitors outnumber their fans at most of their meets. Once a year they come together with runners like themselves and are appreciated for what they do.

Oregon's state-meet crowd is large by cross-country standards. That's because each runner brings along an average of two family members and friends. These supporters care about the race almost as much as the runner does, and dash about the course to grab glimpses of their athlete.

If you want to renew your memories, or to see what you missed, go to a high school cross-country race this fall

This is a feel-good meet to watch, if not to run. The young runners all seem to start at a sprint. Standing close enough to the course to see them sweat and hear them pant, I can feel some of what they feel, both "the thrill of victory, and the agony of defeat."

Several years ago, I watched a favored girl fall back through the field and wind up in an ambulance. In a boys' race, one of the early leaders was reduced to walking the last lap on the track and dropped to last place.

Only two of the runners that day were acquaintances of mine. I'd known their parents since their own teenage years. Their daughter had been injured all season and finished in mid-pack. Their son was expected to win, but his kick failed him and he placed a dejected third.

Without knowing all the kids by name and face, I knew them by what they were feeling. I hurt for those who felt they'd never recover from their failures. And I celebrated with the winners who felt they'd conquered the world.

If you have ever run cross-country and want to renew your memories, or if you want to see what you missed, go to a high-school cross-country race this fall. These teenagers will leave you feeling good about our sport's future as well as their own. They'll show you that competitive running in its purest form is still in great shape.

5K Training Schedule

This training program for the 5K (road, track, or cross-country) spans thirteen weeks, which is three months or one full season of the year. The plan allows you to be flexible in choosing from a range of distances and times, and in deciding which days of the week to run. I recommend that you don't run hard two days in a row, nor rest for more than two straight days.

Prerequisites for entering this program are recent runs of at least 5K (about three miles), racing experience at any distance, and an acquaintance with anaerobic (out-of-breath) running. Your greater experience might allow you to start at a higher level than week one, and to skip some weeks later on. However, if a week seems especially tough to you, repeat it or even back down a level before progressing again.

The 5K program is the same whether you race the distance on the road, track, or cross-country. Take all or most of your fast runs on the same surface on which you'll be racing.

The program's principal ingredients are:

▶ **Longer runs,** to make the race distance seem shorter. Training runs become significantly longer than the 5K race—up to five miles.

▶ **Fast runs,** to make the pace seem more manageable. These runs can be either a race, or a training session at race pace (or slightly faster) at a shorter distance. They can be a straight run of up to two miles, or shorter intervals totaling no more than two miles. Train for speed on the surface you'll be racing—track, road, or cross-country.

▶ **Easy runs,** which are unchallenging in both length and pace. These are best run in modest time periods (about a half hour), and are meant for recovery.

▶ **Rest days,** which don't require total rest. They can include cross-training activity, as long as it leaves you refreshed and ready for your next run.

Week	Longer Runs	Fast Runs	Easy Runs	Rest Days
1	2–3 miles	Up to 1 mile	30 minutes	1 or 2
2	2–3 miles	Up to 1 mile	30 minutes	1 or 2
3	2–3 miles	1–2 mile race	30 minutes	1 or 2
4	3–4 miles	1–1.5 miles	30 minutes	1 or 2
5	3–4 miles	1–1.5 miles	30 minutes	1 or 2
6	3–4 miles	5K race	30 minutes	1 or 2
7	3–4 miles	1–1.5 miles	30 minutes	1 or 2
8	4–5 miles	1–1.5 miles	30 minutes	1 or 2
9	4–5 miles	1–1.5 miles	30 minutes	1 or 2
10	4–5 miles	1–2 mile race	30 minutes	1 or 2
11	4–5 miles	1–1.5 miles	30 minutes	1 or 2
12	3–4 miles	Up to 1 mile	30 minutes	1 or 2
13	None	5K race	30 minutes	2 or 3

10K-ING in a race not too long, not too fast

chapter 20

Perfect Ten

A generation ago, I made the case for ten kilometers as the perfect race distance. During the first running boom of the 1970s and early 1980s, this was the most popular event, accounting for more than half of road races nationwide and most of the biggest crowds.

The 10K has lost its popularity title, replaced in the second running boom of the 1990s and 2000s by the 5K. But I still like the longer race better.

To me the 5K feels too much like a sprint. Or if I decide not to push my pace, it seems to end too soon. I haven't had enough time to fully warm up, or to break out of the human traffic jam that comes with being the most popular racing distance.

I love the 10K for many reasons. First, its distance is familiar. Most runners who race typically train with runs in the half hour to hour range. (This has been my daily "home" for more than thirty years.) And most of these runners can finish a 10K race within that time span.

The challenge of racing the 10K lies in running the familiar distance faster than usual, but not recklessly fast. This race's pace is manageable with speed training that's not excessive in its intensity or

One fast session a week—which can be taken as regular racing—can lead to a satisfying 10K

amount. One fast session a week—which can be taken as regular racing—can lead to a satisfying 10K.

If you enjoy racing, you want to race often. The 10K allows this, because recovery comes quickly. Applying the standard formula of one easy day following each all-out mile, you can safely run a 10K as often as every week (or by using the more conservative day-per-kilometer standard, every other week).

The 10K is a true race, unlike the marathon, which can often resemble a survival march. Yet the 10K is not a mad dash, unlike the 5K and especially the mile.

I spent the early years of my running life training and racing on the track. This netted me a solid set of PRs, a few small-time victories, and a legacy of injuries.

I spent the next several years as a marathoner. This phase of my career enabled me to repeatedly break three hours in the marathon, and to survive runs as long as seventy miles. It also resulted in foot surgery caused by racing too far, too often.

I'm proud of all the times and distances run back then, and don't regret any of the suffering that they produced. But I'm long finished with those efforts.

What I wrote in the 1979 book *Run Farther, Run Faster* is even truer now: "I've been to the extremes of racing. Small, simple five- to ten-mile races are where I've decided to settle down. If I want to make rare trips out from here again, I'm familiar enough with the other neighborhoods to visit them briefly. But this is home."

This "home," which centers on the 10K, might not be as thrilling as the exotic places visited at the extremes of pace and distance. But here I can relax, live comfortably, and avoid much of the frenetic activity that very fast and very long travels involve.

I urge other runners to visit the places I've gone. If nothing else, they make "home" look all the better when you come back to settle down.

Did I Win?

As I walked back to my hotel from the Stampede Roadeo 10K in
Calgary, Alberta, a teenager shouted from across the street, "Did you
win?" He wasn't so much talking to me as showing off for his
three buddies.

The gray in my hair and lines in my face showed him I wasn't
the kind of winner he meant. Nonetheless I answered affirmatively,
nodding my head and walking on without explanation.

During my seminar the day before the race, I'd asked my audience
to do me and themselves a favor. If you're not in the marathon, I said,
please don't say, "I'm only running the 10K." If you're slow, don't say,
"I'm only a mid-pack or back-of-the-pack runner."

You're out there doing the best you can, I told these runners.
You're ahead of the thousands of people who won't or can't do what
you're doing.

I'd gone a long time without practicing what I was speaking and
writing. I hadn't been fulfilling George Sheehan's definition of
winning, which is: do the best you can within the limits of your
current abilities; keep on doing it as long as you can; and don't
apologize for whatever you've done.

An old practice of mine was to run
nearly every race shorter than a marathon
that I attended as a speaker. This habit
had ended for me more than a year before
my Calgary visit. One complication or
another eliminated the races from my
travel weekends, which felt unfinished
without them.

*Do the best you
can within the
limits of your
abilities*

I hadn't done what everyone else had come there to do. I'd left
town without a necessary ego adjustment—a final reminder that I
didn't stand above the crowd, but ran with it.

The race director in Calgary brought me back to my first starting
line in sixteen months, ending my longest racing drought ever. When
I arrived for the weekend, Kelvin Broad outlined my duties.

And instead of asking, "Do you want to run one of our races?" he
gave me my assignment: "You'll run the 10K on Sunday morning."

Even after receiving my marching orders, I thought of ways to slip out of the race. I could start, and then veer off the course early. Or I could run all the way, ever so slowly, and not cross the finish line, so my slowness would remain unrecorded.

But at that starting line I remembered another of George Sheehan's statements: pinning on a race number means you've taken an oath to do your best, whatever that might be.

I ran unnoticed in the crowd, but ran each kilometer faster (or less slowly) than the one before, my old excitement smoldering again. I ran an unremarkable time, but it wouldn't have been possible without that race.

Did I win? Yes, I think so.

10K Training Schedule

This program for the 10K (road, track, or cross-country) spans thirteen weeks, which is three months or one full season of the year. The plan allows you flexibility in choosing from a range of distances and times, and for deciding which days of the week to run. I recommend that you don't run hard two days in a row, nor rest more than two straight days.

Prerequisites for entering the 10K program are recent runs and past races of at least 5K (about three miles). Your greater experience might allow you to start at a higher level than week one, and to skip some weeks later on. However, if a week seems especially tough to you, repeat it or even back down a level before progressing again.

The 10K program is the same whether you race the distance on the road, track, or cross-country. But you need to take all or most of the fast runs on the same surface on which you'll be racing.

The major training ingredients for the 10K are:

▶ **Longer runs,** which become significantly longer than the race—up to eight miles.

▶ **Fast runs,** which are races or training sessions at race pace (or slightly faster) but shorter distance. This training can be a straight run of up to three miles, or shorter intervals totaling no more than three miles.

▶ **Easy runs,** which are unchallenging in both length and pace. These are best run in moderate time periods (about a half hour), and are meant for recovery.

▶ **Rest days,** which don't require total rest. They can include cross-training activity, as long as it leaves you refreshed and ready for your next run.

Week	Longer Runs	Fast Runs	Easy Runs	Rest Days
1	3–4 miles	1–2 miles	30 minutes	1 or 2
2	3–4 miles	1–2 miles	30 minutes	1 or 2
3	4–5 miles	1–2 miles	30 minutes	1 or 2
4	4–5 miles	5K race	30 minutes	1 or 2
5	5–6 miles	1–2 miles	30 minutes	1 or 2
6	5–6 miles	2–3 miles	30 minutes	1 or 2
7	6–7 miles	2–3 miles	30 minutes	1 or 2
8	6–7 miles	5K race	30 minutes	1 or 2
9	6–7 miles	2–3 miles	30 minutes	1 or 2
10	7–8 miles	2–3 miles	30 minutes	1 or 2
11	7–8 miles	2–3 miles	30 minutes	1 or 2
12	4–5 miles	1–2 miles	30 minutes	1 or 2
13	None	10K race	30 minutes	2 or 3

HALF-MARATHONING is more than a cut-rate marathon

Middle Class

In my recent races, I've finished almost exactly in mid-pack. This seems the proper place to be, for one born in the middle of the country at the middle of the century.

If running in mid-pack means being average, mediocre, worst of the best, or best of the worst, then I fit those definitions. But I prefer to think of it as being normal, typical, or moderate in approach.

I had the chance at a race directors' conference in Portland, Oregon, to stand up for middle-of-the-roaders. Les Smith, the director of these directors, asked me to join a panel to talk about where running was headed. I admitted that my crystal ball was notoriously hazy.

I never could've predicted when I took my job with *Runner's World* that the magazine of 2,000 circulation would grow 250 times larger...never would've believed that marathons would have to actually turn away runners...couldn't have guessed that women would be the majority in some race fields...couldn't have imagined running four-and-a-half-hour marathons and finishing in mid-pack.

To these race directors I said, "I don't know any better than you do what will happen in the next ten or twenty years. But here's what I hope will happen."

My wishes centered on those runners in the middle levels of our sport. This is the vast middle class, and I'd like to see their experience and status upgraded. That can happen in three ways:

1. Recognize middle-class runners. They run less than needed to become first-rate, and lack the talent to qualify as elite. But they train far more than needed simply for exercise.

They truly race their races instead of merely running in them. Racing isn't their mission, but neither is a race just another run to finish.

They race to qualify for Boston, to win age-group awards, to better their PRs, and to beat their rivals and pals. Race organizers tend to focus their attention on recruiting elites and increasing their total numbers by filling their ranks with novices. Middle-class runners deserve to be more than afterthoughts, as they are often the events' most loyal supporters.

2. Support mid-size events. Racing has become a numbers game. The bigger the event, the more successful it's rated, and the happier its sponsors are to keep spending.

Races with shrinking numbers of entrants lose sponsor support, and often go out of business. The smallest events are left to operate as no-frills fun-runs, little known even in their own communities.

Mid-size events deserve more endorsement. They offer a better-quality experience than no-frills races, and less crowding and commotion than mega-races.

3. Provide more middle-distance races. Road racing has become polarized. The best-attended events are 5Ks at one end and marathons at the other.

Many short road distances remain popular. But among middle distances—those run by most of us in a little less than an hour to well past three hours—only the half-marathon pulls in big numbers.

We need more races of ten, fifteen, and twenty miles (more 15, 20, 25, and 30Ks), to bridge the gap between the 5K and the marathon.

Half Truths

I like almost everything about the half-marathon (13.1 miles) except its name. No other road distance is known as a fraction of another.

This designation makes the "half" sound like a low-rent marathon, an item discounted fifty percent from the real thing. Too often it's treated that way—as the second-rate event on a two-race program, added as an afterthought for slackers who won't put in a full marathon effort.

Those who do run it can become victims of its name. They think, "If I ran the half-marathon in 2:00, I must be ready to go four hours for the full distance."

No one expects the men's 800-meter world record-holder to run two more laps at the same pace for a 3:23 mile (when the best time ever run is twenty seconds slower). Yet we're tempted to think a runner should be able to hold half-marathon pace for another thirteen miles.

If that were possible, then the U.S. men's record-holder in the half, Mark Curp, would've been a 2:03 marathoner instead of 2:11. The world marathon record would be about 1:59 instead of six minutes slower.

The standard conversion formula between the two distances, for runners equally well trained for both, is to multiply the half-marathon time by 2.1. Put another way, a runner's pace usually slows by five percent when the distance doubles.

The half-marathon is a unique event with its own training and its own rewards

But here I am falling into the very trap I'd intended to avoid. I too am cheapening the half by comparing it to its big brother.

The shorter race is a unique event, with its own special training and pacing requirements, and its own rewards. Don't sell it short because of its name.

I have a wistful fondness for the half-marathon. This distance brought my last significant personal record, mainly because it was never run in the years when I routinely ran faster.

All but one of my PRs are older than my first child, and Sarah is now in her thirties. The lone exception is my PR in the half.

When Sarah was a preschooler, I ran my first half-marathon, barely beating my half-way split time during a full marathon a decade earlier. Okay, that was a cheap mark, but you take whatever you can when your PR-setting years are fading. A little later my record fell by a single second, then never again.

My point here is not that I ran so well, but that this middle distance could be the least tapped yet most promising source of records for most of us mid-pack runners. These races that take between one and three hours to finish can provide little-explored experiences all their own.

The attraction of the half-marathon isn't its similarities to the marathon, but its differences from it:

▶ The distance is not so great that it demands extra-long training runs, as marathons do. Two hours is the most time you need to invest in a long training run, and you can survive a half-marathon on even less. This is a welcome change from spending all of Saturday morning running, and the rest of the weekend semi-comatose from the extreme effort.

▶ Even if you train moderately (with your long run peaking at ten miles, for instance), no wall is likely to stand between you and a half-marathon finish line. So this can be a true race, instead of a survival exercise. For many of us the half marks the end point of running for time and the beginning of struggling just to finish.

▶ When you don't hit a wall, you spend much less time recovering. Dr. Jack Scaff, who in the 1970s founded the still-popular Honolulu Marathon Clinic, told Hawaiian runners that hitting the wall during a race was an injury, and that they needed six weeks to recover just as they would from any other injury. By emerging from a half-marathon uninjured, you can train at this distance or race another after a recovery period of only two weeks.

For several years I traveled to a special pair of Canadian races. I ran a marathon in stages—the first half in Vancouver, and the other half two weeks later in Kelowna. This experience wasn't at all like running a full marathon. It was both easier and faster.

Half-Marathon Training Schedule

This training program for the half-marathon spans thirteen weeks, which is three months or one full season of the year. The plan allows you flexibility in choosing from a range of distances and times, and for deciding which days of the week to run. I recommend that you don't run hard two days in a row, nor rest more than two straight days.

Prerequisites for entering the program are recent runs and past races of at least 10K (about six miles). Your greater experience might enable you to start at a higher level than week one, and to skip some weeks later on. However, if a week seems especially tough to you, repeat it or even back down a level before progressing again.

The key ingredients for training for a half-marathon are:

▶ **Long runs,** which at their peak of twelve miles approach the race's length, but match or exceed projected race time (because of the slower training pace).

▶ **Fast runs,** which are occasional short races or time trials to keep your legs and spirit lively. Limit your distance to 10K.

▶ **Easy runs,** which are unchallenging in both length and pace. These are best run in moderate time periods (of thirty to forty-five minutes), and are meant for recovery.

▶ **Rest days,** which don't require total rest. They can include cross-training activity, as long as it leaves you refreshed and ready for your next run.

Week	Long Runs	Fast Runs	Easy Runs	Rest Days
1	6–7 miles	None	30–45 minutes	1 or 2
2	3–4 miles	None	30–45 minutes	1 or 2
3	7–8 miles	None	30–45 minutes	1 or 2
4	None	5K–10K	30–45 minutes	1 or 2
5	8–9 miles	None	30–45 minutes	1 or 2
6	4–5 miles	None	30–45 minutes	1 or 2
7	9–10 miles	None	30–45 minutes	1 or 2
8	None	5K–10K	30–45 minutes	1 or 2
9	10–11 miles	None	30–45 minutes	1 or 2
10	5–6 miles	None	30–45 minutes	1 or 2
11	11–12 miles	None	30–45 minutes	1 or 2
12	1 hour	None	30–45 minutes	1 or 2
13	Half-marathon	None	30 minutes	2 or 3

MARATHONING at the sport's most historic distance

Marathons Start Early

Running a marathon is mainly a training challenge, in which making it to the starting line is tougher than going the 26.2 miles to the finish. The race takes a few hours. The training lasts several months. For runners beginning to train now, the "victory lap" of marathon day is still a season or two away.

Maybe you can wake up one fine morning and decide to run a 5K or 10K race that day, trusting your typical mileage to carry you through. Try this in a marathon, though, and the distance will quickly reveal your inadequacies.

You can't fake a marathon. Skimp on the training, and the results will be miserable—both during the race, and while enduring its damage afterward. In the marathon, you either pay in advance with training, or pay later with pain.

This elongated training is a big part of the marathon's mystique. Anyone can get excited about the race, but not everyone can endure the training.

Between dream and reality stands that preparation. It separates the dreamers who'd like to run a marathon someday, from the realists who train to go the distance and finally do.

I've trained for marathons dozens of times. From these experiences came my book, simply titled *Marathon Training*.

Runners ask me to explain why my training program differs in key ways from others they've seen. People usually ask:

Q: Can I really train for a marathon in only three months? Your program, which lasts just 100 days, is one of the shortest.

A: To this I must respond with a major disclaimer: those one hundred days don't start until you've run at least ten miles in training. Before that point, you're pre-training. Take as long as you need to reach that starting line.

Q: So you're saying that I can train even less than three months, if my longest current run is already more than ten miles?

A: You can safely begin my program at a training distance about two miles longer than your current long run. If your longest recent run was ten miles, then you can start my program at twelve miles. This lets you either shorten my program's length, or progress more slowly than the plan recommends.

Q: Your long runs go up by two miles at a time, instead of the usual single mile. Is this too big a jump?

A: Because you aren't asked to run long every week, my two-mile increase averages less than 10 percent per week, for the length of the program. I adhere to the widely recommended limit for adding distance.

Q: You only list one run at each distance. Why?

A: This gives you the important sense of steady progress, instead of feeling like you're repeating yourself at a certain level.

Q: You never mention how much total weekly mileage to run. Why not?

A: Counting miles can cause you to run too much on days that should be easy (or off), and can leave you tired for the runs that should really count. Instead, emphasize the long runs and the recovery between them.

Q: Your scheduled long runs end well short of marathon

distance. How can we run the extra distance on race day, if we never train this far?

A: The infectious excitement of race day—when you run with hundreds or thousands of other people and the hoopla you all generate—will give you those final miles.

Q: You recommend running at least a minute per mile slower than marathon pace during long runs. Where does race-day speed come from, if you don't train this fast?

A: You do practice speed; just not on long-run days. Taking long runs too fast makes them too hard to repeat as often as you need them. Train faster on weekends without a long run. Run about half the distance of your long run, but run it faster, or run a 5K or 10K race.

Q: You advise running no more than two marathons a year. Why do I have to wait six months for my next one?

A: You could run another much sooner, but limiting yourself to two per year enables you to do something other than train for and recover from marathons. There is much more to running than this. Give yourself time to sample it all.

The Far Side

Hal Higdon, a runner for more than a half-century, knows what works and why. But as the sport's senior writer at *Runner's World*, he also knows that an article needs the opinions of others. While writing about the long run in marathon training a couple of years ago, he asked me to comment. Parts of our discussion follow:

Q: What is the main purpose of the long run?

A: More and more I see it as an orthopedic test and a dress rehearsal for the race. Your long runs should test your feet and legs, to see if they can carry you the distance. Don't enter the marathon until you've passed your longest test. Make your long run a dress rehearsal, over the same or a similar course, at the same time of day, in the same shoes and clothes, with the same drinks and snacks.

Q: What is the peak long-run training distance for marathoners?

A: For competitive athletes, I recommend running nearly full marathon time over shorter than the marathon distance (slower than race pace, in other words). This approach was nearly standard among marathoners I surveyed for the book, *Road Racers & Their Training.* For the rest of us mid-pack runners, I'd advise, at the very least, running three-fourths of your projected marathon time.

Q: Should you incorporate walking into your long runs, whether or not you plan to walk in the race?

A: Walking breaks are optional. Take them or not, as needed and preferred. If used, incorporate them in the same way in both training and racing. Again, think "dress rehearsal."

Q: What about walking breaks as a strategy for finishing marathons?

A: I'm absolutely sold on it. I wouldn't have attempted my last dozen marathons without these breaks. My legs couldn't have endured non-stop training or the full race distance without walking breaks. Thousands of newcomers would never make it to or through the marathon without these breaks.

Q: How much recovery do you need between long runs?

A: Past programs (including my old ones) recommended taking long runs too often. Now I advise spacing long runs apart by at least two weeks, or as much as a month. After the longest training runs, the recovery period is almost race-like. This makes sense, because the effort of running this far is race-like as well.

Q: How much rest should you take before and/or after long runs, during the regular training week?

A: Resting afterward is most important, if the long run has left you with any soreness. Don't run again until that pain eases, however long that takes. This advice departs from earlier recommendations to run easily for a few days, to flush out lactic-acid build-up in your muscles. But acid build-up isn't the main problem. Muscle trauma is, and that heals most quickly with rest. Light cross-training (such as swimming or cycling) is okay during this period.

Q: Is there any advantage to combining long runs with other types of training on weekends? For example, speed training Saturday and long run Sunday?

A: That would make me miserable, as I recover slowly. I always schedule my long running and short racing on separate weekends. But other runners can manage it. You can race short on Saturday and run long on Sunday, for example.

Q: First-time marathoners don't always know how fast to do long runs, because they don't know how fast they can run a marathon. What do you suggest?

A: I tell them to figure conservatively. The usual formula used for estimating marathon potential is 10K time multiplied by 4.7. Newcomers might multiply by five instead. Example: a fifty-minute 10K equates to a four-hour-ten-minute marathon, which allows time for walking breaks if needed.

Q: How fast should experienced marathoners run their long runs?

A: Marathon racers usually run one to two minutes per mile slower in training than in racing. This was the pace I used when I was at my fastest, when my long-run pace was eight-minute miles and my marathon pace was about six-and-a-half minute miles. Marathon "survivors"—we grizzled old-timers—usually run about the same pace while both training and "racing." That might be the only gear we have!

Marathon Training Schedule

This training program for the marathon spans thirteen weeks, which is three months or one full season of the year. The plan allows you flexibility in choosing from a range of distances and times, and for deciding which days of the week to run. I recommend that you don't run hard two days in a row, and also not rest more than two straight days.

Prerequisites for starting this program are a recent run of at least ten miles, and a past race of 10K or longer. Your greater experience might allow you to start at a higher level than week one, and to skip some weeks later on. However, if a week seems especially tough to you, repeat it or even back down a level before progressing again.

The program's key ingredients are:

▶ **Long runs,** which reach twenty to twenty-two miles. Alternate the long run with one about half that distance, reaching nine to eleven miles, but at a somewhat faster pace.

▶ **Fast runs,** which can be an occasional short race or time trial, to keep your legs and spirit lively. Limit the distance to 10K.

▶ **Easy runs,** which are unchallenging in both length and pace. These are best run in moderate time periods (thirty to forty-five minutes), and are meant for recovery.

▶ **Rest days,** which don't require total rest. They can include cross-training activity, as long as it leaves you refreshed and ready for your next run.

Week	Long Runs	Fast Runs	Easy Runs	Rest Days
1	12–14 miles	None	30–45 minutes	1 or 2
2	6–7 miles	None	30–45 minutes	1 or 2
3	14–16 miles	None	30–45 minutes	1 or 2
4	None	5K–10K	30–45 minutes	1 or 2
5	16–18 miles	None	30–45 minutes	1 or 2
6	8-9 miles	None	30–45 minutes	1 or 2
7	18–20 miles	None	30–45 minutes	1 or 2
8	None	5K–10K	30–45 minutes	1 or 2
9	9–10 miles	None	30–45 minutes	1 or 2
10	20–22 miles	None	30–45 minutes	1 or 2
11	None	5K–10K	30–45 minutes	1 or 2
12	1 hour	None	30 minutes	1 or 2
13	Marathon	None	30 minutes	2 or 3

ULTRARUNNING
where distance is almost limitless

The Great Beyond

John McGee spoke while still under the influence of his longest run ever. He didn't finish the fifty-mile race that he'd conceived in Edmonton, Alberta. But he went far enough to feel elated about the day that took him well beyond what his training should've allowed.

"The ultras could be the future of running," he said while he sat watching other runners continue their five-mile loops. "They pose a new challenge for all of today's marathoners who are looking for something new and different."

I didn't disagree at the time. It's not easy to argue with a lawyer like McGee, even when he's tired.

But thinking about his statement later, I'd say that ultrarunning is less the future of the sport than its past repeating itself at new distances. Today's ultras bear a strong resemblance to yesterday's marathons—small, obscure, and peopled by the sport's fringe element.

Most ultras go unnoticed beyond the pages of their own magazine, *Ultrarunning*, just as marathons went unreported outside of *Long Distance Log* a generation earlier. Ultrarunners are seen as eccentrics and extremists even by other runners, just as marathoners once were.

Today's ultras bear a strong resemblance to yesterday's marathons

Some runners prefer to be different. They like to go where the crowds don't go, to the courses less traveled—which means far different and much tougher than the norm.

Today, "normal" running ends with the marathon. The runners who flock to these events are attracted by the crowds and the excitement they generate, as well as by the chance to run a course proven to be fast.

But in our sport we've always had a certain small group that refuses to do what everyone else does. When running was largely confined to track and cross-country for school athletes, the dissidents broke away and ran on the roads. When shorter road races grew popular, they moved to the marathon... then to road ultras... then to off-road treks.

To find an exclusive race, a runner must now search for one that is usually very steep and very long. Hundred-mile mountain-running races take place across the country, from Virginia's "Old Dominion," to Colorado's "Leadville's Trail 100," to California's "Western States," satisfying the urge to be different.

The size of the group allowed to start is often limited by extreme qualifying standards, and by how many runners the mountain trails can support. This situation suits the entered athletes just fine; they want their club to stay exclusive.

If ultras are to grow into "the future of running," I believe that they must take a different course than ever-longer, ever-tougher. They must take a different direction from the avant-garde of ultrarunning— to easier ultras, if that's possible.

For ultras to grow, their organizers need to provide more races, such as 50K to 50 miles, to offer a more accessible level of competition above the marathon. Organizers need to bring ultras down to flatter trails and roads, which emphasize running and not mountain-climbing ability. Some organizer needs to create a North American counterpart to the 54-mile "Comrades" race in South Africa, which most American ultrarunners dream of running.

I confess I don't think it's likely that any of this will happen. But then again, in the 1960s, I never would've thought that marathons would grow and go where they've gone.

Stop and Go Longer

Ken Crutchlow inspired me to try walking breaks. I introduced him in Chapter 3 as a British adventurer whose feats included running from Los Angeles to San Francisco, 550 miles in ten days.

Talking with him after his finish, I asked how he could do this with almost no training. "Five-mile bursts," he said. "That's how I ran it, five miles at a time with a bit of rest between the runs. Never would have made it otherwise."

What proved good enough for the untrained Crutchlow seemed good enough for mildly trained me. A few weeks later, I entered a hundred-mile race near Sacramento, California, to test his technique.

My longest run ever had been thirty-two miles. My longest recently (just one week before) had been a marathon. This should've set my distance limit at about fifty miles, but Crutchlow convinced me to try to double that distance.

The course was a two-and-a-half-mile lap through a suburban housing development. I started by running five miles at a time, resting for five minutes between these efforts. I carried on that way through fifty miles. Then I dropped down to two-and-a-half-mile runs—one lap of the course—with resting breaks in between.

This practice brought jibes from fellow runners. "You're dropping out already?" asked one early in the race. "With ninety-five miles to go?"

Instead of taking walking breaks between running segments, I gave myself resting breaks—actually sitting an average of five minutes, drinking and snacking, before resuming running at my usual pace exactly where I'd left off. I wanted to say I'd run the full distance.

Midnight passed. Lights in houses along the route flickered out. Four other runners remained on the course somewhere, but I hadn't seen any of them for hours.

I'd never felt so alone. Nothing I'd ever done in running seemed quite so senseless as running these laps by myself in the darkness after I'd already run so many.

A lone official stood, recording laps, in a golf-course parking lot that marked the start and end of each lap. I sat down there for my break after my seventieth mile, and couldn't get back up. The thought of going on was too depressing. I mumbled to the scorer, "That's it for me. Write 'DNF' [Did Not Finish] on your sheet."

Another runner, Peter Mattei, sprawled in the back of his station wagon. He was only resting, not dropping out.

"What do you mean you're quitting?" asked Mattei. "You can't stop now. You only have thirty miles to go."

He was serious. Compared to the seventy we'd already run, another thirty didn't sound like much. I had six to seven more hours of running to go. But I couldn't face even six or seven more minutes.

I was very tired of running. But to my surprise I wasn't overly tired from running—even after fourteen hours. I'd been more tired after all of my marathons. I would've been almost as tired if I'd stayed out at a party until 2:30 in the morning.

Ken Crutchlow was right. By taking long runs in short stretches, you can fend off physical fatigue all day. Mental fatigue from trying to run all night? Well, that's a problem Crutchlow must've solved somehow too.

I never solved it, never running more than thirty-five miles in a race again. But this experience taught me that taking breaks can make possible what seems impossible.

Old Way of Walking

I can laugh off charges that I'm less of a real runner for taking walking breaks. But my humor wanes when attacks on people I know and respect grow personal.

Jeff Galloway is the best-known proponent of mixing walking with running. This allows him to draw much of the praise when walking breaks work, but also requires him to field much of the criticism from non-believers.

A would-be Olympic Trials qualifier grumbled in *Runner's World* online about "Gallowalkers" cluttering up the course. I'm mystified about how people who take twice as long as he does to finish could get in this runner's way. But mostly I'm upset that he uses Galloway's name in a negative label.

By taking walk breaks on long runs you can fend off physical fatigue

Disagree with Galloway if you wish. But don't question his wisdom, commitment, and talent. He's smart, strong, and skilled enough to have made the 1972 Olympic team in the 10,000 meters, to have run more than a hundred marathons, and to have gently guided thousands of runners into doing more than they might have dreamed.

Galloway carries on a proud tradition, long popular in the ultras, to do what you need to keep on going. You can hardly call these people less dedicated athletes.

Jeff Hagen, a dentist by profession, won many hundred-mile and twenty-four-hour runs in his fifties. He described his deeds in an article for *Marathon & Beyond* magazine, which explained his way of walking in races.

In twenty-four-hour races, he walked for longer periods than the minute-at-a-time that Jeff Galloway and others generally recommend. Hagen's strategy arose from tips he picked up in a mountaineering class.

"One of these [mountaineering] principles held that taking frequent rest breaks, of three to five minutes each, was more efficient and effective than taking shorter or longer breaks," he wrote in *M&B*. "I was taught that less than three minutes did not provide adequate rest, while more than five minutes resulted in little additional benefit and wasted valuable time.

"Applying this to walking breaks [during a long run] suggests that breaks of less than a minute might not be as effective as those in the three- to five-minute range. This concept has been reported in research found in the running literature."

In my own research, I looked back at the writings of a godfather of walking breaks: Tom Osler, mathematics professor, top ultrarunner in the 1970s, and author of the 1978 *Serious Runner's Handbook*. His book underlined his own five-minute recommendation.

Osler promised readers they could double the length of their longest non-stop run, without trying twice as hard, by breaking for walks early and often. Osler typically ran for twenty-five minutes and walked for five in his medium-length ultras, which meant calling timeout at about three-mile (5K) intervals. In really long races, he'd shorten the length of his running intervals, but kept his walking time at five minutes.

Osler's way of walking rates another look from runners like me, whose marathons qualify as our "ultras."

50K Training Schedule

This training program for the 50K spans thirteen weeks, which is three months or one full season of the year. The plan allows you flexibility in choosing from a range of distances and times, and for deciding which days of the week to run. I recommend that you not run hard two days in a row, and also not rest more than two straight days.

Prerequisites for entering this program are a recent run of at least fifteen miles and a past marathon.

Your greater experience might allow you to start at a level higher than week one, and to skip some weeks later on. However, if a week seems especially tough to you, repeat it or even back down a level before progressing again.

The program's major ingredients are:

▶ **Long runs,** which peak at the marathon distance of 26.2 miles. It's best to run this distance in an actual marathon, at least a month before your 50K. On alternate weeks, run half the long-run distance, but at a faster pace.

▶ **Fast runs,** which can be an occasional short race or time trial, to keep your legs and spirit lively. Limit your distance to a half-marathon.

▶ **Easy runs,** which are unchallenging in both length and pace. These are best run in moderate time periods (thirty to sixty minutes), and are meant for recovery.

▶ **Rest days,** which don't require total rest. They can include cross-training activity, as long as it leaves you refreshed and ready for your next run.

Week	Long Runs	Fast Runs	Easy Runs	Rest Days
1	16–18 miles	None	30–60 minutes	1 or 2
2	8–9 miles	None	30–60 minutes	1 or 2
3	18–20 miles	None	30–60 minutes	1 or 2
4	None	10K–Half-marathon	30–60 minutes	1 or 2
5	20–22 miles	None	30–60 minutes	1 or 2
6	10–11 miles	None	30–60 minutes	1 or 2
7	22–24 miles	None	30–60 minutes	1 or 2
8	10–11 miles	None	30–60 minutes	1 or 2
9	Marathon	None	30–60 minutes	1 or 2
10	12–13 miles	None	30–60 minutes	1 or 2
11	10–11 miles	None	30–60 minutes	1 or 2
12	1 hour	None	30 minutes	1 or 2
13	50K race	None	30 minutes	2 or 3

FUN-RACING
after your final PR

chapter

24

Retiring Type

If you have the itch to race, go ahead and scratch it. It doesn't matter if you race fast or slow; long, short, or middle-distance; race from the front, in the middle, or at the back. What matters is only that you give it your all.

Keep racing until you don't need it anymore. This might mean completing a single race, running five to ten years' worth of weekly races, or racing for a lifetime.

Some runners can never quit racing. George Sheehan raced until he couldn't run anymore. He ran his last race, a ten-miler, little more than a year before cancer took his life just shy of his seventy-fifth birthday.

Runner's World founder Bob Anderson said in his mid-fifties, "If I didn't race, I wouldn't run."

To these two runners, "retire" was as dirty a word as "quit."

I once thought I'd never quit racing. It was too rewarding a challenge to ever give up. Turns out, though, that I am the retiring type. I haven't really raced since 1980.

My last race—my last full and honest effort under true racing conditions, that is—came in the "Artichoke Capital of the World,"

Castroville, California. I had no clue while "beating my age," with a thirty-six minute, thirty-five second (36:35) 10K shortly after my thirty-seventh birthday, that this race would mark my finish line. I'd never again come within three minutes of that time.

The ability to race fairly fast didn't suddenly desert me. Nor did an injury settle in for a permanent stay. Life just had other plans for me. A move cost me a set of racing and traveling companions I was never able to replace. I changed jobs once, and then again. A handicapped child came along, and a marriage ended.

All of this combined to render racing almost irrelevant. I did no more than dabble in it, going through the old motions more slowly.

I quit wanting to train long and fast, which is what racing requires. I stopped wanting to push hard, which is what racing is about. Those urges have never returned. My runs have become a way of venting pressure rather than turning it up.

I've accepted retirement with no regrets. I had my time, and it was a good long time. Typically, a runner earns five to ten good years of racing. Mine lasted twenty-two years, with twenty separating my first PR from my last.

This isn't to say that races have lost all their attraction. I still run slowly in races, and probably always will. There's much to be said for just being there, taking part. But I've long since quit really racing, and probably never will race again.

There's much to be said for just being there

If racing excites you and keeps you going, race with all your heart. Collect those PRs, gather those memories, enjoy those years of pushing your speed and distance limits. Race until you don't need it anymore, and then retire.

I haven't truly raced for a long time now, for half my running lifetime. I don't feel the need. I've collected all the PRs I'll ever win, gathered enough memories to last several lifetimes, and enjoyed pushing my speed and distance as far as they would stretch.

So I'm retired. Not from running, of course, and not even from going to races. I'm retired only from the challenging and rewarding, pressured and painful act of racing—and from training to race that way.

This isn't to say that I've abandoned all fast and long training. I do both regularly, just not nearly as hard nor as often as before. I don't train this way to race better, but to keep in touch with the miler and marathoner I once was.

Past Fast

Time cuts two ways for a runner in a race. Time can make you a winner when you set personal records. Or time can beat you when it ticks faster than you run.

Keep racing until you don't need it anymore

Time's blessings turn most harshly into curses when your PRs become permanent. You push as hard as before, but your times are slower. A crisis looms when you ask yourself, "Why race anymore?" and you can't find any good reason to continue.

You read so much about training for PRs and about celebrating these private victories. Yet you see so little written about what to do after you set your last PR—a fact of running that you'll eventually have to face.

You plan to be a lifer in this sport, right? You need to know, then, that life is much longer than the period for PRs.

If you're still in those PR-setting years, enjoy the excitement while it lasts. While it won't last forever, you can still stay on a running-for-a-lifetime course.

What should you do when you eventually slow down?

More than half of my running life has occurred after I set my last PR. I have some words of advice from the other side of the PR hill— along with some words of comfort. No abyss awaits you when your improvement ends. I can tell you with certainty that you can still enjoy racing and running after your PRs have ended.

I've found other ways than running my best times to make racing satisfying. Here are four ways for the post-PR runner to enjoy races:

1. Run in races without racing them. This means running at your everyday pace. But you may wonder: why bother going to a race if I can do the same training without traveling?

I have plenty of reasons: you can join hundreds or thousands of like-minded folks who reclaim the streets from cars. You can accept drinks and cheers and T-shirts. You can do a good deed by pacing someone else to a PR. You can reward yourself for maintaining your physical fitness.

2. Start a new set of records. When the old ones become unbeatable, what's to stop you from starting over? Instead of setting lifetime goals, consider shorter time periods. Aim for PRs in your current ten-year or five-year age group. Or just try to run faster for a particular course or distance than you did last year, or in your last race of the same type.

3. Adopt a new racing specialty. Racing takes wildly diverse forms, and few runners sample them all at once. This leaves much unexplored territory for record-setting. If you hit your time wall in standard road races, try ultras, or trail runs, or cross-country, or track. Or simply race a distance you haven't run before.

4. Appreciate racing's timeless values. Improving your times isn't the only reason to race. In fact, that can become one of the lesser reasons. A good and honest effort counts the most, and you can't check that on a watch. You have to feel it.

Jack Foster, a New Zealander who held the world masters' marathon record for almost two decades, said as he eventually slowed down, "Only my times have changed. All the other experiences of racing that attracted me initially are the same as they always have been, and they still appeal to me."

The times of racing must slip eventually. But the feelings of racing never have to change.

Running the Good Race

It's not what I wanted to hear with more than half the race left to run. I hadn't yet made the turn for home on an out-and-back course, when a runner heading back shouted to me, "If you know so much about running, what are you doing way back there?"

You might think that after such a put-down, I wouldn't dare show my face at another race. But I keep coming back. I've tried to stop many times, yet couldn't stay "retired" for long.

Racing still attracts me, though for different reasons than those during my years of chasing PRs and prizes. Those aren't the only possible payoffs on race days.

My PRs stand like tombstones—monuments to the racer I was thirty years ago. I no longer contend for any age-group prizes. I probably never will again, unless I make it to the ninety-plus category by outlasting—instead of out-running—most of my competition. In my sixties, I'm easing back through the field.

My race times are slower than they've ever been. And my race distances are shorter than they've been in a long time, usually just 5K to 10K.

So what's the payoff from racing? To find other rewards, I had to step out of the PRs shadow and out of the search for the perfect race.

The personal record is one of this sport's greatest treasures. It gives every runner a way to win. But like any item of great value, PRs are scarce. They don't fall consistently, and they don't keep falling forever.

The perfect race is even scarcer than the personal record

Another name for personal record is lifetime best. We runners hope for long lives. After you've run your fastest times, you might start searching for the "perfect race."

The perfect race is even scarcer than the personal record. Inveterate racer George Sheehan described perfection this way, using the marathon as his example:

"The perfect marathon is like the perfect wave, and every marathoner keeps looking for it. On that day he will run his best pace all the way, and when he comes to the twenty-mile mark he will feel as if he just started and what he has gone through was just a warmup. Then he will float through those last six miles, strong and full of running."

You'll have but a few race days—at all distances, over an entire racing career—when your health, talent, training, experience, and enthusiasm, and the circumstances of weather, course, and competition converge perfectly. I haven't enjoyed one of those days since the 1960s.

Someday you'll reach a point when you realize that you've already run your perfect races. After you've experienced that kind of perfection for the last time, how should you measure your current successes?

If racing excites you and keeps you going, race with all your heart

You revise your standards. Instead of aiming for the perfect race, you go for a good one. Instead of striving for a lifetime best, you shorten your sights.

You might simply compare what you do on race day with what you would do on a normal training day. The infectious excitement of race day can bring out your best, which is far better than you might imagine it to be.

Forget about PRs. Think about the distances and paces you typically run by yourself. Now look at what you can achieve in a race.

You can probably run at least one minute per mile faster than you normally do in training, or you can hold your usual pace for twice the distance. That's what I count on, and it's always satisfying.

Sometimes both effects come at once, both faster and farther. That's when racing is truly magical.

Extra speed and distance aren't the only definitions of success in racing. Consider two others:

▶ **Pacing.** To run a good race, you should finish faster than you start, ideally with the first mile as your slowest and the last one as your fastest.

▶ **Passing.** In a good race, hardly anyone passes you after the opening rush. You do most of the passing instead, not because you specifically aim to beat others, but because your pacing is right.

All-time great races are rare, but running a good one is possible anytime. That doesn't mean that the good ones are guaranteed, however. There are no guarantees in racing, and that element of uncertainty is one of its most enduring attractions.

What am I doing way back in the field? Same as anyone ahead or behind me—I'm finding out what I can do today.

Part Three

Running Long

Injuries can be good for you. The bigger they are, the better they can be—if the pain eventually lets up and allows you to run again. I'd go so far as to say that you don't truly become a runner until you've endured an injury. You don't fully appreciate running until you've almost lost it.

My first major injury was good for me. After suffering from it for a year, I turned to longer and slower running—which led to longer and faster racing that lasted from the mid-1960s to the early '70s.

Unfortunately, I overdid the racing—going too far, too fast, too often. My left foot signalled its reluctance to continue like this when a lump of calcium formed on the top of my heel bone. The more I ran and raced with it, the bigger it grew and the more it hurt.

Finally I stopped racing and went to a doctor. He gave me the conventional advice of that era: if it hurts to run, rest. If that doesn't work, stop running and find yourself another activity.

I found another doctor. This one, a podiatrist, said that rest would never cure my problem. He showed me an X-ray of the bony growth cutting into my Achilles tendon, and told me the only cure would be surgery.

I went under his knife, hoping for the best but fearing that running could be over for me. Happily it wasn't.

My left foot quickly regained most of its strength and flexibility. But this scare permanently changed my views about running and my approaches to it. Mostly I would never again take it for granted.

My running didn't end with that injury. The rest of my running life began then, and in many ways has been the best and certainly the longest part.

That surgery occurred more than half my lifetime ago. I've gone from the 1970s to the 2000s with no recurrence of that injury, and with no other injury threatening my running future.

My runs today are much slower and shorter than before that injury, but I'm also healthier and happier. I almost never wake up in the morning unable or unwilling to run. I almost never finish a run without feeling better for having taken it.

I don't regret a single hard or long mile from my racing past. Even the speed- and distance-induced injuries make good memories for what they taught me.

Nearly all my runs are easy now. I've never stopped running in races, but have long since quit taking my results seriously. I refuse to let my past PRs haunt my present running.

My views about running are both longer and shorter than they used to be. Once I looked no farther than the next race's finish line; now I see only the ultimate line that we all hope to reach as late as possible. Once I trained for races weeks or months away; now I look no farther ahead than my next run.

I hope you reach this last, longest, and best stage of a runner's life, after enjoying all that the two earlier stages had to offer.

EASING out of routines too hard and fast

chapter 25

Off-the-Job Training

Many of us wear the label "serious runner" as a badge of honor and courage, and sometimes it is. But I took running really seriously for only one year, and it was a disaster.

If I'd kept trying that hard, you wouldn't be reading this page now. I would've stopped running after that awful year, and the next forty-plus years wouldn't have happened as they did.

My career as a racer peaked in 1961, as a high school senior, when running was still a delightful new plaything. Later that year, as a college freshman, running became my job, but my racing career soon hit bottom.

I didn't go to Drake University to establish a business profession, to join campus organizations, to form friendships, or to find a future wife. I went there to major in running.

Drake paid me well for that. I went there on a full scholarship, then (as now) wrongly called a "free ride." The ride wasn't free. We runners paid for it by training two hours every afternoon of the school year, and racing almost every week.

The burden of having to earn my "ride" weighed heavily on me. So did being surrounded by teammates who were also opponents.

Running can be a wonderful hobby but a terrible job

I came to Drake as one of the fastest runners in my state. But so did everyone else on the team, and some came from faster states than Iowa.

We had to prove ourselves all over again, to each other and to ourselves. This started right away, as every training run became a race.

In our first true race, our coach, Bob Karnes, lined us up to race a mile before a Saturday football crowd. I expected to run at least as fast as the PR I'd left off with the previous spring.

But I ran ten seconds slower. Never mind that I'd done better only a few times before, and had never started a season this well.

My standards had gone up … way up … too high up. That day I fell into a pattern of self-flagellation over "bad" races. At first I beat up on myself only on paper, in my running journal. Later the abuse became physical.

After a slower-than-hoped race that October, I ripped off my spikes and ran a series of mad dashes on the crushed-brick track, in bare feet. You could call it a "punishment run."

The effect was the opposite of my intent. From then on, my racing went from not bad to truly bad to worse.

My mile time that freshman year slowed by almost half a minute from what I'd run in high school. And by majoring in running, I hadn't made time for proper studying. My grade-point average barely kept me eligible to run.

I had to get out of my job. And I did, as soon as the last race ended the following spring. I quit training and saw no reason ever to start again.

My early retirement, at age nineteen, lasted only a month. One day in early summer, my dad dropped me at a swimming pool a few miles from home. He couldn't pick me up later, and with no other ride, I started walking … and then running.

That run, short as it was, produced a life-changing plan for me. I'd return to Drake, but give up my scholarship in exchange for the freedom to train in ways that worked better for me.

Coach Karnes readily accepted my plan, because he had nothing to lose. He hadn't gotten any mileage from me anyway, and now had a "ride" to give someone new. Anything I could contribute to his team would be a bonus.

I called the restart a "new career." It featured a new approach in which running wasn't vocational—and a new set of records.

In my sophomore year, I broke most of my old PRs. Better yet, I became a true student—making good grades, making time to learn a trade by working on the school newspaper, and making friends who weren't runners.

Writing about running later became my job. But the running itself was never again more than a hobby.

The point of this confession is that running can be a wonderful hobby but a terrible job. It can suffer when it gets too serious.

More Better Runs

Old habits die slowly. I spent the first half of my running life training to race by racing often and hard. Since then, I haven't truly raced for almost twenty-five years.

Yet for most of that time I've kept training like a racer—scaling down distances and speeds, yes, but sticking with the same old pattern: alternating hard and easy days, running long runs twice the length (or more) of usual ones, adding fast runs up to two minutes a mile quicker than usual.

But eventually I realized that training this way did me few favors. It had trained me for races that no longer mattered much. And my one major run a week had caused my many minor ones to suffer, cutting some of them short and canceling others.

My quest became to simplify all of my running. I needed to weed out complications and to make my runs more alike—to make the long runs shorter, the short ones longer, the fast ones slower, and the slow ones faster.

The first step in my campaign was to stop training for one great day that might never come. The second was to start making each running day a little better.

My quest became to simplify all of my running

The more days I run, the happier I am. If I feel more energy and less pain on certain days, and can run a little extra, I'm happier yet. I don't need a race day, or even a long or fast day, to feel satisfied.

So am I advising you never to race, and never to train at race-like effort? Not at all. I highly recommend racing to anyone who hasn't tried it, and who hasn't stopped improving.

What I'm saying here is that hard racing isn't for everyone, even though much of the advice written in our sport (my past work included) is framed for runners who race.

In this section, I'm writing for the rest of us: those who have moved beyond racing, who run in races without racing them, who are between racing seasons, and who don't race and don't plan to start. I'm speaking for those who want to run nearly every day. And for those who don't mind running the same way most days, since that frees us from wondering whether we should run at all or how we should run.

This is not a scaled-down version of race-training programs, which dictate some runs to be much longer and faster than others, and compensate with some easier days off. My non-racer's training program aims to make more days the same, and more runs better.

If this approach appeals to you, put each element of your current running routine to these two tests:

▶ Is this what I'd want to run if I didn't have to do it to prepare for a race? If it isn't, then choose the runs that you look forward to, and discard those you dread.

▶ Could I take these runs nearly every day of the week? If one day's rest isn't enough between your runs, then tone down their length and pace until you can repeat them daily and indefinitely.

The ex-racer or non-racer has no greater or more distant goal than to run well each time. Running is "training" only for the run of the moment and the next one to come.

Easy Writer

Writing attracts me for most of the same reasons that running does. Both create something from nothing—words on blank paper in one case, miles on empty roads in the other.

In both, your results just about equal your efforts—both in the big event and in the practice leading up to it. Both are solo, in the sense that no one can do your work for you.

Bernie Greene of Silver Spring, Maryland, shares my twin passions. He isn't a writer by profession; he's a U.S. government statistician. But he contributes regularly to various running magazines, and takes his avocation seriously, even in mostly humorous pieces.

Greene is one of the few people who ever ask me specific questions about our favorite sedentary activity, which also happens to be my job. One of his many e-mail messages asked, "Is writing as easy for you as it looks?"

It isn't easy for him, he added. "Gawd, I'm forever revising, editing, tweaking, and even then I'm not quite satisfied."

Is my writing easy? Not at one level. But it is at another.

There are two sides to writing, just as there are two sides to running. The public side is publication for the writer, and racing for the runner. The private side is practice for the writer, and training for the runner.

The public writing that Greene mentioned is the only type that our readers ever see. It's hard work for the same reasons that a race is, because it reveals exactly who we are at our best.

As a public writer, I work hard at making it look easy (to borrow a phrase from George Sheehan). Like Bernie Greene, I fuss over the wording of my pieces to make them sound casually conversational. Then I still think, when the published piece appears, "This could've been better."

As an old-time runner, I pretend that race results no longer matter, but they do. I still run as well as my current training and talent allow, casual as my efforts might appear. I still think of how my public running could've been better.

The other side of both activities is the private daily writings and runs. These are truly easy most of the time, or should be if they are to

My private running is short and slow so I don't tear myself down beyond overnight repair

remain everlastingly satisfying. Effort, concentration, and especially self-criticism all must ease.

My private writing is a daily journal page that no one else sees, at least not in its raw form. I can't fuss over these entries as if they were bound for publication, because that would be too much work, too often.

This writing is almost as easy as talking to myself. The results range from dreadful, to routine, to (on odd occasions) worth dressing up and going public with in a column or book.

My private running is usually short and slow. I don't run any harder because I don't want to tear myself down beyond overnight repair.

These runs can be almost as easy as walking. They can range from awful, to routine, to (at rare moments) worth taking to a race.

The easy running, like the easy writing, isn't pretty. But both serve as low-stress private practice for the hard, public efforts to follow.

SIMPLIFYING the running to what matters most

Long-Distance Learning

Teaching and coaching are endurance activities, reaching far in distance and time. The teacher-coach can't imagine who will grab hold of the lessons and run with them—or how far.

It's never too late to thank an old teacher-coach, and we're never too old to find a new one. I was approaching age sixty and was a running teacher myself when I discovered a coach who taught me important lessons without knowing he had.

Jack Farrell didn't coach a team anymore, having retired after a brilliant career at Thousand Oaks High School in southern California. Instead he taught other coaches who read his articles on the web and heard him speak at coaching clinics.

"It's a thrill to get to share my ideas with a new crop of coaches," said Farrell. "Theoretically I still contradict virtually every other clinic speaker, and I relish the role of maverick."

In the early 1990s, Farrell returned from a coaching sabbatical with new ideas to try. "I spent a good many years working with young runners and assigning killer workouts, followed by easy recovery runs," he wrote. "The athletes using this approach seemed to run too hard on the hard day and then were relatively 'trashed' on the recovery day."

Farrell decided the old hard-day/easy-day pattern had to go. He reduced training to its simplest and most effective terms:

▶ **Run about the same distance nearly every day,** with beginners running as few as two miles.

▶ **Add distance slowly,** by about one mile per month, with team veterans peaking at eight miles.

▶ **Race frequently,** at about one minute per mile faster in a 5K than current training pace, which improves gradually with better fitness.

Farrell's runners took no really long runs nor worked through intense interval sessions. Their speed training came mostly in races.

Too simplistic, you say? Look at the results.

Boys' teams from Thousand Oaks won their state cross-country championships in 1993 and '94, and ranked as high as second nationally. One girl from Thousand Oaks ran even better than that.

Farrell wrote, "In the 1995 season, her fourth year utilizing these training principles, Kim Mortensen won the National Cross-Country Championship. During the 1996 track season Kim posted nation-leading times in the 1600, 3000, and 3200." The 3200 time remained a national high-school record in 2004.

One good test of any training method is how adaptable it is to runners of wide-ranging ages, abilities, and ambitions. I couldn't be less like Farrell's former athletes. They were young enough to be my grandchildren, and they trained to race while I had little urge to race anymore.

Yet with only slight modifications, I adapted Farrell's program for high-school runners to meet my current needs and wishes as an elder:

▶ Run no harder on any one day than it would be possible to run almost every day.

▶ Add five minutes (about half a mile) to daily runs each month, until they peak at about an hour.

▶ Race a 5K or 10K once a month, at least one minute per mile faster than training pace.

My races are longer but less frequent than those of Farrell's kids. My racing has become almost an after-thought instead of the main reason to run.

But I haven't lost the occasional urge to run a little longer or a little faster. So I still reserve one day most weeks for roughly simulating my old races. On that day I train in one of two ways:

▶ Running beyond my usual one-hour limit, often while adding one-minute walking breaks that have become standard in my recent half-marathons and marathons.

▶ Running less than my usual half-hour minimum, but for a measured distance, running at least one minute per mile faster than my norm. (This after a thorough warm-up.)

My results? In racing terms, my clocked times aren't worth mentioning, but in health and enjoyment terms, I have better times than I've had in decades.

Farrell, the self-proclaimed "maverick," proved that his methods work with young runners. He also taught a long-ago graduate that he wasn't too old to learn something new.

Simple Times

My heroes have always been runners older than myself. Though I can't grow younger, I can age better, and these heroes show me who I'd like to grow up to be.

I found a hero in Ed Whitlock. In 2001, the British-born Canadian had just become the oldest runner ever to break three hours in a marathon, dipping all the way to 2:52 at the age of sixty-nine.

Remarkable as his time was, it was incidental to my admiration of Whitlock. I came to admire him not for how fast he raced his marathons, but for how he trained for them.

He hadn't needed to turn himself into a techno-runner to become as good as he was. In an era when the theory and practice of running has grown increasingly (and often frustratingly) complex, his approach has been utterly and refreshingly simple.

Whitlock's program included no intervals or tempo runs. He
didn't follow a hard-easy plan, didn't cross-train, didn't stretch or lift,
didn't wear a heart monitor. He trained alone, three laps to a mile,
around and around a cemetery in his Ontario hometown.

His only goal, he said, was "to go out there and put in the time."
This he did, for two hours a day at a leisurely nine minutes per mile.
Nevertheless he raced his marathon at a pace almost two-and-a-half
minutes faster.

He only deviated from this routine on race days, which came
around every week or two. Races were his speed-training substitute.
He ran these short distances as much as three minutes per mile faster
than his everyday pace.

My running was fastest—and healthiest—when it was simplest

I stopped running Whitlock-
like times at half his age. Now my
glorified-shuffle daily runs rarely
reach half the length of his.

I didn't look up to Whitlock for
his numerical achievements, but for
the simplicity supporting them. He
reminded me that my running was
also fastest—and healthiest—when it was simplest.

My best year of many years was 1968—before our sport became
sophisticated, and before I knew any of what I know now. I was running better as a road racer than I ever had, though my career was
already a decade old and 400 races along.

My magic spell began after I dropped out of a marathon (and
decided I wasn't meant to be a marathoner). The spell ended less than
a year later, when I revoked my retirement from the marathon.

When I was marathon-free, I was also injury- and illness-free. I
ran twenty races, as short as one mile and as long as 30K (about nineteen miles). Seven of them resulted in permanent PRs. Seven more
races led to my fastest track times since college, when I'd trained
exclusively for track.

My approach was Whitlock-simple. I could fill a page with the
names of techniques and tactics, practices and products that I didn't
use (most hadn't been invented yet) and apparently didn't need.

Instead, I just:

▶ Ran easily, steadily, and consistently for nearly an hour a day

▶ Raced hard, fast, and often

▶ Ran longer and slower, for about two hours, on non-race weekends

In 1968, I'd stumbled onto my best mix of easy distance and hard racing. Not knowing how good this combination was for me, I stumbled out of it again.

The many complexities of modern running soon followed. I would never run as well again, though I was only twenty-five when my golden year ended, and I'd race on hundreds of more occasions.

I can't live off the good old times. But their simple ways are still good ways to live.

My hero Whitlock didn't speak my final line here, but he moved me to write it. The more complicated the rest of life becomes, the simpler running needs to be.

Simply Superb

September 28, 2003, was one of the greatest days ever for marathoners. The two-hour-and-five-minute (2:05) barrier fell twice in the same race, to Kenyans Paul Tergat (2:04:55) and Sammy Korir (2:04:56) in the Berlin Marathon. Andres Espinoza of Mexico ran the first sub-2:10 for masters, by a lot, with 2:08:46.

Yet none of them had provided my greatest thrill that Sunday. I'd cheered loudest for someone else who went where no other marathoner had gone before: Ed Whitlock.

When I first wrote about Whitlock (see the preceding section), he'd become at age sixty-nine the oldest marathoner to break three hours. The wait for him to run sub-three-hours at age seventy-plus wouldn't last long, I figured.

His first try, soon after turning seventy, fell a tantalizing twenty-five seconds short. He could've decided that was his last try.

The more complicated the rest of life becomes, the simpler running needs to be

Injuries come easily and heal slowly at his age, perhaps especially for such superstars, the runners who race the hardest. Whitlock had a knee problem, which caused him to pass his seventy-first and seventy-second birthdays without running another marathon.

Finally he could train again. "I started in the winter with ten-minute runs, each week adding four or five minutes for each day's run and gradually building up," he said.

By summer, Whitlock was back to normal running, which is to say his characteristically simple regimen. Whitlock ran two hours most days, in three laps per mile around a cemetery. He avoided streets because "cars tend to aim at you, whereas in the cemetery they're a more docile lot."

"On the streets, I always start speeding up," he complained, while in the graveyard "my only objective is that I have to go out for two hours, so I might as well take it easy." He only sped up when it counted—in the races he ran twenty-five to thirty times a year.

Whitlock's runs reached two hours again in July. "Since then I also got in some longer ones," he told me. "A few at three hours, pretty well all LSD [Long Slow Distance], and all on my small cemetery loop."

He reported racing nineteen times since the spring, at distances of 1500 meters to a half-marathon. These had once again made him "race-tough" in ways that standard speed training might not have.

"My Crim Race [in Flint, Michigan] at 1:02:25 [6:15 pace for ten miles] in late August gave me hope," he said before running the 2003 Toronto Waterfront Marathon in late September. "I would have wished for another month of preparation, but hopefully everything will go well."

It did. He ran 2:59:08 at the age of seventy-two. Score one more victory for simplicity.

WRITING the running history you make yourself

Personal Records

You don't say no to an FBI agent. When one told me to keep a written record of my running, I said, "Right away, sir."

Fred Wilt was one of J. Edgar Hoover's feds, but I didn't get to know him through his day job. Wilt, a former Olympic athlete himself, moonlighted as a running coach and author.

His first book, *How They Train*, reached me as an impressionable sixteen-year-old. Wilt recommended in his summary chapter that "Runners should keep a logbook or diary describing all their running and racing in detail. This allows them to review the data to see which training techniques are working and which ones aren't."

My diary-keeping began immediately. The first day's entry on a sheet of lined notebook paper read: "11/11/59: 2-mile road run, slow."

That was all I wrote about a run that was hardly worth noting. But it was the quiet launch of an enduring habit, and the earliest tangible sign of a career to come.

This logbook I began writing on Veterans' Day 1959 continues to this day. The record that Fred Wilt urged me to keep has taught me more about how to be a runner than anyone else's book ever could.

It also taught me how to be a writer, and taught me more than a little about how to live my life.

A writing journal evolved out of my running diary. Soon after I began the logbook, words of observation and opinion started to appear—then sentences, paragraphs, and whole stories.

The diary recorded training for running; the journal became training for writing. They still share the same daily page.

This private journal led within a year to making my writing public—first in newspapers, then in magazines and newsletters, and later in books and on a website. Plenty of my writing is published, but much more remains unseen.

Some of this writing has to do with the subject that earns my paychecks—running. But more deals with whatever subject thrills or troubles me at the time. In that sense, much of my writing is training for living. I draw from more than 15,000 days of diary-keeping and journal- writing to offer tips for adopting and perfecting running principles and methods.

A private diary works well simply as a runner's record, but it can serve in wider ways by growing into a writer's journal. Here are some of my suggestions about how to keep a running journal:

Keep It Simple

The easier it is to keep your record book, the more likely you are to settle into the long-term habit of logging in. Start by reducing log-book information to the few items that mean the most to you— such as the type and length of your daily run in distance or time, your pulse rate, your monthly weight, and any unusual happenings while training. Adopt a consistent format for quick comparisons of different days.

My daily page still starts as that first one did in 1959. At the top goes a cryptic notation of the day's running, with a time period instead of a distance (a typical entry: "6/3/04—30 min. with mile in 7:23").

I'll note if my pace is faster than usual, or if an injury slows me down. This notation leaves a factual record of physical efforts that day, available for review and analysis later without interference from my flawed memory.

If you're only keeping statistical records, a calendar with large blocks of space will work nicely, as long as it's tacked to a wall in your home. But the calendar won't travel or store well. A notebook works better for this purpose.

I now keep my diary/journal on my computer, because that's the standard tool of my trade and I'm more comfortable typing than writing by hand. Thousands of my earlier pages were scribbled on paper, though, and I still recommend that practice. Notebook paper and pens are much cheaper and more portable than the smallest of laptops.

> *The easier it is to keep your record book, the more likely you are to settle into the long-term habit of logging in*

Keep It Short

Let's say you already spend an hour each day on running and supplemental exercises. You may wonder how and when you'll find even more time to write about your running.

The most common excuse I hear for not running is, "I don't have time." The same is said for writing. But you aren't given the time; you have to make it if these activities are important and satisfying to you.

The time requirements are modest for both running and writing. A runner, for instance, can pack training into as few as twenty minutes. And you can record the essentials of your training session in the time it takes you to read this paragraph. Writing a journal entry takes longer, but still not excessively so.

After my morning run, I write at the beginning of my workday at my desk. I fill about one typed page, in an average time of twenty minutes. I intentionally keep my session short, because I don't want it to seem like a second job, and do want to look forward to more of the same the next day. In this way, I've yet to lose interest in my hobby.

Keep It Practical

The great value of your factual diary entries is the trail they trace. Days of running would otherwise leave behind what would appear to be mostly random footsteps.

You can't take much direction from them at first. But as the weeks, months, and years add up, these steps form a trail that points two ways. It shows where you've been, and where you might go next.

Analyze your accumulating data over extended periods of time to judge your results. The longer you maintain your diary, the clearer your patterns of response to running become—and the clearer your thoughts about it become.

I typically make an accounting at the end of each month. A couple of weeks would be too short a period to show how much (or little) I've accomplished.

For instance, I might run long on a Sunday and again the following Saturday. So my mileage that week would appear misleadingly high. Temporary lows might come from a brief illness or a business trip.

Tallying by the month levels these artificial highs and lows. I compute daily averages to compare my performance from month to month. You can do the same with your own running—as well as with figures such as body weight—to keep watch on long-term trends.

Keep It Personal

The practical section above focused on keeping a logbook or diary. Next I hope you'll consider journal writing, which can happen when you start to analyze and explain the numbers in your diary.

It might strike you as odd to write a daily letter to yourself, meant for no one but you to read. This might seem to be one small step removed from talking out loud to yourself. But once you start, I bet you'll discover that it can be interesting, helpful, and simply fun.

Keep your journal personal, which doesn't have to mean strictly private. You might later select and sanitize certain passages to share with others. But don't write with that goal in mind, because it will alter your style and content. You write differently when you feel eyes looking over your shoulder than when the page is intended for your eyes only.

In my journal I employ a let-it-rip form of writing. I use few or no notes, I have little idea at the start where the piece will wind up, and I go as fast as my hand will move from the top to the bottom of the page.

Don't try to make each page perfect

I don't try to make each page perfect. I leave bad spelling and grammar uncorrected, and facts unchecked. This isn't the time to stop and revise the material. Editing can come later if the material earns the right to go public.

It also isn't the time for modesty or good manners. These are our pages. We can write anything we want here, honestly and personally, without angering, shocking, or boring anyone.

Keep It Going

The longer the diary-journal continues, the greater its bulk and the higher its value. Store your records in a safe place, treating them as the precious volumes they will become in time. Their ultimate value is as a personal library of dreams and memories.

You can open your ongoing book to any old page, and bring a day back to life. You can call up a mental videotape and, from a few lines on the page, recreate all you did and felt that day. These recordings give substance and permanence to your efforts that otherwise would be as fleeting as the moment, and to your experiences that would be as invisible as footprints on pavement.

Writing can attract us for the same reasons that running does. Both running and writing are personal in the sense that no one else can run the miles or write the lines for you, and no one can know how much the results mean to you.

In my office stands a bookcase filled with more than forty binders, each representing a year's worth of personal writing. On a nearby shelf rest all the books I've written and edited for publication.

If, in the case of fire, I had to choose between the two sets of books, it would be no contest. I'd haul out the diary-journals that tell the truest story of my life.

Talking Books

In 2002, Eric Steiner, a regular contributor to *Northwest Running* magazine, was the first journalist to interview me at length about producing and preserving running books. He sorted through my ramblings to produce a concise and coherent article. Here are some highlights from our exchange:

E.S.: Who among running writers have you looked to for guidance over the years, or simply fawned over?

J.H.: As a writer-speaker, no one approaches George Sheehan as my role model/mentor/father-figure/friend. I knew him before he was *the* George Sheehan, so I never held him in the awe that many of his readers and listeners did.

My first reaction to Hal Higdon was more fawning. He was already an established writer and running celebrity when I met him. I was a sixteen-year-old and he was an old man of twenty-nine.

Kenny Moore is my age-mate, but I look to him as the elder statesman and epitome of running-writing talent. All of us writers in this sport do.

E.S.: Which books by other writers did you like the best, or influenced you most? Can you pick your top five?

J.H.: Nothing against the authors of recent hot-sellers, but none breaks into my list of all-time favorites. My most treasured books came out too early to sell well, and in some cases they weren't even well written. Their strength was that they spoke the greatest truths to me at exactly the right time.

My early favorites had lasting effects, because they reached me at my most receptive age, when their theories were new and pleading to be tested. These first life-changing books, in the order I read them, were:

1. *Franz Stampfl on Running*, which introduced me to Roger Bannister's concept of interval training. This led me to Bannister's autobiography, *The Four-Minute Mile*, which bordered on poetry.

2. *Commonsense Athletics* by Arthur Newton, the true father of long slow distance (LSD), whose ideas heavily influenced my book on that subject a decade later.

3. *How They Train*, Fred Wilt's account compiling what dozens of accomplished runners really did in training.

4. *How to Become a Champion* by Percy Cerutty, an eccentric whose ideas have proven in years to be less wild as they first sounded.

5. *Run to the Top* by Arthur Lydiard, the one book that changed the running world's—and my own—training the most.

E.S.: You've now published more than two dozen books of your own. Which do you like best?

J.H.: That's kind of like asking which of my three children is my favorite. Each book, like each child, is unique and incomparable.

Did I Win?, my biography of George Sheehan, probably contains my most heartfelt writing, because it came together shortly after my good friend's death. But that was really his book, not mine. I was a conduit for his story.

My journals tell the truest story of my life

Of my own books, *The Long Run Solution* stands out as my truest statement of how I feel about running. It's not by chance that my current book [this one] adopts *Solution's* format and updates its material.

TALKING with runners about running and more

Talkathons

Two of the best reasons to run have little to do with staying in shape or training to race. These companion attractions are thinking and talking.

Team running enables you to talk freely with friends, while solo running allows a heart-to-heart talk with yourself. Both opportunities have become scarce in a world long on loud noises and short on calm voices.

Running alone with my thoughts is my choice most days. This hour a day is all mine—time away from the phone, radio, and computer that share my office, time to clear away mental clutter so worthwhile thoughts can bubble up. I don't carry a pen and pad while running, but usually come back from a run with ideas begging to be put on paper.

George Sheehan, one of the sport's all-time great writers, said he did his best "writing" away from his desk—while running. He treasured the solitary times "when I've been able to withdraw from the world and be inside myself. Such moments can open doors impervious to force or guile."

Talking with other runners for my work fills the rest of my day, so I feel little need to actually run with them. If I worked outside the sport, I'd need to talk my way into a running partnership or group.

Something in the act of running together—the rhythm, the sweat, the common purpose, the stripping of outer roles and inner restraints—loosens up one set of muscles more than all others. Those are the jaw muscles. Listen to two or more runners talking, and you'll never again believe that long-distance runners are a lonely breed.

Dr. Sheehan balanced aloneness with togetherness. He once wrote that talking on the run "frees me from the polysyllabic jargon of my profession, removes me from the kind of talk which aims at concealing rather than revealing what is in my heart. For me no time passes faster than when running with a companion. An hour of conversation on the run is one of the quickest and most satisfying hours ever spent."

Two of the best reasons for running, according to Sheehan, are contemplation and conversation. His third reason was competition, which he defined not as competing against others but as joining them to bring out better efforts than we could ever make alone.

A daily run is as different from a race as a private chat is from a public lecture. Conversing is easy, just as taking a casual run is. Speaking before a group is as hard and fearsome as racing, but the audience brings out the speaker's best lectures just as a race crowd brings out the best runs.

Even Sheehan, perhaps the most skilled speaker this sport has known, paced and stewed before his lectures. But once onstage, he spoke calmly and beautifully.

No hour passed faster than one at a Sheehan talk, and he left his listeners wanting more. They would cluster around him for another hour before letting him leave the hall.

He drew his largest crowds and longest ovations at the Boston Marathon. One year there, after he'd autographed his last book and answered his last question, we left the room together.

"That was quite a show," I said. He agreed, but added, "At times like this, I have to remind myself that a few blocks from here, I'm just another skinny Irishman."

I may look like just another gnome in glasses, but talking with my running buddies tells me I'm more than that.

Talking with running partners who know you best and care about you most—and sometimes just having a good talk with yourself as you run—tells you who you really are. No time is better spent.

Words to Run By

Every special interest develops its own jargon, its insider language. Runnerspeak is so much my natural language, I forget that everyone doesn't speak it fluently. A new reader of *Runner's World* complained, "I marked twenty-six words in my first issue that are foreign to me."

I need to realize too that language evolves. Wording that served one running generation doesn't necessarily carry over to the next.

When I started running, some descriptions already sounded quaint, if not silly. Runners were "harriers," "thinclads," or "spikesters." I gagged when a headline writer called us "cinderfellas."

Long retired are most of those terms, along with others from my early years in the sport. Gone the way of cinder tracks and the broad jump are "warm-ups" for flat-soled training shoes and "sweats" for long-sleeved, long-legged training suits.

Runnerspeak keeps changing. The following list can serve as a dual lesson—to show newer runners how we used to talk, and to update us older runners on today's common usages.

Old: I put in 100 miles a week.
New: I train 100 miles a month.

Old: Our long, slow runs are at seven minutes per mile.
New: Our short, fast runs are at seven-minute pace.

Old: My hard runs are at race pace.
New: My hard runs push the anaerobic threshold.

Old: I'm running a time trial.
New: I've scheduled a tempo run.

Old: My stopwatch tells me how fast I run.
New: My heart-rate monitor sets my tempo.

Old: I'm running ten interval quarters for speed work.
New: 5K races are my speed training.

Old: This is an easy day.
New: It's my recovery day.

Old: I'm resting today.
New: This is a cross-training day.

Old: It's a small race with fewer than 100 runners.
New: It's small with just 1,000 entrants.

Old: The entry fee is high at $5.
New: It's a bargain at $50.

Old: The distance is 10,000 meters.
New: It's a 10K.

Old: Where do you pin your race number?
New: Your bib goes on the front.

Old: Stand at the starting line.
*New: Stand behind the appropriate pace sign, in back of
        the start banner.*

Old: I plan to go out fast.
New: I'll walk until the traffic clears.

Old: Pick up the pace.
New: Throw in a surge.

Old: I finished strong.
New: I ran negative splits.

Old: The officials gave me 30:01, but my watch read 29:59.
New: My watch said 30:01, but my chip time was 29:59.

Old: My marathon time goal is three hours.
New: My goal time is four hours.

Old: Drink plenty of water.
New: Replace your fluids.

Old: He's dropping out.
New: She's taking a walking break.

Old: I'm making a pit stop in the woods.
New: I'll wait in line at the Porta Potti.

Old: It's nice to see a few girls coming to races.
New: Look at all those women.

Old: I love to beat the young guys under age twenty.
New: I get a kick out of beating all the youngsters under forty.

Old: Who won?
New: Which Kenyan won this time?

Old: She hit the wall.
New: She bonked.

Old: Don't eat during a run or you'll get cramps.
New: Eat energy bars or gels to keep from bonking.

Old: Train in your race T-shirts to show everyone what
    you've done.
*New: Never run in a cotton T-shirt because it doesn't wick your
    sweat away from your skin.*

Old: Where can a runner find good shoes?
New: How do I decide which shoe is best from all these choices?

Old: That's the number-one-rated shoe.
*New: It's a good stability shoe if you need motion control, but bad
    if you require more cushioning.*

Old: Are your feet flat?
New: Do you pronate?

Old: My knee hurts.
New: You might have an IT [iliotibial] band injury.

Old: Arthur Lydiard is my training guru.
New: I follow Jeff Galloway's advice.

Old: My heroes are the old-timers Billy (Mills) and Buddy (Edelen).
*New: I admire the old-timers Billy (Rodgers) and Joanie (Benoit
    Samuelson).*

Don't Ask Me

My favorite part of going on the road to talk to runners is to listen to
them. That is, to hear their questions at the end of my lectures. I don't
have all the answers, or even a majority of them, but pondering the
questions is still a worthwhile exercise.

While flying to one scheduled appearance, I filled my time by
writing my own list of questions.

Why, if people who run beyond 26.2 miles are called "ultra-marathoners," aren't those who run less called "submarathoners"? Why, if we have biathletes, duathletes, and triathletes, aren't running specialists called "monoathletes"?

Why are older runners called "masters," a term that denotes skill rather than age? Why does the public persist in calling runners the despised J-word (joggers), which is like referring to skiers as "sliders" or golfers as "swingers"?

Why haven't we coined a better term than the "half-marathon," the only distance known as a portion of another distance which implies that it is inferior to it? Why can't we replace the half-marathon with a 20K?

Why do we race by kilometers but still take splits and average our pace by miles, which sound slower and come up less often than kilometers? Why do we train by miles, when kilometers would add up faster and make totals greater?

Why can't we find a classier term for walking breaks than "run/walk"? How about "interval racing" or "Gallowalks" instead? Why, if walking breaks are so beneficial, do runners training on roads still run in circles while waiting for stoplights to change?

Why are there so few races in the great gap between the half-marathon and marathon, when such in-between races could make excellent training for these events? Why does cross-country remain a sport for school kids, when adults' aging legs need the break from hard macadam roads more than young legs do?

Why do watches give times in hundredths of a second, when official off-track times always round up to the nearest full second? Why, if watches split times into hundredths, do runners talk of their own times by rounding them down to the lower full minute?

Why does it seem that our favorite model of running shoe is always the one to disappear from the marketplace? Why do so many of today's finest running shoes come with the round laces that don't stay tied as well as the flat ones?

Why don't more running shorts come with bigger pockets for carrying gel and bar snacks?

Why does a runner who professes belief in the "listen to your body" mantra nevertheless take painkillers to quiet his or her body's messages? Why does the body lie about how good or bad it feels right before a run, or especially a race?

Why, if male athletes are "jocks," aren't women athletes named for an item of apparel? Why, if women are equal to men in races, are the men's results almost always listed first in news reports?

Why are the too-fast starters and the late-race bonkers at races nearly always men? Why, if women organize Races for the Cure to combat breast cancer, don't men produce a similarly popular series of races for fighting prostate cancer?

Why, if "to finish is to win," do finishers risk bodily harm to themselves and others to move up from 1002nd to 1001st place? Why, if "everyone's a winner," do races still keep score and give prizes to a select few of these winners?

Meet and Greet

We met as runners do on a sidewalk, passing briefly within arm's length of each other. As is my habit, I greeted her with a small wave and the single word, "Morning."

She glanced at me, from the corners of her eyes without turning her head, and said nothing in return. This was the look she might've given a homeless drifter gone too long between washings, and coming too close to bum spare change. It was a don't-bother-me response.

This isn't the way one runner should greet another. It certainly wasn't how we used to signal such meetings in an earlier, more innocent era.

The old custom of greeting every runner who passes, just because he or she happens to be running, is almost obsolete. The traditional brief but friendly exchange between runners has rapidly faded, and that's a shame.

When runners were few, we all knew each other in our communities. If not by name, we knew one another by our reasons for running and our approaches to it.

But we didn't stop to talk. That too was part of the custom We wouldn't interrupt anyone's run for extended chit-chat. A simple word or two in passing—or just an unspoken smile, wave, or nod of recognition—would do. A small gesture was enough to signify that we weren't alone, that we shared experiences and secrets with a wide community of runners.

Then the running population exploded. The streets and sidewalks grew crowded with us, and we runners grew more diverse in background and purpose. Runners now form more of a city than a community.

Much has improved with our sport's growth. But one unfortunate casualty has been the sense of connection between runners who don't otherwise know each other.

Rarely these days does another runner initiate a greeting toward me. Even eye contact comes grudgingly.

I'm a creature of old habit, though, and still greet every runner I meet. Nine in ten do respond, often with surprised looks that seem to convey: Who are you, and how do you know me?

I'm happy to say that the woman I mentioned earlier, who refused to acknowledge me, is the exception. She and a few others like her do cast looks of irritation (usually men who don't want me to interfere with their focus) or suspicion (usually women who wonder why a strange man would speak to them). But to give a greeting and receive nothing in return is discouraging and a bit embarrassing.

In these circumstances, I respond with another comment. It's louder than my first, in case my greeting went unheard and because I'm now shouting back over my shoulder. "And you have a nice day too."

This seldom has any effect on a reluctant greeter. But it helps me feel that I'm doing my part to keep alive one of the finer old customs of running.

The greeting of one runner by another makes our world a warmer place. It keeps our sense of community intact. It says, "I know why you're here, and I'm happy that you are."

DEFENDING all runners' right to feel good

Running's Health

My local newspaper in Eugene, Oregon, the *Register-Guard*, reacted curiously to the 2001 return of the National Track Championships to Track City, U.S.A. The sports section lavished as many as six pages a day on the meet.

Yet the front page that Sunday led off with a negative story headlined "Popularity of Running Tails Off, Slows to a Walk." This erroneous claim demanded and received the following rebuttal from me, in my letter to the editor:

Most of my mornings start with a run. I follow this with another favorite morning habit, reading your newspaper.

Imagine my surprise to pick up Sunday's paper and learn that running is a dying, damaging activity. The anecdotes and statistics seem to support these claims, but they are misleading. I say this as one who has run for forty-some years (more than half of them in Eugene), who writes about the sport for a living, and who travels the country meeting with runners.

Your article props up the tailing-off theory by reporting a decline in the number of runners and in the sales of running shoes. I've read the census figures and offer a different take on them.

Most of the drop has occurred among marginal "runners" who had only one foot in the activity anyway. They ran less than three times a week and no more than a mile or two at a time. Those who run more and more often are more likely to keep running.

Imagine my surprise to pick up Sunday's paper and learn that running is a dying, damaging activity

Interpreting the shoe-sales figures: As many as half the pairs sold aren't worn by runners. Blame changes in footwear fashion, not a dwindling runner count, for the decline in these sales.

Better measures of the running population are the numbers of [running] magazines and books sold. Only true runners buy them.

Circulation of the largest magazine, *Runner's World*, tops 500,000. Books on the sport are more numerous and sell better than ever before.

"The difference between a jogger and a true runner," said the sport's finest writer, George Sheehan, "is an entry form." Entries at U.S. road races grow each year, according to the national Road Running Information Center in Santa Barbara [California]. More than a quarter-million Americans run at least one marathon annually.

True, the number of road races in Eugene has slipped. These events haven't disappeared, though, but just moved north to the Portland area.

More than 12,000 runners enter the annual Portland Marathon and its shorter companion events on one day in October. More than 30,000 try the five-kilometer Race for the Cure in Portland.

As for the suggestion that running is inherently bad for the legs, it's interesting that your article mentions Eugenean Janet Heinonen. She has run at least thirty miles a week for forty years, and her knees and hips still work just fine.

Runners do get hurt. These injuries usually result from training mistakes—too far, too fast, too often.

The problems nearly always ease if the error is detected and corrected. Very few injuries need be retirement-provoking.

Running is basically a health-giving activity, and running's health is undoubtedly sound. It's true nationally and here in Eugene, where the movement took its first steps four decades ago.

America's Best

America's top long-distance runners can't win. No matter which way they turn, they run into critics.

If they run against world all-stars, the slower Americans are seen as not competitive. If they don't run in the same races, they're considered to be ducking the best competition.

If they enter races open to all, they don't win any money and can't support themselves in the style required of modern athletes. If they enter Americans-only races where they can earn a paycheck, they're seen as supporting exclusionary events that reward mediocrity.

If they don't win, they're told they haven't trained hard enough. If they train harder, get hurt, and can't race, they're told they don't know how to prepare properly.

If they run fast, they're told how many of the world's runners are faster. If they're the fastest Americans, they're told how many past U.S. runners were faster.

Critics of today's American runners are numerous and noxious. They take to newspapers, magazines, and websites to hurl charges that runners are unskilled, ill-trained, and under-motivated. The message they send to our top runners is, "You're no good, you'll never be any good, so don't bother."

This message stinks. It discourages honest effort and the celebration of success in ways lesser runners are allowed to measure it.

Running is breeding its own annoying fans, like those of the big-time team sports who live to shout "We're number one!" and to attack athletes who dare to disappoint them. The All-American ethic is: to win at all, you must win it all—the World Series, Super Bowl, Olympic gold, or Boston Marathon. Anything less turns the fan into a critic and the "loser" into a failure.

Running defines winning better that. Winning is being there, and trying to perform better than you did the last time, or better than you ever have before. Winning can mean beating other runners, yes, but it mainly means meeting or exceeding your own goals.

This definition of winning as running a personal best should not suddenly be canceled out when runners leap into national- and world-class arenas. They still deserve to celebrate and be celebrated for improvement, no matter what their rank in time or place.

American runners can't do the impossible; they can't live the sort of lives that many of their African counterparts have lived. They can't go back in time to choose different parents, to be born in a different place in different circumstances, to grow up at high altitude, to run miles to school and back every day, to eat only homegrown foods, and so on.

The top Americans can only do what all runners can: make the most of talent given and training done. None of America's best runners would accept less, and none of their critics should expect more.

Different Worlds

Old friends can agree to disagree, and remain pals. Jeff Johnson and I have been disagreeing for almost forty years, since he questioned a 1966 article I'd written in my Iowa running-club newsletter about slowing and lengthening my training.

Johnson and I had run "all-comers" track meets together one summer in the early 1960s. He was a Stanford student, and I'd come to the West Coast from Iowa to run every race I could.

That summer deepened our love for the sport so much that we've never left it. Running gave both of us careers, though each of us took a different direction.

Johnson once sold Tiger shoes, then helped found Nike, and later coached club athletes with elite ambitions. I still do what I started that summer, which is to write for magazines.

We've stayed friendly for four decades. But that isn't to say that we've always agreed on the subject of running.

Several years ago, he objected to a story of mine in which I stated that the current shortage of world-class U.S. runners didn't trouble me. "The U.S. leads the world where it really counts—in distance-running participation," I wrote.

Johnson compared this to an educator saying, "The U.S. has more people than ever reading at the fourth-grade level, even though we produce fewer scientists. Nevertheless this is evidence that the U.S. leads the world where it really counts."

He added, "I think it possible that you and other popularizers of our sport are partly responsible for this decline in quality by dumbing down what it takes to get to the top. For the last quarter-century the running publications have sought to expand their markets (a not-unreasonable goal) by preaching that running is easy and fun, that you can walk your way to a marathon finish, etc. All of this is true, but little or none of it aids in the advancement of performance."

I don't know whether the writings of Jeff Galloway, myself, and other running writers have affected America's running elite at all. But I can say for certain that our collective messages have smartened up our main audience of mainstream runners. Many are former athletic illiterates, who've since triumphed if only by lifting themselves to a "fourth-grade" running level.

My amiable disagreement with Johnson reminds me that all of us runners don't think alike. Running today is really two distinct sports, with a growing gulf between them.

On one side are the major- and minor-leaguers: the pros, semi-pros, and amateurs who live like pros. On the other side are the rest of us, who run races but have no more in common with the pros than rec-league basketball players do with NBA stars. (A third group of runners never races, and its sport is like shooting hoops alone in the driveway.)

The mixing of the two worlds at races is an illusion. They and we share little else there but a common course. For instance:

▶ They outrun 99.9 percent of all runners. We outnumber them a thousand to one.

▶ They're athletes. We're just runners.

▶ They're largely young. We're mostly middle-aged and older.

▶ They race long and fast. We race long.

▶ They race for place and time. We race for time.

▶ They're paid to race. We pay to race.

▶ They train to race. We race to spice up our training.

▶ They plan their day around training. We squeeze training into the rest of our day.

▶ They train as much as they can. We train as little as we can get by with.

▶ They're featured in magazines. We read those magazines.

Critiquing Critics

I vowed a long time ago not to speak badly of other runners' running. But how do I respond when runners criticize the running of others? By critiquing the critics, do I become one myself?

It's hard to remain silent amid the rising volume of negativity in our sport. You have to wonder why anyone would worry much about how other people run, or run-walk—especially if these are the slow-pokes that "real runners," if they're as fast as they claim to be, would hardly see.

Do they have all their own running problems solved? Were they never slow themselves? And do they think they'll never slow down?

Running commentators aren't immune from the wider problem in general sports reporting. They easily can be sucked into this attack mode of chat rooms, talk-radio shows, and Sport Centers.

Critics can speak or write, publishers can print, and broadcasters can air whatever they wish. That's their right.

But that doesn't mean we have to read or listen to them. I've cut off a growing number of commentators, publications, and websites that vilify runners. I deny them access to me, and suggest that you do the same to those that anger or depress you.

The best way to stop such negativity from affecting or infecting us is to turn it off at its source. Canceling those subscriptions and steering clear of those websites may encourage larger audiences to do the same, drying up the critics before they do too much damage.

More than fifty years ago, folksinger-poet Woody Guthrie penned a paragraph that is more timely now than ever, and could stand as the best defense against the rising volume of runner-against-runner criticism. Guthrie wrote:

"I hate a song that makes you think you're born to lose, no good to nobody, no good for nothin', because you're either too young or too old, too fat or too thin, too this or that. I'm out to sing the songs that'll make you take pride in yourself."

I prefer the stories that lift us up rather than bring us down. What about you?

TRAVELING on runs across distance and time

Terrible Tourist

Travel can be instructional, and you can learn as much about yourself from your time on the road as you do about your destinations. What I learned about myself on one driving trip wasn't pretty. I traveled with a traditional runner's mindset—that is, to cover ground quickly—and that was no way to tour through country so scenic.

The trip was my idea. My proposal shocked my wife, Barbara, because it was so out of character for me. We rarely travel together outside the running circuit.

"Let's drive to Idaho and Montana," I said. "Those are two of the six states I've never visited."

"How long do you want to take?" she asked. She's the great tourist in our family, having visited more countries than I have states.

"Oh, three or four days," I said, pulling out a map and tracking the most direct route across Idaho, barely touching the nearest point in Montana.

"No, no," Barbara protested. "We can't drive all that way and not see Yellowstone National Park and the Grand Tetons. We have to spend at least a week."

She thinks any trip lasting less than a week is hardly worth taking. Hurrying doesn't allow her to see enough to satisfy her explorer's curiosity.

We compromised between our travel styles. Barbara agreed to limit our time on the road to one week. I agreed to stay off the interstate highways and to take close looks at those two national parks.

I freely admit here that my wife was right. The sights were spectacular and not to be missed. But I also confess that I don't enjoy traveling the way she does.

Despite the splendid change of scene, the best parts of my days were taking my usual morning run, in a new place each day, and settling into a motel each evening, plugging in my laptop, and sitting down to my usual writing. I'd brought much of the baggage of my home life along with me.

That trip taught me that I'm a terrible tourist. I feel little urge to be one at all. I'm happy with home and all that goes on there, and don't want to leave it except when duty calls.

The least attractive trait I discovered about myself on the trip was my strong streak of workaholism. My reaction at journey's end was, "Hooray, it's over. I can finally get back to work."

Maybe I should put a more positive spin on my response. Maybe I enjoy being home so much because my everyday life resembles a permanent vacation—with little to do but run and write, and all day to do it.

Lost Weekend

Standing in my street clothes in Birmingham, Alabama, in 1999, watching the half-marathoners leave me behind at the starting line, I felt like a fraud. I'd lectured them on preparation the night before. Now they were running, and I wasn't.

This was especially embarrassing because I'd ignored the runner's first rule of air travel: never pack your running shoes in a bag you're going to check. Always wear or carry them.

How many times have I given that advice? Too many times to count. You'd think that after flying to running events since the 1960s, I'd know better than to let my shoes out of my sight.

Mine was a three-legged journey to Birmingham. I'd waved good-bye to my bag in Eugene—and didn't see it again until five days later.

That was my first trip with my new laptop computer. The carry-on bag didn't have room for both my computer and my shoes, so the laptop won the space.

My checked bag must have gone to Birmingham, England. The airline couldn't retrieve it during my stay in Alabama, so I lost my weekend of running.

I didn't run one step. Not my usual jetlag-clearing session on arrival, and not my planned half-marathon the next day. Two big zeroes went down in my diary, because I'd forgotten the runner's basic rule of packing.

"We have lots of shoes," said Valerie McLean, trying to reassure me. She owned the running store Trak Shak that organized the race.

She would've given me a good deal on any shoes in her store. But running a half-marathon in untested shoes is a risky venture. I wouldn't trust a pair of shoes I hadn't tested while training. And running in shoes without my orthotics, the custom-made inserts molded to my feet, is like trying to read without my bifocals. It's possible but very difficult.

I might run in new shoes with my inserts, or maybe in old ones without them, but not in new shoes without inserts. That would be a foolhardy combination, especially at the distance of a half-marathon.

When I returned to the airport to head home, I heard my name called and was told, "Your bag just arrived." "Then check it in again," I said, still dejected at missing the race. So of course my bag then disappeared, with my shoes still inside, for another three days. The lost weekend dragged on.

I can't emphasize enough: wear your running shoes onto the plane, stuff them in a carry-on, or even drape them over your shoulder. Just don't check them!

Miles from Somewhere

The mileposts displayed higher and higher numbers as I ran north: 351, 352, 353. This is one long trail, I thought blissfully. I know it leads to Omaha, Nebraska, but where does it start—St. Louis, Missouri?

It's known as the Wabash Trace, a former rail line recently converted by the Rails to Trails Conservancy into a walking/running/biking path. We runners should all be lucky enough have a trail like this in our hometowns.

I grew up in the tiny, miles-from-nowhere town of Coin, Iowa. As a child, I placed pennies to be flattened on the Wabash tracks. I knew bedtime had come when the 9:25 Wabash freight train's whistle blew.

My earliest endurance activity was walking the tracks to the fishing and swimming holes along the river. I helped save a friend from falling off a railroad bridge, but lost a dog in another mishap.

The railroad abandoned the line shortly after our family moved away in the early 1960s. For thirty-some years, the roadbed lay idle and became choked with weeds.

The Trace was more than a decade in the making. So when it was finally finished, I was eager to run on it through Coin for the first time in 2000. I'd heard that the locals were pleasantly surprised by the people the trail attracted. They were health-conscious, environmentally friendly, and upscale, bringing cash into an area sorely needing it. Coin now welcomes these visitors with a shower room and a covered picnic area at its Community Center.

I immediately liked everything about the Trace: the surface of finely crushed rock over a dirt base; the bridges, much like the old river crossings I'd walked shaky-legged as a kid, but now with solid bases and safety railings; the signs, including "No Hunting" and mile markers, starting from who-knows-where; the grade, as trains required that hills be gentle; the quiet, with wind singing in the bare trees this late-fall day.

I ran out and back for an hour total, and saw only one cyclist. This path deserved much more of our kind of traffic.

By the end of my hour, I'd already planned a future multi-day run, or a one-day bike ride, to Omaha at milepost 400 or so. And who knows, maybe someday I'll even head south to find the location of mile 0.

Seeing Ghosts

I don't just believe in ghosts, I visit them often. They're visible only to me but are clearly there, everywhere I've ever gone and remembered. "Ghost" is another word for "memory." The longer our memories, the greater our population of ghosts.

Many of mine live in the San Francisco Bay Area of Northern California. I first visited there in 1963. My first running job came there, first long race, first marriage, first child, first book (like another type of child), and first home purchase.

That home was in Sunnyvale. I lived there for less than a year, and I hadn't thought much about the place in decades.

Pleasant business recently took me back to Sunnyvale, which now sits in the heart of Silicon Valley. My host offered to drive me past my old home. We didn't need directions. Once on those streets again, my mental GPS clicked on.

Our condo development had been new when we moved in. It looked like it had been well cared for ever since. On the grounds, saplings had grown into tall, shade-giving trees.

No one there could see my ghosts, including the current residents who were living with them in their condo.

If anyone had seen me loitering about, they would've eyed me suspiciously. They couldn't have known that I was visiting my younger self, or that my youngest daughter took her first steps here, or that an early book of mine was penned within those rooms.

Driving back to my hotel, even older ghosts awakened. A long, straight, heavily traveled road stretched toward Los Altos. That was where *Track & Field News* had launched me onto my career path, and where *Runner's World* would set up shop.

We passed a Sunnyvale high school. My first long race, the National Championship 30K, had started and finished on the Fremont High track in the summer of 1963. In that race I'd tripled my previous longest run, and wouldn't run any farther for another four years.

I realized that the kids now using that track not only weren't born yet in 1963; many of their parents weren't either. But my ghost remains alive and well there, forever young.

WATCHING and supporting the runs of others

Living the Afterlife

A slight middle-aged man sitting in front of me at the 2001 N.C.A.A. Track Championships looked vaguely familiar. He wore a baseball cap pulled low over his thin face.

When he spoke to a seatmate in Arabic-accented English, recognition finally clicked in. He was Said Aouita. He said he'd come to Eugene for the Prefontaine Classic (the international, Olympic-level meet), and had stayed another week to see the collegians run.

For those who don't remember him, his name is pronounced "Sah-EED Oh-WEE-tah." In the mid-1980s, this Moroccan was the first to run under thirteen minutes in the 5000 meters, and a close second under 3:30 in the 1500 meters.

Now in his forties, he was thoroughly engrossed in the N.C.A.A. meet, scribbling copious notes in his program. He sat almost completely unnoticed by the crowd around him, seeming content in his anonymity.

That's how it should be, I thought. Aouita had his time. Now it was someone else's turn at the glory—including the current Moroccan-born world record–setters he'd inspired, Hicham El Guerrouj and Khalid Khannouchi.

Runners fast and fortunate enough to reach the top spend only a few years there. Most of them peak in their late twenties and early thirties.

Then where do these champions go? What do they do with their next fifty or sixty years, after the cheering stops?

Many more unnoticed, ex-great runners roam the world than celebrated current ones. The same week that I spotted Said Aouita in Eugene, I saw three more past winners at the Steamboat Marathon in Steamboat Springs, Colorado.

Lisa Rainsberger was there, too. You might remember her as Lisa Weidenbach, who three times in a row in 1984, 1988, and 1992, missed the Olympic Marathon team by only one place. Her serious racing years are long past, but she doesn't look back with regret.

"I'm living in Colorado Springs and training marathoners there," she told me. "We brought forty of them to this weekend's race."

Rainsberger pointed to her young daughter, Katie. "This is my first medal," she said, in reference to the difficult pregnancy she'd had with her first child. "And this is my second," she added, pointing to her growing belly. "It's a boy, due this fall."

At Steamboat, a bearded mountain man stood in the finish chutes, directing traffic. Most likely not one finisher in a hundred knew him as Benji Durden.

He'd made the 1980 U.S. Olympic Team, but couldn't compete because of the U.S. boycott against the Moscow Games. Then Durden ran a 2:09 marathon and went on to reach the first World Championships in 1983.

"I haven't raced in years," he said, "but I'm at a race almost every weekend. Last year Amie [his wife] and I handled forty-six events."

One of the runners Durden guided into a chute at Steamboat was running under an assumed name. The announcer read it without commenting on her true identity.

I'll honor her wish to remain anonymous by not disclosing it here. She was one of America's all-time greats, and she ran a forty-three-minute 10K that day.

I bet she was thinking: I like being out here running, and I don't mind doing it slowly. I just don't want to be singled out for it.

The ex-stars in my story all appear to be living well in their athletic afterlife. They keep running, keep working, keep watching the sport—only in a much quieter and less visible way than before.

Runners on Parade

Mornings don't start much better than this one. I hadn't run a step for two Sundays in a row. But what I'd seen would inspire my running and writing for some time to come.

Both these Sundays several years ago had started with marathons— first in Portland, Oregon, and then in Victoria, British Columbia. I'd finished my work earlier, as I'd given talks and taken runs on the marathon courses (at a fraction of their total length) on the days before.

Sundays were my days off from running. All I had to do was watch other people go about their business.

The day in Portland started with an early wake-up call. It came not from an operator downstairs at the Hilton, but from a runner in the next room, as he flushed the toilet and turned on the shower. Who else but a runner would be up as early as 5:45 on a Sunday?

Runners throughout the hotel and elsewhere were awaking for the dawn start of the marathon. I looked out the window an hour before the seven o'clock race time and saw runners warming up. I wished they'd realize that this distance already required more than enough steps, without wasting any beforehand.

At the start, I watched more than 5,000 marathoners pass, and their parade filled me with unexpected emotion. While talking to a stranger, I had to break off my conversation for fear my voice would choke.

Later that morning my wife Barbara asked, "Did you see anyone you knew at the starting line?"

"Only one I knew by name," I said. Then I added, "But you might say I knew all 5,000 by what it took them to get here, what it will take to get through their marathon, and what they will take away from this day as lessons and memories."

This thought was what had almost choked me up. More of the same followed a week later.

On Saturday at the Royal Victoria Marathon, I was asked a hundred or so times, "Are you running tomorrow?"

I responded no, and explained why in my speech at that night's banquet.

"Someone has to stand and cheer for you," I said. "There's a lot to be said for watching you run."

Without the tunnel vision required of a runner on race day, as a spectator I can see the full field. I've watched thousands of these parades, and yet the sight never fails to stir me.

My early wake-up call on Sunday morning came from runners in nearby rooms at the Grand Pacific Hotel. An hour before the race, I looked down at the street beside the Inner Harbour and saw runners wasting steps in typical fashion with warm-ups an hour before the start.

Standing a block into the marathon course, I scanned the eager, happy, concerned athletes passing by, and could only name two. But I felt I knew all 3,000 by the long-term project they now were starting to finish. I felt moved again.

A True Fan

A marathon viewer can give encouragement to the runners, and also take inspiration from them. Having favorites to cheer for adds to the thrill.

No one in the 1999 National Capital Marathon in Ottawa inspired me more than Ernie DeCaro from Auburn, New York. The year before, he'd undergone surgery for cancer that had taken the gluteus muscles of his left buttock. His condition was serious, but he could still joke, "I now have official certification that I'm a half-assed runner."

He had run and raced for years, but had never tried a marathon until New York City's the same year as his surgery. After finishing that one he'd written, "My thoughts go immediately to next time."

National Capital came next for DeCaro. After corresponding for more than a year, we met for the first time at this race.

We walked from the expo to our hotel on Saturday, splashing through a rainstorm. "We're almost there," I told him and his running partner, who responded, "That sounds like one of the lies that spectators tell you during a marathon."

This is not a beauty contest or a style show, but a survival test

I understood what she meant. Sometimes observers shout specifics, such as, "Only one mile to go."

But distance and time become elastic when you're racing. Early miles seem to pass in a few minutes each, while the last mile feels like it's half an hour long.

A related lie is, "It's all downhill from here." The last mile always seems uphill, no matter what the topo map might show. But my favorite lie is, "You're looking good." No one looks his or her best at the end of a marathon, especially a rainy one.

You're not supposed to look good. This is not a beauty contest or a style show, but a survival test.

Don Kardong once wrote, "Do you want to see how you'll look twenty years from now? Glance in a mirror right after you finish a marathon."

A rare truth-telling spectator asked me late in one race, "Are you okay? You don't look so good." I must have appeared to need a 911 call.

DeCaro's partner recalled a sign that a spectator had held up in the final miles of a New York City Marathon. It read, "Remember, you chose to do this." And not only had they chosen, but they'd paid for the privilege of pushing themselves this far.

I took a position about a kilometer from the finish. My view was better here than at the finish line, and surrounding voices were quieter.

I kept most of my cheers neutral, with "Way to go" or "Good job," or I just clapped.

It doesn't matter what you say, if anything. Runners only want to know that someone, loud or silent, cares about what they're doing.

When DeCaro passed, I couldn't resist shouting those three great lies: "Almost there … downhill from here … looking good!" He bettered his PR by nearly half an hour—and that's the truth.

End of the Road

To the uninitiated and uninvolved, this spot has the look of a hospital emergency room on a day of disasters. It's the finish line of a long race. The longer the race, the more startling the sights.

Runners have made their final push across this line and their last gestures to the crowd. Now they start to walk away from it all, as well as they're able, in their first few moments after their last running steps.

An observer can't help but notice the runners who look the worst. They wear a thousand-meter stare, unaware of anyone around them. They limp, stagger, weave, or lean on other runners for support. They bend, doubled over, from pain or fatigue. They bleed or vomit.

Officials triage the cases, sending those most at-risk to the medical tent. The others shuffle toward the comforts of foil space-blankets, drinks, and foods.

An ugly scene, you say? Only if you don't look beyond the suffering. If you do, you'll come to see that behind the finish line is a strangely beautiful place to watch a race.

Behind the finish line is a strangely beautiful place to watch a race

When not racing myself, I sometimes stand there. In the fall of 2003, I positioned myself at the finish lines of two marathons, one just a week after the other.

Casual visitors are as unwelcome in the chutes as they are in a busy emergency room. The serious business of recording results must be done here, and even the runners are hustled away as quickly as possible. But special passes enabled me to get in everyone's way at both the Portland and Royal Victoria marathons.

Les Smith, Portland Marathon director, conducts a seminar each year for other race directors. He ends with an invitation to observe any and all facets of his operation.

I took great interest in this year's race, as about a dozen of my students were running, along with many more friends. What better place to greet them than at the end of the road?

Rob Reid, the race director of the Royal Victoria Marathon, taught me the value of this practice. He's made it his custom, and I'd like to see other race directors copy it.

He stands just past the finish line, to shake runners' hands and thank them for coming. Reid invited me to join him at the finish.

You quickly get over any squeamishness or reluctance to intrude on a personal moment. The runners don't seem to care how they look or act, so why should you?

Here you see them at their most honest, all poses stripped away. Their hair and clothes are a mess. The young look old and the old look ancient.

Here you see the whole range of emotions and actions. Runners shout, swear, shrug, smile, or sob. You can't tell at that moment if they are expressing defeat, relief, or joy.

I seemed to be invisible to most of the runners, and rightly so. But occasionally one responded to my good wishes.

Lorne Sundby was an e-mail acquaintance of mine from Edmonton in Alberta, Canada. I'd met him only a couple of times before, at other finish lines.

In Victoria, Sundby gave me a sweaty hug and yelled, "I qualified for Boston!" I was honored to be with him at that beautiful moment, when his effort began turning into both memories and hopes.

AGING *actively,*
on the run or
at a walk

chapter
32

On the Road Again

Highway 169 in Iowa passes near the bridges of Madison County.
The book and movie by that name were make-believe, but the bridges
themselves are real.

I paid a brief visit to Route 169 in the summer of 2003, not to
view a covered bridge, but to set foot on a highway once traveled by
an amazing friend of mine. Paul Reese ran along this road while
crossing Iowa, south to north, in 1995.

Five years earlier, Reese had run across the United States. Age
seventy-three at the time, he's the oldest to make this journey.

The next-to-last line in *Ten Million Steps*, Reese's book about his
adventure, read, "One of the secrets of aging gracefully is always to
have something to look forward to."

Reese looked ahead to running across each of the states he'd
missed the first time he'd crossed the country. This he accomplished
in two stages, starting with those west of the Mississippi, and following with the eastern states plus Alaska and Hawaii.

He'd passed his eightieth birthday before bagging his final state.
Two more books—*Go East, Old Man*, and *The Old Man and the Road*—
came out of those trips.

By then he and wife Elaine had sold the motor home that she had driven all those miles in support of his efforts. "This was always a team effort," he said, and at that point it looked like such big efforts had ended.

Reese lowered his sights, but they remained plenty high for someone past age eighty. He completed his "last" marathon at Honolulu several times over.

We don't have to surrender, at any age, to life's hard knocks

The December 2002 marathon in Hawaii seemed as if it really would be his last. Soon afterward, he ruptured a disk in his back. This left him on crutches through March, and walking with a cane through April, the month he turned eighty-six.

Reese's first career was as a Marine officer. I once referred to him as an "ex-Marine," and he firmly informed me, "There are no ex-Marines." The toughness that carried him through two wars still served him well.

While injured, he plotted his next campaign. "One of my regrets is that I haven't traveled by foot from Canada to Mexico," he said. "That regret evaporated in May, when Elaine decided we should acquire a camper van and embark on more road adventures."

After they bought a Road Trek, Elaine said to her husband, "I suppose now you'll want to do your Canada-to-Mexico thing." To which her husband replied, "Brilliant suggestion!"

In July 2003, they stood at the Canadian border in Montana. Twenty-six days and 292 miles later, they reached the southern end of that state. The others would follow in separate stages, as time and health allowed.

"This trek reeked with conservatism," Reese said, "as my goal was walking a mere eleven miles per day. But because the longest distance I'd gone since the Honolulu Marathon in December was eight miles, and that only once, I wasn't sure how I'd fare.

"My hope was that the walk would be good therapy for both my physical and emotional health. No way, if I'd stayed home, would I have done so much exercise. This proved to be true. As the days passed, I did grow stronger, and was even able to do some running."

He reported, "Montana was a party for me. Having been semi-crippled the first four months of the year, I reveled in just being able to walk. Being vintage eighty-six, having lost three close friends in the past five months, and having seen other friends of my age beset with physical problems, I savored being alive and in control of all my faculties."

The lesson we can learn from Paul Reese's latest feat is that we don't have to surrender, at any age, to life's hard knocks. His back injury certainly wasn't his final hit.

Life's Ultrarunners

It's not just the races that demand attention to pacing. A runner's career does too.

We run differently in races where the finish line is visible at the start, than in those where the end is dozens of miles away. And we pace ourselves differently when running as if we can finish in a few minutes, than when we feel we may not finish within a few hours.

A question about pace came to me from a runner named Jack Gaskill. He asked about his individual runs, but my answer had more to do with pacing his career.

"I really like the idea of going slower, not worrying about the time it takes me to finish a race," wrote Gaskill. "Am I crazy for wanting to run slower? I feel almost guilty for not training the way the rest of the world perceives that I should."

My reply: "If you want to run indefinitely, you should adopt a relaxed pace that will keep you healthy and happy. You should view your running lifetime as an ultramarathon."

Twice within three weeks in 1999, I spoke to groups of life's ultrarunners in my hometown of Eugene. The first group was the Fifty-Plus Fitness Association, an organization that promotes active aging, and the other was a local Rotary Club. On both occasions, I was one of the younger folks present.

At both I told similar stories. I talked about having older heroes, because we can't grow younger but we can always age better. I talked about not admiring winning racers as much as runners who never

Pacing is a matter of perspective—you can go out hard to finish quickly, or hold back to last a long time

stop running. I talked about hearing Old John Kelley once say, "It isn't what you once did that really counts, but what you keep doing."

In both talks I told of meeting Whitey Sheridan at a race in Hamilton, Ontario. It happened to coincide with my fortieth anniversary as a runner, so I asked my lecture audience there, "Has anyone here been at this longer than I have?"

Sheridan had been running almost thirty years longer. He gave me a look that said: Keep at it, kid. You're just getting started.

My forty-fifth running anniversary rolled around in 2003, and my forty-fifth anniversary of daily diary-writing came the year after. I remain a mid-packer in both activities, and have the numbers to prove it.

At the 1994 New York City Marathon, I finished in the exact middle of the pack—14,500th out of 29,000 runners. The fact is, I don't work hard enough to rate any better. My running and writing rarely top more than an hour apiece each day.

My gently paced hours keep piling up, though, and good things keep coming from them. I haven't outrun or outwritten many people, but I've outlasted generations of faster and more talented starters by adopting an ultrarunner's pace.

Pacing is a matter of perspective. You can go out hard to finish quickly, or hold back to last a long time. You can rush toward a visible finish line, or work slowly toward one that is out of sight.

Those older Fifty-Plus Fitness and Rotary people I stood among are life's ultrarunners. They are smart, patient, and fortunate enough to be winning by outlasting others who might have sped past them in their early miles.

Aging Agendas

Nothing illustrates the rush of years more than a long-delayed visit to an old hometown. Seeing friends again after all that time puts a face on our aging.

For about a decade in the 1960s and '70s, I lived on the outskirts of Stanford University's campus in northern California. Those were also my best years as a road racer, and not by chance. Races abounded in the San Francisco Bay Area, at a time when they still were scarce in most other places.

Runners were abundant there too. That's how I really got to know the friendliness of the long-distance runner. Groups of us took long runs together on Saturdays, then met again Sunday mornings in friendly competition.

In the late 1970s, I left that area and those friends. Since then I'd seen too little of them, and many of us had completely fallen out of touch.

So I was glad to go back for the first time in too many years, when the Fifty-Plus Fitness Association invited me to speak at its race.

The race-weekend events at Stanford included a day of workshops, an awards banquet, and an 8K run. I can't recall spending many better weekends, as the gap between my past and present narrowed there.

The surface changes in some old friends were startling to me, as I'm sure mine were to them. But we quickly looked past physical appearances as we rediscovered the same people we'd known before.

Inevitably some stories were sad. My longest-time friend in the area now cared for his wife with advanced Alzheimer's...a former ultrarunner now wore a pacemaker and defibrillator in his chest... an eighty-seven-year-old lay critically ill in Stanford Hospital.

But good news and positive views far outweighed the rest. I reconnected with my close friend Paul Reese, who I hadn't seen in years. In his lecture, he said that a key to aging well is to "always have an agenda." I'd edited the three books he'd written, and now in his eighties, he planned to write his fourth.

Two other longtime friends, Jim O'Neil and Ruth Anderson, also attended that event. Both were in their seventies, and both had marked on their agendas trips to the World Masters Championships.

Neither had missed any of these every-other-year meets since they began in 1975.

My most gratifying reunion at Stanford was with Bob Anderson. We hadn't been in touch since he sold *Runner's World* magazine in 1985.

I'd heard that Anderson still raced well, and now saw him finish fifth in the Fifty-Plus 8K. He ran better times in his fifties than he did when we worked together at his magazine.

"Working in the sport worked against my own running," he said. "I didn't have enough time to train or, frankly, all that much interest in doing it. Now I'm free to do what I couldn't do back then."

Anderson stated his agenda numerically. He still had 5K and 10K times he wanted to beat.

He and many others I met at Fifty-Plus illustrated the best way to age. That's to keep looking forward, not to increasingly gaze backward.

LSD Lives

My firstborn book awakened from a long hibernation to find itself in middle age. That's to say that *Long Slow Distance*, my first slim book that was published in 1969 and slipped out of print shortly thereafter, is now available free online at http://joehenderson.com/lsdbook.

I've written a new introduction and a new conclusion, but except for my original typos, left everything in between as it was.

The book focused on the experiences of six accomplished runners. Now I'm happy to report that, thirty-five years later, they've all aged well in our sport. From the new conclusion of *Long Slow Distance*, here are some notes explaining how these older runners have managed so successfully:

Training trends have gone through many pendulum swings, from high mileage at low speed to the reverse, between the late 1960s and the early 2000s. LSD, by an assortment of names, has come into and fallen out of favor several times over the decades.

I've made the case for this type of running and will let it stand as written. But I can't leave without updating the lives of the six profiled runners. We were born no later than 1947. We live three on the East Coast and three on the West. Running has stayed with us all through the years since *LSD*'s publication.

▶ Amby Burfoot was then a recent Boston Marathon winner and the second-fastest marathoner in U.S. history. He peaked young as a runner, with his 2:14 marathon at age twenty-two standing as his permanent PR. His afterword to *LSD* hinted at another latent talent—as a writer. His first *Runner's World* article (about Bill Rodgers) appeared in 1975, and soon thereafter Amby contributed regularly to the magazine. Eventually he became its longest-serving editor.

Burfoot celebrates his Boston win on each five-year anniversary by running the race again. He regularly acts as a pace-team leader at marathons, reliably running within seconds of four hours.

▶ Bob Deines was a fourth-place finisher at age twenty-one in the 1968 Olympic Trials Marathon. His training served him even better in ultras than in marathons. In 1970, the year after *LSD*'s publication, he won a national title while setting a U.S. record for fifty miles.

Deines's life course then took him away from high-level running, and he wound up working as a carpenter in Willits, California. That physical labor added muscle to his frame, yet he still ran marathons in the 2:40s while weighing thirty pounds more than before. Deines has since written and taken photos for an environmental-activist publication.

▶ Tom Osler was then a sub-2:30 marathoner and national champion at several road distances. He moved deeply into ultras, running races lasting as long as forty-eight hours. His *Serious Runner's Handbook* was one of the finest instructional texts ever written about our sport. In it he became one of the first writers to recommend breaking up long runs with brief walks.

Osler has remained an avid racer, with nearly 2,000 finishes to his credit. He suffered a stroke in 2003, but recovered and returned to racing. He has also thrived in the field of education, and is currently a math professor at Rowan University in Glassboro, New Jersey.

▶ Ed Winrow, who was born in 1937, was the eldest of the pro-filed runners. He was then winding down his successful racing career, and moved on to one of the most important and gratifying jobs anyone can do—passing on his experience and enthusiasm to the next generation.

After coaching at Valparaiso University in Indiana, he led college teams in Brockport, New York, and Mansfield, Pennsylvania. His own son, Kip, ran at the college level. Winrow competed in short triathlons in the 1990s, until two serious bike crashes ended that phase. He lives in retirement in Brooklyn, New York.

▶ Jeff Kroot was and still is my closest friend among the runners featured in *LSD*. He's now a prominent architect who has served as mayor of San Anselmo, California.

Kroot improved his marathon PR to 2:45:00 in 1975, then eased out of racing when the Bay Area events grew too big for his liking. He continues to run regularly and remains a loyal fan of track and field, the sport he used to photograph professionally.

▶ I was then a staff writer at *Track & Field News*, which published *LSD*. Within a few months of the book's release, I became editor of the newly renamed and relocated magazine *Runner's World*. Many more books have followed my original one, most of them expanding on variations of the LSD concept.

I moved to Eugene, Oregon, in the early 1980s, and now teach running classes at the University of Oregon. I'm urging youngsters to slow down their training, but that's as hard a sell now as it was in 1969.

LASTING on the runs you never want to end

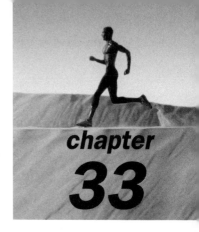

Keeping On

Among runners, streaking isn't the 1970s fad of running unclad in public. It's the largely private practice of running day after week after month after year, without a single miss.

I'm a reformed streaker. Or should I say "recovering" streaker? I admit that anyone who has written at least a diary page every day for more than thirty years hasn't yet rooted streaking out of his life. He's only redirected it.

My last and longest running streak of almost five years ended in 1987, and I've never felt any urge to revive it. But I retain some fascination with successful streakers, who keep going for years, enjoying full running lives.

James Raia also observes them with professional interest. A couple of years ago, the writer from Sacramento, California, told me, "I'm working on an article about running streaks. I've interviewed a few folks who are thirty-year daily runners. Do you have any thoughts about streaks?"

I began by telling Raia of my former habit. "While I'm a recovering streaker, I still admire and often write about those who keep going far longer and under much tougher conditions than I ever did."

The two streakers I've followed most closely are Mark Covert and Ron Hill. Both were high-class runners at one time, so they have more than their streaks going for them.

Covert is a Southern Californian, now coaching at Antelope Valley College. He was one of America's top runners in his early twenties, and missed the Olympic Marathon team by only a few places in 1972.

Covert's streak began in July 1968. For the life of it, he has averaged more than seventy-mile weeks.

The biggest threats to his streak have been: a broken bone in his foot, which he encased in a work boot and ran his minimum three miles; running on the deck of a cruise ship during a tropical storm, while crew members took bets on his being washed overboard; hemorrhoid surgery, which still didn't stop him from going out the next day.

Ron Hill is the international king of streakers, as far as anyone knows. This British runner began in December 1964, when he was becoming a world-class racer. He would be the second man to break 2:10 in the marathon, after Derek Clayton.

Hill insists that his streak continues today, though he now defines a "run" rather loosely. He requires only one mile, at any pace.

He has needed to dip that low a couple of times: after a car crash when he broke his sternum, and after bunion surgery when he finished his mile in twenty-seven minutes on crutches the next day.

Getting Out More Often

Have you run today, or will you run before day's end? I can say with certainty that Maryland's Bob Ray will tally another day in his logbook. He's America's champion streaker. Since April 1967, this retired postal worker from Maryland has run the most days without a break.

George Hancock, a streaker himself who keep records on fellow never-miss runners, can name dozens of Americans who haven't skipped one day since 1980. They always show up for work, no matter what forces conspire to stop them.

These are the Cal Ripkens of running. Ripken didn't miss a single baseball game with the Baltimore Orioles for more than fifteen seasons. Admirable as his feat was, Ripken didn't have to play games year-round, or even daily during the season. Streaking runners get no off-season, no rain-outs, and no travel days to rest. (They also have no big-league curveballs to hit, no sellout crowds to please, and no seven-figure salaries to earn.)

Anyone who waits to run until the day is just right will never be more than a part-time, fair-weather runner

The truest mark of pros in any specialty isn't how much money they make, if any, but how well they continue to do their job on difficult days. Anyone can do well when blessed with good health, solid training, high spirits, and unpressured time. But only pros keep showing up and giving their all when conditions aren't ideal.

Anyone can run on a day when the sky is blue, the temperature mild, and the air still. Anyone can run after a good night's sleep, free of injuries, on a fine course, with no need to hurry home.

Not just anyone will get up and go when running conditions shout, "Forget it!" There are days when other duties shove the run into the dark hours ... when the course is dictated by convenience, not beauty ... when the temperature falls or rises, the sky drops rain or snow, or the wind howls ... when the runner feels sleep-deprived or hungover ... when the runner's tight or sore legs beg for a respite.

On these days the streakers, the blue-collar workers, the pros of running, go to work as always. They go out when they feel like staying home, knowing they're likely to feel better afterward than before, knowing they can find good runs even on bad days.

Semi-streakers plan days of rest, but don't miss their scheduled days of running. They never ask themselves, "Will I run today?" They never say, "Not this morning; I have a headache," or, "The day's too nasty; I'll wait till tomorrow." They run as planned.

What runners do, or don't do, on those days defines them as either devotees or dabblers. Anyone who waits to run until the day is just right will never be more than a part-time, fair-weather runner.

Have you run today? Will you?

Off Days

When you love to run, you hate to stop. The hardest days to face are the easiest ones, when running is absent. You want to run, not rest.

I know. I never took a voluntary day off, beginning in my youth (when recovery comes quickly) and stretching into my forties (when efforts can be as big as they ever were, but recovery takes longer).

During my last and longest streak, my everyday runs took a lot out of my running. I avoided any of those runs—hilly runs, off-road runs, group runs, races—that would put my streak at risk.

But the types of runs I missed were the very runs that had first attracted me to the sport. They'd been my peak experiences in running, and I've happily welcomed them back now that I'm recovering in valleys of rest. I've come to realize that "rest" is not surrender to sloth.

I took a long time to learn that a weekly day of rest is important for both body and soul

Credit George Sheehan for teaching me this lesson at last. Sheehan preached and practiced every-other-day running. He sacrificed neither training quantity nor race quality in the process.

When Sheehan made this switch in his fifties, his mileage stayed the same. He simply ran twice as long, half as often. His most dramatic result was a 3:01 marathon PR at age sixty-one.

I'd long accepted the training principle of mixing easy days with the hard. I had to take the next, harder step to accept the ultimate in easy: rest.

Like many converts to a new practice, I veered from one extreme to the other: from having never missed a day to skipping every other.

Skipping that many days was too many for me. Never mind that I'd doubled the length of my remaining runs. Resting as many days as I ran seemed to disqualify me as a real runner.

I gradually worked out an agreeable compromise between enough rest and too much. This became one day off each week. It usually fell on a Sunday, so my mother would've been proud.

Back where we came from in small-town Iowa, Mom observed the Biblical day of rest, refusing to indulge in any commercial or entertainment venture, and urging us children to abstain as well. But Dad and us kids were less observant.

I took a long time to learn that a weekly day of rest is important for both body and soul. It keeps me from backsliding into never-ending streaking. But more than that, it provides a day for reflecting on the week past and recharging for the one to come.

If you love running too much to stop, if you think rest is equal to surrender, please consider the following tips from a former streaker. Believe me when I tell you that one of the keys to continuing as a runner is knowing when to stop.

▶ **Earn a rest with a big effort.** On the final day of your week, run farther or faster than normal, or far and fast in a race. Then welcome a day off (or two or more days, if that run was really hard), knowing that it will provide a quicker and safer recovery than trying to "run out" stiffness and fatigue.

▶ **Make your rest day a floating day.** Sundays are sacred only in the religious sense. Your rest could come the Monday after a race, or the Wednesday of a business trip, or the Saturday after a stressful work week—or simply as an unscheduled day when running gets squeezed out by higher priorities. Save your rest for the day you need it most.

▶ **Take a rest day for your family and friends, if not for yourself.** They'll appreciate not having to delay a meal or an outing while you finish a run. On your rest day, give them the time you'd normally spend away from them.

Patient Pace

One year while walking to the start of the Portland Marathon, I passed a church. Chiseled in concrete on its wall were the words, "Run with patience the race set before you."

I wasn't well enough versed in the Bible to place this line (it's in Hebrews), but I knew it spoke wisely to runners.

Races are exercises in patience. They're long in the planning, preparation, and execution. Gratification is long in coming.

You work through what the British call "bad patches" to reach a better place. This is true not just in training for and running in races, but through your runner's lifetime.

Injuries and illnesses can often test your patience. You can't rush recovery; you must hold back, do what's possible, and wait for better days ahead.

Clearly you need to pace yourself. The letters in "pace" start and end the word "patience," and signify what the longer word is all about.

Pacing isn't just for racing or training; it's for all your years of running. You don't run the first mile of a marathon in six minutes if you're planning to finish at an average of eight.

One year in a longtime-runner's life is like a mile in a marathon. You can't push the pace too hard in any one season or year, if you still expect to run strongly next year, or a decade or more down the road.

In training, racing, and living, you can either push hard for a short period, or back off and stay relaxed for the long haul. Rare is the runner who can handle an intense pace for a long period.

Taking a long-term view is most important during a "bad-patch" period. Your urge is to break through the problem, pick up the pace, and make up for lost time.

But this is a time to keep your pace within your comfort zone. Let progress come gradually, instead of trying to hurry it.

Run at a peaceful pace. Did you know that the Italian word for peace is pronounced "paw-chay" and spelled "pace"?

COPING
by running through the hard realities

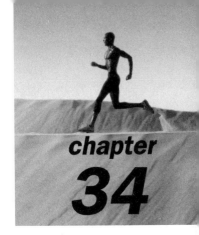

Re-Birthday

I have a long-standing habit of dedicating each of my marathons to someone special. These races demand so much from my limited training that I seek outside help.

Sometimes I've worn the person's name on my shirt. Other times I've penned it on the underside of the bill of my cap.

At the 1999 Las Vegas Marathon, I carried the letters "LCH" and the numbers "2-16-83." The initials are my daughter Leslie's. The date isn't her birthday, as she was born in September 1982. February 16th, 1983, is her re-birthday.

She was born with Down's syndrome, which was shocking enough. Then we learned that she also had a heart defect common to Down's babies. She was born big, at almost eight pounds, but gained little weight during her early months.

Surgery was risky, we were told. But without it she wouldn't survive to see her first birthday.

She weighed only ten pounds when we checked her into a Portland hospital for her operation. She nearly died there when her heart stopped in the recovery room. Doctors wouldn't let her go, ripping open their sutures and applying direct cardiac massage to restart her tiny heart.

That evening in the ICU, her mother and I were allowed to see Leslie for the first time after her operation. Her surgeon said, "She's quite unstable now, and the next few hours will be critical."

We were also told that she was too young and too drugged to realize what was happening to her. But she was awake, barely visible amid the technology, when we entered her room. Her readouts immediately began to normalize when she saw faces she recognized.

Complications followed. Her new heart valve chewed up her red blood cells, leaving her anemic and requiring transfusions for several months.

Leslie fought past her traumatic start in life. She learned to sit up, then to walk, and eventually to run. She now does some reading and writing, and though she can't speak, she's fluent in sign language.

Doctors said in 1983 that she probably would need twice-a-year checkups for the rest of her life. She might require another heart operation upon reaching her teens.

Now in her twenties, she hasn't yet needed more surgery, so far has shown her repaired heart is still working fine, and goes years between checkups. She doesn't know the reason for the scar down the center of her chest.

Whenever I felt disheartened during that Las Vegas Marathon sixteen years after her surgery, I thought of Leslie and how much tougher her road had been. Then I touched her initials on my hat brim in celebration of her re-birthday.

Father George

George Sheehan was one of the best-loved writers and speakers in running history. And he was my best friend in the business, sport, and passion that we shared.

Our connection spanned the entire twenty-five years of his writing career, from his first newspaper column to his last book. I recruited him to write his long-running column in *Runner's World*, and assisted him with all but one of his books.

I humbly and proudly stood in his shadow on numerous stages at running events. We talked by phone hundreds of times a year, and traded equal numbers of letters.

My office has the look of a shrine to Sheehan. In a file drawer are most of the columns he wrote, many of them unpublished in any running magazine. On a bookshelf are all of his books.

In one of them, *This Running Life*, Sheehan wrote, "I will not last forever. But I am damn well going to know I have been here." Later in that same book he noted: "There is nothing more certain than the defeat of a man who gives up. And, I might add, the victory of one who will not."

These lines took on new meaning when he learned in 1986 that he had a terminal illness and, his doctors warned, only months to live. He fought his cancer to the finish, which he didn't reach until almost eight years after his diagnosis. He ran scores of races, wrote dozens of columns, gave countless speeches, and completed three books in those years.

On a wall behind my desk is a photo of him that still looks over my shoulder. Beside it is a medal from his memorial race, the 1994 George Sheehan Classic in Red Bank, New Jersey, inscribed on the back with one of his lines: "Winning is never having to say I quit." He didn't—not until his final book, *Going the Distance*, was finished in his final week and he told me by phone, "I'm ready to go now."

Soon after his death, a publisher asked me to write a biography of Sheehan, and quickly. Its title posed the question that he often asked of himself: Did I Win?

Writing never comes easily. If it isn't hard, it usually isn't much good. Sheehan himself rewrote each of his pieces several times. "I work very hard at making it look easy," he liked to say.

I'd written my other books that way. Each chapter had been a long, slow slog toward making it a quick and easy read.

But the book about Sheehan came easily. I'd sit down in the morning with few or no notes beside me, and my hands would fly over the computer keyboard. First drafts often stood up as final works. It was as if Sheehan stood at my shoulder, dictating his material to take down. Nothing like this had ever happened to me before, and I never expect it to happen again. There was only one George Sheehan who could give me that much help.

Sheehan keeps winning because, long after his death, his words keep informing and inspiring runners. He would delight in the irony of this.

In *Dr. Sheehan on Running*, the book of his that I still like the best, he explained his penchant for quoting history's master thinkers—from Socrates to Santayana—in his own writing and speaking.

"My family rarely gives me any credit for original thought," he wrote. "When a topic comes under discussion at the dinner table, someone is likely to turn to me and ask, 'What would Bucky Fuller say about that?'"

Sheehan himself became a valued source of quotable quotes. He gave voice to what other runners thought, felt, or sensed, but couldn't find the words to express themselves as well as he could.

Name any subject related to the running experience—and many subjects far removed from sports—and this master thinker had found just the right words to describe it. His friends and fans would ask one another, "What would George Sheehan say about that?"

His answers survive. To a runner and a wordsmith, that's the ultimate form of winning.

November to Remember

Drake University Coach Bob Karnes told our team when the 1963 season began, "If you win the conference title, that'll earn you a trip to the Nationals." We won, and he made good on his promise.

Our team never flew to meets. We drove.

Our plan was to leave Des Moines on Saturday, two days before the Monday race in East Lansing, Michigan. My plan for that Friday afternoon was to do laundry, then take an easy run.

The news that shook the world came to me in the most mundane of settings: an off-campus Laundromat, where a radio shouted to be heard over the sloshing and spinning of washers and dryers. All background noise seemed to vanish with the announcement, "We interrupt this program for a news bulletin from Dallas ..." America would all but stand still for the next few days, to absorb the shock of the Kennedy assassination.

"It was hard to think of something so unimportant as running today, but I had to run out some of my bottled-up emotions," reads my diary from a time when I wrote only a one-sentence comment each day. The killing of the president was the worst national crisis of my life at that time, yet I never mentioned it by name. My diary's daily notes from that period read as if I didn't notice or care what had happened:

Saturday the 23rd: "They postponed the race one day."

Sunday the 24th: "We're really leaving [for Michigan] this time."

Monday the 25th (the national day of mourning): "Run relaxed and fast all the way—even if I'm last, which I very well could be for awhile."

Tuesday the 26th: "Very interesting race, this N.C.A.A., even if I was buried in 119th [of 165 finishers]."

My memories of running that weekend are so hazy that I must check my diary to fill the gaps in my recollection. But even forty years later, I can still remember the smallest details of that tragic murder in late November. I was so shaken that I used the race as an escape from hard reality.

Why Running Still Matters

The day when everything changed began the same as all days did for me. I woke up early on September 11th, 2001, but kept the radio and television off for the first hour. I didn't know then that the world as we'd known it was crumbling.

The morning's silence, and its peace, ended just before I went out to run. I listened, stunned, to the bulletins on the news. Each report sounded worse than the one before.

In the following days I heard from many runners. They were about equally split between those who ran but felt guilty about it, and those who couldn't bring themselves to run because it seemed suddenly unimportant, even disrespectful.

My day's run was slow to start. But I never thought about not starting it, and never felt the act of running trivialized the tragedy. To head out on a day like that wasn't heartless or selfish—it was just the opposite. I wasn't going out to play, but to mourn. My run opened my heart to the pain of others.

No one could run away from a tragedy this immense. But a hard, mind-numbing effort could act as a brief respite, out of reach of the horrendous, non-stop news that threatened to overwhelm me.

Running can serve us better by enabling us to run with a problem rather than away from it. A run can turn down the volume and slow the pace of events—away from our radio, TV, computer, phone, job— and can let us stare the problem in the face.

Such runs can be wrenching, as tears and fears rise up with nothing to deflect them. This is a necessary part of healing, since letting ourselves feel our worst helps us start to feel better.

We could find solace by walking or cycling, or just sitting quietly in a beautiful place. But when bad times happen, we're most likely to turn to running, because running is a friend we know so well.

Some tragedies are national ones, which we all must endure together. More often we suffer from personal blows, and those we must recover from on our own.

My father died suddenly and much too young in 1971. That loss hit me so hard that I couldn't write a word about it, or anything else, for a long time.

Yet in those darkest of days, I never missed a run. My dad was a former runner himself, and a lifelong fan of the sport. But I didn't comfort myself by thinking, "He would've wanted me to keep running."

That would have been a minor truth. The major reason I kept running was because I needed it, then more than ever.

Running when you're hurting inside can really help. It can't solve the world's problems, nor can it make your own disappear. What running on those days can do is allow you to step away from ground zero, look inside yourself, and sort through your thoughts and emotions before coming back to wrestle with tough new realities. That's why running still matters—more than ever.

ENJOYING *whatever you can do as a runner*

Running in Circles

The best runner in my family asks me without words, but with his glances: Why are you so slow?

We're an odd couple. He's tall for his type, and I'm short ... he's thin, and I'm, uh, less so ... he's young, and I'm old ... he's a sprinter, and I'm a distance runner.

Our bond is our shared status as retired racers. Before joining our family, he briefly worked as a professional runner—on the greyhound track.

Buzz was born to run; it's his whole reason for being. His breed has been developed for a single purpose—to run extremely fast, in short races, for the pleasure and profit of dog-racing fans.

When instinct kicks in, Buzz bolts into high gear and dashes ahead for a minute or two, before dropping back to my much slower pace.

Since Buzz has joined me on my runs, I've run a lot more laps—slower and bigger ones than he might otherwise run, but laps just the same.

For decades I plotted running courses that never duplicated themselves. Some were out-and-backs, but a route looks different when you reverse directions. Usually I'd run a single large loop, with new scenery every step of the way.

A course never looks quite the same way twice

Buzz has reduced my range. Running safely with him means using fewer and shorter routes, with multiple laps per day or multiple repeats per week.

Neither of us minds repeating ourselves. After all, repeating ourselves is what runners do.

Ours is a life of constant reruns. We're always circling back to where we started, then starting all over again. Even if we don't run extra laps one day, we'll surely come back for more of the same another day soon.

Anyone who thinks this sounds boring doesn't have a runner's mindset, or hasn't chosen courses well. To a runner on just the right route, each repetition of the course has a comfortable sameness. Yet each run there also seems a little different from any other.

Some runners choose to run the same route each day, and savor its familiarity. I have about half a dozen regular running routes in Eugene, so Buzz and I run each of them about once a week.

Our favorite is Pre's Trail, named in memory of Steve Prefontaine, one of America's greatest distance runners. It winds around a former garbage dump converted into a riverside park. I first ran here more than thirty years ago, when a marathon passed through.

I've lived nearby for more than twenty years, and probably have averaged one run a week on Pre's Trail. That's more than 1,000 repetitions, and I haven't yet tired of the course.

Where is your favorite place to run? That may be a question you don't often hear.

We think and talk about the whats and hows (especially the how-fars and how-fasts) of running. But the wheres seldom come up, beyond where a next race might be.

Yet your home courses are where you spend dozens to hundreds of hours a year. You must choose them well.

Plot routes that start and finish in the same spot, that you can reach quickly and easily from home or office, and that you can run in all weather and light conditions. These might not be the fastest, easiest, or prettiest routes. But you can run them because they're convenient, familiar, and safe.

Someone who doesn't know your courses as you do might think you'd tire of them after the ninety-ninth repetition. Not so.

A course never looks quite the same way twice. The combinations of season, light, weather, and your own feelings and thoughts there, are ever-changing.

Happy Talk

An early book of mine opened with a description of a morning visit to my doctor's office. I greeted the receptionist cheerily. Her coffee hadn't yet done its job, and she said grumpily, "My, aren't you Mr. Bubbles today!"

Another thirty years of living has popped some of my bubbles. But I still feel happier than the typical sixty-something man on the street.

Running helps keep me that way. I've made a habit of looking for and clinging to ways of running happily. My list of these fifty ways starts with someone else's line. Crosby, Stills, and Nash didn't write and sing their song, "Suite: Judy Blue Eyes," for runners, but it offers sound advice for longtimers facing their inevitable slowdown:

1. Don't let the past remind you of what you are not now.

2. Start a fresh set of PRs every five to ten years.

3. If you can't outrun many other runners, take pleasure in outlasting lots of them.

4. Instead of counting those who "beat" you, look at all those who dropped out, planned to start and never did, and can't or won't run at all.

5. Set low race goals, the least you'd like to accomplish, then surprise yourself with how far you exceed that minimum standard.

6. Pick heroes and favorites and follow their results.

7. Meet a celebrity runner and see that he or she is more like you than different.

8. Don't think that these elite runners owe you entertainment.

9. Let stories of top runners instruct and inspire you, but not intimidate you.

10. Read the writers who think what you've thought and who put it in words.

11. Say "hi" to a passing runner who you don't know, but who may greet you in return.

12. Give a call or send a note to celebrate a runner's triumph or to sympathize with trouble.

13. Offer running advice to someone who asks for it.

14. If you spend your days surrounded by people, run alone.

15. If you're a loner all day, run with a partner or group.

16. Run by time for an unknown distance, so you aren't haunted by a known pace.

17. Or run a known distance without wearing a watch.

18. Combine distance and time only in races and hard training, when it really counts.

19. Take pride in the minutes of running adding up on your watch and in your logbook, knowing that only you could have put them there.

20. Set your watch to zero before each run, knowing it's time to start over.

21. Find a new course, or vary an old one.

22. Drive to a prime running spot for a change of scene, instead of running the same well-worn path from your front door.

23. Go where cars don't.

24. Shake off jet-lag and explore a new city on foot, soon after arrival.

25. Make a mini-vacation of a trip to a race.

26. Iron out an irritating wrinkle in your running routine.

27. Keep your training plan simple enough to write on a three-by-five-inch card, if not a Post-It Note.

28. Decide how you feel after warming up for a mile, not before you start, when your body tells lies.

29. Finish a run feeling better than when you started.

30. Finish a race faster than you began.

31. Earn your shower by getting good and sweaty.

32. Earn a day (or more) off after a hard run.

33. Return eagerly from time off.

34. Push the right buttons to solve an injury riddle.

35. Appreciate all runs more after missing some.

36. Run into the dawn of a new day.

37. Run at noon to break up a long workday.

38. Run in the evening to calm down from a hard business day.

39. Run to work up an appetite or to work off a meal.

40. Run on days when weather conditions keep fair-weather runners indoors.

41. Adapt to the weather instead of griping about its eccentricities.

42. Go out in winter during its peak daylight hours.

43. Strip down to minimum clothing after a long winter of overdressing.

44. Wait to run in the cool of darkness after a hot summer's day.

45. Run to feel the first chill of fall after a long summer.

46. Bring to a race someone who helped get you there.

47. Run a relay race with a team that depends on you and celebrates with you.

48. Volunteer at a race to help others run easier and better.

49. Keep the non-runners closest to you unburdened by your running, and you'll feel happier yourself.

50. Run with a dog to see what true happiness is.

No Mile Wasted

Ask me about my normal daily run and the answer won't impress you. Tell me you run longer and faster, and I'll accept that; most runners do. But try to tell me that my runs lack "quality," or worse, count only as "junk miles," and I'll give you an argument. Here it comes.

For as long as I've been running easy and writing its praises, I've heard critics claiming such runs are a waste of time and effort. That's how they responded to my first book, *Long Slow Distance*,

One critic with a long memory called me recently to comment on a column of mine. The stranger said, "I'm happy to see your metamorphosis from the person who promoted long slow distance [LSD] to admitting you were wrong."

Wrong? Did I say I was wrong?

"I tried LSD," the caller continued, "and so did many others who ran with me at the time. All it did was make us long slow racers."

Then came his unkindest cut of all: "LSD was a cancer that ravaged the sport for a long time, and you were the person who spread it. I praise you for having the nerve to renounce it."

Renounce Long Slow Distance? I don't think so.

I've only retired the term, not the concept. LSD had become misleading, because it invited runners to stack up their highest possible mileage at their slowest possible pace. But too much distance can do as much damage as too much speed. So I've since substituted less catchy but more accurate words, such as "gentle" and "relaxed" running.

My shift to a slower gear wasn't meant to improve my racing, but to escape the damages of excessive speed training. The other runners featured in my LSD book did the same. To our surprise and delight, all six of us improved our times as a result.

Our improvement didn't come from any inherent magic in slower running; it came from easier running. It let us refresh ourselves between hard efforts, instead of staying forever tired.

I was slow to see that slower running was less a training system than a recovery system. We raced better by staying healthier and happier, not by training harder.

The standard way to judge a running program's success is by a runner's racing results. When runners aim for racing's biggest payoffs, no training seems too hard and no sacrifice too great.

Running can grant its rewards instantly and regularly

But another way to judge a program's value is to ask yourself: Would I still run this way if it had no racing payoff? The runners in my LSD book didn't keep racing better indefinitely; no one does. But we kept running, and keep doing it, in our own relaxed way.

You can view your runs as either vocational or recreational, as a job or a hobby, as work or play. "Serious" training falls on the left side of those word-pairings. My running leans far to the right.

Working implies doing something because you must, without welcoming the job. It suggests tolerating a distasteful task to earn an eventual reward.

But what if that payoff never comes, or if it's smaller than expected? Would you feel that all your time and effort had been wasted?

Running isn't my second job. No one pays me or forces me to do it. It's my hobby, and I choose to find my rewards in a maximum number of runs.

To me, "junk miles" are those run reluctantly today, only to invest in a better tomorrow. This seems like counting the hours until quitting time, the days until the weekend, the weeks until vacation, the years until retirement. Always working toward a distant finish line might mean missing the fun in the here and now.

Running can grant its rewards instantly and regularly. Ask me about my runs, and I'll tell you they're nothing special—except in the quiet, wonderful ways that all runs are special. Any run anyone has wanted to take and enjoyed taking is never wasted.

Conclusion

The highest and lowest points of my writing life both came within six days of each other in December 2003, while this book was in its early miles. The extremes might have fallen on the same day, if I'd picked up my phone messages while traveling. The thrill of the high helped ease the pain of the low.

As it turned out, I'd picked the right writing hero, and was visiting his birthplace at exactly the right time. This was John Steinbeck, and his former home in Salinas, California. I never met him during his life (he died in 1968), but a writer's words can reach well beyond his grave.

Steinbeck's *Grapes of Wrath* was the first book I'd ever read outside of class assignments or of the genre of sports. It wasn't his fiction that moved me the most, but his collection of letters and the journals that he kept while writing his novels.

From his private musings I learned what writing can mean to a writer. For Steinbeck it wasn't a job or even a career. It was a calling, a passion, even an obsession.

He wrote because he could and had to. For every public word he wrote, he penned hundreds or thousands that no one had ever read. He felt about writing as I did about running, and as I would come to feel about writing about running.

Steinbeck had grown up in Salinas, the hometown that had vilified him for writing unflatteringly about it. Now it promotes his birthplace as its top tourist attraction.

There's the Steinbeck House, the Steinbeck Library, the Steinbeck gravesite, and now the National Steinbeck Center. My wife Barbara and I took a tour of those sites in December, walking where he walked and sitting where he sat.

We ate lunch in the dining room of his Victorian house, where volunteers now serve meals to raise funds to preserve it. The narrow, steep stairwell to his room upstairs is closed to the public. But we could see the steps he'd climbed hundreds of times to his bedroom, where he might have written his first sentences.

The nearby Steinbeck Center opened about five years earlier, as a memorial to his life's work. My big thrill there was seeing pages he'd written by hand.

Most of these were photocopies, all encased in plastic. But the words looked to me exactly as they had to him while he wrote them, and I came as close as possible to touching them.

I came home from this high point in my writing life to plunge to the lowest. This came as a call from the new editor at *Runner's World*.

He said that my column, which had appeared for 250 months straight, had "run its course." It didn't fit into his plans for the "new" *Runner's World*, and he was retiring the column and me, its writer.

I could only say that this wouldn't be the end of my writing. Not even close.

John Steinbeck continues to teach and inspire me. A sign at the National Steinbeck Center, posted on the wall at the exit, reads, "I nearly always write, just as I nearly always breathe."

I can say with certainty that as long as I'm breathing, I'll be writing about running. If nothing else, I'll continue my daily diary, where my private words far outnumber my public. There, I write as Steinbeck did, because it's what I can and must do, even when no one's looking.

I can make no better statement than this about my running.

—Joe Henderson

2004

Glossary

Running, like many other fields of endeavor, has a working language of its own. This jargon identifies the speaker as a runner to a fellow insider. Here defined are key words and phrases used in this book and in conversation among runners.

A

Achilles. A long, thin tendon connecting the heel bone with the calf muscles in the back of the leg. It's a major source of runners' injuries.

Active rest. The middle ground between a running day and a total-rest day. A runner "rests" actively with low-intensity alternate activity such as a walk or bike ride.

Addiction. A condition runners claim they achieve after a few months of building up to a few miles of running at a time. Once they reach the point where it feels worse not to run than to do it, they're addicted. Generally this is a positive state, but it can hurt runners who "must" run when they shouldn't.

Aerobic. With a small "a," it means with oxygen or near-normal breathing during a run. (Its opposite is anaerobic, without oxygen or gasping for air while running.) With a capital "A" and plural, Aerobics refers to the exercise program established by Dr. Kenneth Cooper, relying on activities (including running, walking, bicycling, swimming) that supply large, steady doses of oxygen.

Aerobic capacity. A scientific measure of endurance fitness. This is calculated in volume of oxygen consumed at maximum aerobic effort, or "VO_2-max."

Aerobic (or anaerobic, or lactate) threshold. Training done at the borderline where aerobic and anaerobic efforts meet. This is intense training.

Age-group. Races subdivide their fields by age for awards and records purposes. The major divisions are junior (under 20), open (20 to 34 or 39), and masters (35 or 40 and up). Further breakdowns usually come at five-year intervals: 15–19, 20–24, etc.

Aided courses. Those that, while accurately measured, are unacceptable for records because of a net-downhill slope. In the U.S. the difference in elevation between the start and finish can't exceed one meter for each kilometer of the race (for instance, ten meters in a 10K).

All-comers. Informal track meets open to all, regardless of age, affiliation, or ability. They are track's equivalent to everyone's-welcome road races.

AquaJogging. A now-generic term for running in water, supported by a flotation belt. The most popular device that allows this training is the AquaJogger.

Asics. The Japanese shoe company, formerly known as "Tiger," helped revolutionize running shoe-making in the 1960s. Early importers of these shoes to the U.S. later founded Nike.

B

Bandit. Someone who runs a race without properly registering or paying an entry fee. Also known in some circles as a "turkey."

Bannister. Roger Bannister from England ran the most famous time in track history, the first sub-four-minute mile in 1954.

Base. The runner's endurance foundation, built by running long distances at relatively comfortable paces over a lengthy span of time.

Bay to Breakers. This twelve-kilometer race across San Francisco has long been America's largest, boasting starting fields of about 100,000 at its peak.

Bear. Once the most commonly used term for hitting the wall, tightening up or running out of energy—as in, "The bear jumped on my back." Nowadays it's often called "bonking."

Benoit. U.S. runner Joan Benoit (now Samuelson), winner of the first Olympic Marathon for women in 1984.

Bib. Formerly called simply a "race number"; identifies the runner and advertises for the sponsor.

Bikila. Abebe Bikila of Ethiopia is the greatest Olympic marathoner, the first to win twice (1960 and '64). In the first he ran barefoot, the second (in shoes) shortly after an appendectomy.

BMI. Body-mass index, a number arrived at through a combination of weight and height. It's a more reliable fitness indicator than weight alone.

Biomechanics. The way runners move. To coaches, it applies the efficiency of running form. To foot doctors, it's the angles and forces with which the feet and legs strike the ground.

Body composition. This is a measurement of body fat, expressed as a percentage of total weight. Like BMI, body fat is a far better measure of fitness than weight alone.

Bonk. A term lifted from bicycle racing, describing the feeling of hitting the wall for reasons of inadequate training, poor pacing, or improper nutrition/hydration.

Boston Marathon. The most renowned long-distance race in the U.S.; dates from 1897.

Brooks. This shoe company was especially prominent during the first running boom of the 1970s.

C

Carbohydrate-loading. A diet-juggling technique to increase staying power in a long race. It includes eating mainly high-energy starchy and sugary foods during the last few days before a big event.

Certified. A race course that is guaranteed accurate in distance. Strict measurement standards are dictated by the sport's governing bodies.

Chicago Marathon. If Boston is the oldest and New York City traditionally the biggest, Chicago has in recent years become the fastest of the major U.S. marathons. Several world records have been set there.

Chondromalacia. This injury strikes so often in this sport that it's also known as "runner's knee." Wear and tear to cartilage causes pain beneath the kneecap.

Chronograph. A fancy name for a watch on which time can be stopped. Today's runners feel naked without a digital stopwatch on their wrist.

Chute. Where the racing ends and runners are funneled down to single file for timing and scoring purposes.

Clydesdale. A division of races that gives special recognition to heavier runners. The men are Clydesdales, while women compete in the Athena category.

Collapse point. This training/racing theory holds that runners will hit the wall at a point about three times the average length of their daily runs. A marathoner, then, would need to average almost nine miles a day in training.

Cooldown. Post-run activity such as slow running, walking, and stretching that gradually eases the body back to rest. Often curiously called a "warmdown," which is the opposite of its intent.

Cooper. Kenneth Cooper, M.D., the developer of the Aerobics system, author of many books on the subject, and one of the greatest forces in the running-for-fitness movement.

Cross-country. Running and racing on natural surfaces—grass, dirt, beach, etc. Cross-country racing is mainly an autumn sport in the U.S.

Cross-training. Activities that supplement or substitute for running. These include related aerobic exercises such as swimming and bicycling, and complementary ones that build strength and promote flexibility.

D

Depletion run. The final long, or short, hard run before a big race, taken as part of the carbohydrate-loading routine.

DNF. An aborted run. The letters stand for "did not finish."

DOMS. Stands for "delayed-onset muscle soreness." It's well known to marathoners, whose soreness peaks a day or two after the race.

Doubling. Running more than one race at the same event, usually on the same day. This most often happens at track meets, where the distances are fairly short.

Duathlon. As most often contested, this is a "triathlon" without the swim. A common format: run-bike-run.

E

Electrolytes. The minerals in the foods we eat and liquids we drink. Potassium, magnesium, and sodium are the most important to runners because these substances are lost in sweat.

Endorphins. Natural opiates produced during long runs. Thought to contribute to "runner's high" and the addictive properties of this activity.

Energy bars and gels. These products have proliferated since the second running boom of the 1990s onward, with PowerBar and GU being early leaders. They allow runners to consume useful calories immediately before and after, and even during, training or racing.

Exercise physiology. The study of the body's inner workings during activity has produced many practical breakthroughs. One is what to drink and how often while running long.

Expo. A companion event held alongside a race, allowing runners to shop for products, listen to speakers, and meet the celebrities of the sport.

F

Fartlek. This strange-sounding word is Swedish for "speed play." It's training with free-form changes of pace, as opposed to the rigidity of interval sessions.

Fitness. Not a synonym for "health." Health is a mere absence of disease, a passive state. Fitness is the ability to put one's health to use in an active way.

Five-K. The most popular racing distance on the roads. Whether expressed as "5K," "five kilometers," "5000 meters" or "3.1 miles," the length is the same.

Fixx. Jim Fixx, the sport's all-time best-selling author (for his *Complete Book of Running*), who's unfortunately better remembered for dying of a heart attack while running.

Flats. A name once applied to all non-spiked running shoes. Now the term is limited to lightweight "racing flats."

Flexibility. Running tends to stiffen leg muscles, yet their ability to move freely (flexibly) is a measure of fitness. Runners are advised to adopt supplemental exercises for this purpose.

Form. How a runner moves is also known as "style," "technique," or "biomechanics."

Fun-running. The approach that emphasizes neither physical fitness nor serious competition, but running for enjoyment. Some informal races also go by the name "fun-runs."

G

Gallowalks. A technique, which Jeff Galloway made popular, of taking walk breaks during a long run to extend the distance and ease the stress. A typical pattern is a run of about a mile followed by a minute walk during a marathon.

Gels. Two meanings to runners: one is the gels that runners consume for energy, the other a cushioning material used in some shoes.

Gore-Tex. An early miracle fiber in running clothing, which both "breathes" and protects against cold or wet weather.

Glycogen. The fuel of choice for the distance-running body. A high-carbohydrate diet helps store this substance, and training helps the runner use it efficiently.

H

Half. A short way of saying "half-marathon," as in, "I'm running the half today, not the full." The half-marathon is just that—midway to the marathon—at 13.1 miles or 21.1 kilometers.

Hard/easy. This theory of training, popularized by the late University of Oregon coach Bill Bowerman, holds that after each hard effort there must be adequate recovery. Bowerman recommended one to three easy days after each hard one.

Heart-rate monitor. A device for measuring effort by pulse. Many runners prefer to gauge their pace by the heartbeats rather than by time.

Heat exhaustion and stroke. The most serious threats to a runner's health and life. These medical conditions, caused by running too long or hard in hot and humid weather, require immediate professional attention.

Hyperthermia and hypothermia. The first refers to overheating, the second to overexposure to cold. Both are risks to runners in extreme temperatures.

Hydration. The scientific-sounding way to talk about drinking.

I

IAAF. The International Association of Athletic Federations, governing body of running worldwide.

Intervals. Training that traditionally alternates rather short and fast runs on the track with periods of recovery (by easy running, walking, or rest). However, walk breaks during long road runs are also an application of the interval principle.

I.T. band. The iliotibial band on the outside of the knee (and extending up the leg from there) is often injured by runners.

J

Jog. This term, widely despised by runners, has no exact definition. It can be a slow run, or it can be a term that distinguishes "joggers" (exercisers) from "runners" for whom this is recreation and competition.

Jogbra. One of the products having the most to do with freeing women to run comfortably.

Junior. The age category for runners age nineteen and younger. In international competition, a junior can't turn twenty within that same calendar year.

Junk miles. A pejorative for miles run slowly, with little training benefit but simply to pad the daily or weekly mileage total.

K

K. Short for "kilometer," which is 1000 meters or 1094 yards or about five-eighths of a mile. Most road races are run at kilometer distances, as in the 5K or 10K.

Kick. Upping the speed at the end of a run or race.

L

Lactic acid and lactate. A chemical by-product resulting from severe effort and leading to muscle fatigue. Anaerobic running is mainly to blame.

Lap. In terms of running routes, this is one that repeats itself. As in, "I ran a four-lap course."

LSD. To runners, the initials stand for "long slow distance," a way of training with steady runs at gentle paces.

Loop. A course that starts and finishes in the same place.

Lydiard. Arthur Lydiard, a New Zealand coach, changed running with the international successes that the athletes from his small country achieved in the 1960s. Lydiard promoted long-distance training even for track runners.

M

Marathon. A word widely misused to cover any endurance contest. In running it means only the classic races of 26 miles, 385 yards (or 42.195 kilometers).

Masters. The branch of age-group competition generally limited to runners forty and older. Some events drop the age limit to thirty-five, and have a "sub-masters" division for athletes as young as thirty.

N

NCAA. The National Collegiate Athletic Association, which oversees most track (outdoor and indoor) and cross-country competition among U.S. universities and colleges.

Negative splits. This is the heady experience of finishing a race at a faster pace than you started it, which usually means passing runners instead of being passed.

Nike. The shoemaking giant began as a running company, with ex-University of Oregon runner Phil Knight going into business alongside his former coach Bill Bowerman.

O

Open. Two meanings: races open to everyone, and the open age-division that falls between the juniors (nineteen and under) and masters (thirty-five or forty and older).

Online registration. The predominant way of signing up for races in the Internet era is on a website.

Orthotics. Custom-made shoe inserts designed to protect against foot and leg injuries. These are most commonly prescribed by podiatrists.

Out-and-back. A running course that travels to a turnaround point and then reverses itself to return to the starting point.

Overuse. These are injuries caused by the running itself. Not by "accidents" or poor equipment, but by going too far, too fast, too often.

Oxygen debt. Some runs take the breath away. The "debt" from these short, fast runs is repaid with the heavy breathing afterward.

P

Pace. Two meanings: numerical, as in the average pace per mile or kilometer during a run, and tactical, as in how well a runner paces himself or herself.

Pace groups. Most often in marathons, an experienced pacer leads runners trying to achieve a certain time goal such as 4:00 or 4:30.

Peaking. Reaching the best racing fitness of the season, the year, or a lifetime. Training peaks in this period in distance, pace, or both.

Periodization. A tongue-twisting way of saying, run one way during one period and another in the next. Taken in proper sequence—say, endurance, strength, speed, racing—theoretically leads to peak performance at the right time.

Phidippides. The first marathoner, according to Greek legend. His ancient run from Marathon to Athens inspired the first modern Olympic Marathon.

Pitstops. Bathroom breaks during a run, whether planned or not, and with proper facilities or not.

Plantar fascitis. A injury to the heel and arch, made stubborn by the fact that each footfall subjects the affected area to full impact.

Podiatrists. These foot doctors are the runner's first line of defense against many of the injuries that interrupt training and racing.

Point-to-point. A course that starts one place and finishes another, never repeating itself.

PR. In the U.S. it means "personal record." Elsewhere the term "PB" ("personal best") is more common. Either way it's an all-important measure of success that doesn't require beating anyone else.

Q

Qualifying times. They're rare in road races anywhere short of the Olympics, World Championships, and Olympic Trials. The main U.S. race with time standard for entry is the Boston Marathon.

Quality miles. This term is synonymous with "fast," and the opposite of "junk miles."

Quarters. American shorthand for "quarter-mile intervals." Usually called "quarters" even when run as one lap on a 400-meter track.

R

Rabbits. Pace-setters, assigned to break the wind and ease the efforts of the runners who follow closely. On the track the rabbit usually drops out. Pace-leaders in marathons go all the way.

Rosie. "Pulling a Rosie" means cheating by cutting a race course short. It's named for Rosie Ruiz, who "won" a Boston Marathon by taking a streetcar.

RRCA. Road Runners Club of America, a confederation of hundreds of local running clubs, does much of the grassroots organizing in the U.S.

Runner's high. The good feeling that can come during a run and hang on afterward. Thought to be related to endorphin production.

Running booms. There have been two in the U.S. The first began in the early 1970s, the second about two decades later. Both led to huge jumps in numbers of runners.

RW. *Runner's World*, the most prominent of the running magazines for nearly forty years. It has expanded from its U.S. base to publish separate editions in several other countries.

S

Sharpening. Training that brings runners to their racing peak. This term usually applies to speed, which is sharpened after a base of endurance is laid down.

Sheehan. George Sheehan, M.D., was one of running's most-read writers and best-loved speakers. He died in 1993, but his words live on.

Shinsplints. Several different injuries can fit this inexact description. It brings pain to the front of the leg, most often in new runners.

Shorter. Frank Shorter is the only U.S. man to win an Olympic Marathon outright (without earlier finishers being disqualified). He gets credit for touching off the first running boom.

Specificity. It means that the training must resemble closely the racing. Runners get better at racing fast by training fast, racing long by training long, racing hills by training hills.

Spikes. Shoes for track training and racing, featuring surface-grabbing soles.

Splits. Intermediate times taken during a run—at mile or kilometer points, for instance.

Sports medicine. While conventional medicine stresses the treatment of disease and the preservaton of health, sports medicine operates on a higher plane. It emphasizes gaining and maintaining fitness for maximum performance.

Stitch. A sharp pain in the side, occurring while running. It's usually related to faulty breathing, diet, or running form.

Streaking. No, not running naked. In this case it means going as long as possible without missing a day's run.

Strength. Runners develop strength imbalances—strong in the legs, weak above the waist. Weight training and similar exercises mainly aim to balance the fitness. Great strength is most directly helpful to sprinters who rely on explosive muscular power.

Stress fracture. A hairline break in a bone—most commonly a small bone in the foot or in the shin. This generally occurs from the stress of running rather than from an accident.

Stress test. Evaluation of the heart's capacity for work, made while exercising at a vigorous level. This test is recommended for beginning runners of early middle age and beyond, and those with existing cardiovascular conditions.

Surge. A sudden, brief increase in pace. Surges can be used as a training technique or, in races, as a tactical tool.

Survival shuffle. The running form and pace that a runner slips into after hitting the wall.

Sweats. Can mean any suit of long pants and long-sleeved shirt worn in cold weather, but now more commonly referring to unstylish outerwear of loose-fitting cotton.

T

Talk test. This tells runners if their pace is right for building endurance. If they can talk (or whistle or sing) normally, they aren't going too fast.

Tangents. The shortest possible route to run on a road is a straight line—the tangent. Taking it saves distance and time.

Taper. Cutting back on the amount and intensity of running to gather energy and enthusiasm for a big effort. Racers taper from a day to a week or more before a major race.

Tartan. One of the earliest artificial-track surfaces. Today such tracks are often called "Tartan" even when another company produces them.

Tempo run. Running at race pace in training, but only for a portion of racing distance. Say, a fast 3K to 5K run before a 10K race.

Tendinitis. Inflamed and sore tendons. In runners the Achilles and knee are the most common sites for this injury.

Ten-K. The 10-kilometer road race; when run on the track it's called "10,000 meters." In miles it's 6.2.

Time trial. A race-like effort but taken as a test in training, without the usual trappings of racing.

Triathlon. The swim-bike-run combination appeals to some runners as a competitive opportunity. Triathlon's other two phases also provide two of the best cross-training options.

U

Ultras. Races longer than the standard marathon. The first standard distance beyond is 50 kilometers (31.1 miles).

USATF. The United States Track and Field Federation, which governs much of running in this country.

V

Vo$_2$-max. A measure of the body's ability to take in and process oxygen—also known as "maximal oxygen uptake." The reading is expressed in milliliters of oxygen per kilogram of weight per minute.

W

Walk breaks. An application of interval training, which splits a big piece of work into smaller and more manageable pieces. Walk breaks are increasingly popular among marathoners, both in training and in the event itself.

Wall. The point in a long run or race when the pace slows dramatically or ends for that day. Causes are inadequate training, improper pacing, depleted nutrients, or dehydration.

Warmup. Pre-run or early run activities that warm the muscles and establish running rhythm. Walking and slow running serve this purpose the best, stretching exercises the least.

Y

Yoga. Gentle, slow stretching exercises such as those used in yoga help correct the muscle tightness common to runners.

Z

Zatopek. Czech Emil Zatopek did what no other Olympian ever has: he won the 5000, 10,000, and marathon at the Games. His triple came in the same Olympics, in 1952.

Chapter Notes

Here are footnotes and after-thoughts, added advice and extra tables.
The chance to give practical tips and to tell stories doesn't end until
the final page.

1. TEACHING

I now teach three classes at the University of Oregon, titled: Jog/Run
(also called "Running 101"), 5K Training, and 10K Training. Each lasts
a term of about ten weeks.

One class picks up where the former leaves off. Many runners take
the full series, then graduate to training for half-marathons and
marathons on their own.

If you teach or would like to teach an organized program of this
type, I can supply class outlines and training schedules that might
assist you. E-mail me through my website: www.joehenderson.com

2. LEARNING

Note that my Running 101 class begins with a one-mile test. Though
I mention Kenneth Cooper, M.D., as inspiring this test, he recommends a slightly longer run of one-and-a-half miles or twelve minutes
for distance.

While one mile might not be quite as accurate an aerobic test
physiologically, I think it is far superior psychologically. Every
American runner (and many in the metric world) knows what a
mile time means, and will come to use the mile as a standard unit of
pacing for all distances.

Fitness values that I put on the mile follow. These apply to students
in their late teens and early twenties. Add thirty seconds for ages
30–39, 1:00 for 40–49, 1:30 for 50–59, 2:00 for 50–59, 2:30 for 60-plus:

Group	High fitness	Average fitness	Low fitness
women	sub-7:00	7:00 to 8:29	8:30-plus
men	sub-6:00	6:00 to 7:29	7:30-plus

This mile is run on a track or other accurately measured, flat
course. The goal, as in all running, is individual improvement from
one of these mile tests to the next. My students begin and end their
term this way.

3. STARTING

The introductory schedule in this book varies little from the one in my 1976 book, *The Long Run Solution* (which is long out of print). The principles underlying that program still apply today.

One objection that new runners sometimes voice: "Why don't you tell me how far I should run? Minutes don't means as much to me as miles (or kilometers)."

I still favor running by time. But if you insist on knowing distances, here are the conversion factors.

Most new runners, or run-walkers, can go two to three miles (3K to 5K) in the prescribed thirty-minute time period. On a standard track, most can run a quarter-mile or 400-meter lap in two to three minutes.

A one-minute run, then, would cover about one-third of a lap. A five-minute run would extend about two laps.

4. PROGRESSING

Progress has come most visibly in the creation and expansion of organizations that serve runners. Several of the most significant, along with their website addresses, are:

▶ United States Track and Field Federation (www.usatf.org). The national governing body for track, road, and cross-country racing promotes competition for athletes from very young to quite old, as well as fielding elite teams for the Olympic Games and World Championships.

▶ Road Runners Club of America (www.rrca.org). This "club of clubs" comprises hundreds of local groups with hundreds of thousands of members. These clubs do much of the grassroots organizing and promoting of U.S. running.

▶ American Running Association (www.americanrunning.org)—the former National Jogging Association has as its most important services the publication of an advice-oriented newsletter and a referral list of running-savvy medical professionals.

▶ Team in Training (www.teamintraining.org). TNT was one of the earliest and remains the largest group training runners to enter races as a fund-raising effort. The charity here is the Leukemia and Lymphoma Society, which benefits by millions of dollars a year.

▶ Race for the Cure (www.raceforthecure.com). Races contribute portions of their proceeds to many good causes. None gives more than the "Cure" series, which aids the Susan B. Komen Foundation for breast-cancer research.

5. SCHEDULING

Watches for runners abound. They range from simple to complex, from cheap to pricey. I lean toward simplicity and economy.

My watches, plus those loaned to students and given to some as prizes, come from a certain discount store with a star symbol in the middle of its name. These watches do a perfectly adequate job of runtiming for as little as $5.

6. MOVING

One lesson I've learned from teaching running classes is that you can't trust your first impression of a new runner. One who doesn't look like you think a runner "should" could go the fastest.

A woman student showed me running form that was … let's just say it was far from fluid. Runners in my class who didn't know her by name identified her by that form, calling her "The Prancer."

I never tried to change this young woman's form. If the quirks didn't trouble her, they shouldn't bother me. She already could outrun all the women in class—and most of the men—and she wound up qualifying for the Boston Marathon shortly after that term ended. You might say, "Think how much better she would have run with better form." I say in reply, that form she'd practiced since age two isn't going to change much now.

7. EXERCISING

I'm of a mixed mind about stretching exercises. I caution against overstretching (either being too aggressive with the stretches and risking injury, or taking time away from the run to stretch). Yet I stretch regularly, if briefly.

Without getting into descriptions of my individual exercises, I'll just outline the general routine. I stretch after the run, keeping the time short and the exercises simple.

The routine lasts three to five minutes and contains no more than five exercises. None requires sitting or lying down on the cold, wet, dirty ground, or using any props (such as leaning on a wall). The exercises stretch me from the top down, neck to ankles in that order.

8. WEATHERING

The best training tool in our house is an indoor-outdoor thermometer. It tells me before leaving the house each morning how to dress for the conditions outside.

Temperature is only a starting point, of course. Precipitation, humidity, and wind also figure in the how-it-will-feel equation. I could check all that in a weather report on the computer, but can learn almost as much by sticking my head out the door.

Since I drive to many of the runs, my car resembles a locker room. It holds all the extra clothes needed for abrupt weather changes.

For my family's peace of mind, if not my own, I've taken to wearing an ID bracelet (from www.roadID.com) on all runs—listing name, address, and phone numbers. My favorite hat, jacket, and shoes all come with reflective strips for safer running in hours of darkness.

9. DRESSING

The shoe companies made possible the first running boom, by making the runs more comfortable for a wider variety of people. Today's leading manufacturers (with their web addresses) are: Adidas (www.adidas.com), Asics (www.asicstiger.com), Brooks (www.brooks sports.com), Mizuno (www.mizunousa.com), New Balance (www.newbalance.com), Nike (www.nike.com), Puma (www.puma.com), and Reebok (www.reebok.com).

Having good shoes available is only the beginning. You must then find the model, from a confusing array, that is right for your foot type, mileage, speed, and surface. Buy a shoe that will fit correctly and feel good WHILE RUNNING (not just while standing in the store), and know when it's time to retire a worn-out pair.

If you've found a model you love, you're unlikely to find the same one next time. Most of the companies replace the good ones from their product lines too soon.

10. FUELING

Diet stands alongside religion and politics as a battleground issue. Contradictory viewpoints have their true believers.

I generally sit out the "holy war" over general nutrition. Instead I point readers to books that can both cover this subject at length and appeal to their personal dietary leanings. You have plenty of choices here.

My advice is limited to aspects of nutrition that have the most direct and measureable effects on running performance: the weight we carry, what and how much we drink, the timing and size of meals relative to training and racing, identifying food allergies and intolerances, and which products might boost or sustain energy while running.

On that first matter, weight, there are better ways of judging what's right for you than stepping on the scales. One is to have your body-fat checked, which requires expert help. Or you can check your own body-mass index (BMI). This reading combines your height and weight. Several calculators reside on the web. Type "Body Mass Index" into your browser.

A related matter, rapid weight loss, isn't a plus. If you drop two pounds (1kg) or more from one day to the next, this usually signals dehydration rather than fat loss.

11. HEALING

An injury, minor to serious, visits almost every runner eventually. But we vary in how we hurt ourselves.

New runners get hurt differently than oldtimers. The most "popular" injuries among my student novices are shin and iliotibial band (outside of the knee) pain. Longtime runners get more wear-and-tear injuries, such as "runner's knee" (pain under the kneecap).

Short-fast runs injure in different ways than long-slow runs. Speed injuries tend to strike the leg muscles and Achilles tendons of the feet. Distance injuries are more likely to attack the knees or hips, or to appear as stress fractures of foot or leg bones.

Injuries also vary by foot type. A so-called "rigid" foot with a high arch (which mine is) is predisposed to Achilles tendon and calf-muscle problems (my longtime bugaboos). A "floppy" foot with a low arch carries a weakness for plantar fasciitis (under the foot) and knee pain.

Choosing the right shoes for your needs minimizes many of these ailments. So does adjusting the speed-distance-recovery balance in your running program.

12. WINNING

New runners need measurable victories the most. That's why I find many ways to reward my students other than by who crosses the finish line first. Three ways to win prizes are:

▶ Improvement. The runner with the biggest leap forward from one test run to the next is a winner.

▶ Slow/fast run. It's a run-by-time on an out-and-back course. Students go out for a specified time (six to fifteen minutes, depending on the class), then return the same way. Lead runners at the turn suddenly become last, and the last become leaders. Everyone has an equal chance to finish first, with that runner winning the day's prize.

▶ Handicap run. This aims again to equalize the finish by letting the slowest runners start first and the fastest go last to play catch-up.

13. RACING

Race distances are mostly metric. Here are conversions for the most popular events:

Racing distance	Miles/meters
1000 meters (1K)	0.62 mile
1500 meters (1.5K)	0.93 mile
1 mile	1609 meters (1.61K)
3000 meters (3K)	1.86 miles
2 miles	3219 meters (3.22K)
5 kilometers	3.11 miles
8 kilometers	4.97 miles
5 miles	8.05 kilometers
10 kilometers	6.21 miles
12 kilometers	7.46 miles
15 kilometers	9.32 miles
10 miles	16.09 kilometers
20 kilometers	12.43 miles
Half-marathon (21.1K)	13.11 miles
15 miles	24.14 kilometers
25 kilometers	15.54 miles
30 kilometers	18.64 miles
20 miles	32.19 kilometers
Marathon (42.2K)	26.22 miles
50 kilometers	31.11 miles

14. JOINING

The 5K is the typical entry point into racing. The most beginner-friendly events are the big ones. No 5K's are bigger in the U.S. than the Races for the Cure (www.raceforthecure.com), which support the fight against breast cancer. Some but not all of these races are limited to women.

Many runners become racers on the job. That is, they enter a Chase Corporate Challenge event (www.jpmorganchasecc.com) with their company team. These races are most often three-and-a-half miles, or 5.9K.

15. TRAINING

My advice to students matches my own practice: on most runs seek a relaxed pace that is one to two minutes per mile (about 40 to 80 seconds per kilometer) slower than you could race that same distance. Here are a few comparisons, racing versus training:

Race pace per mile (per kilometer)	Relaxed training pace per mile (per kilometer)
5:00 (3:06)	6:00 to 7:00 (3:44 to 4:20)
6:00 (3:44)	7:00 to 8:00 (4:20 to 4:58)
7:00 (4:20)	8:00 to 9:00 (4:58 to 5:35)
8:00 (4:58)	9:00 to 10:00 (5:35 to 6:12)
9:00 (5:35)	10:00 to 11:00 (6:12 to 6:50)
10:00 (6:12)	11:00 to 12:00 (6:50 to 7:26)

16. PACING

My one experiment with a heart-rate monitor ended early when my guesses at the pulse rate closely matched the digital readout on my wrist. If you aren't yet so tuned in to the physical effects of your efforts, a monitor can serve you well. Its greatest value, I think, is giving you permission to make your easy days easier. Runners tend to overexert on those days, and the monitor sets a numerical limit on effort.

17. PREVIEWING

You can predict racing performance at one distance from recent results at longer or shorter distances. As the distance doubles (from 5K to 10K, for instance), multiply the time by 2.1. The same standard works in reverse, dividing by 2.1 as the distance drops by half. Here are multiplication/division factors for several combinations of racing distances:

Races compared	Multiply or divide by
1500 to 3000 meters	2.1
1 to 2 miles	2.1
3000 to 5000 meters	1.7
5K to 10K	2.1
8K (5 miles) to 10K	1.3
10K to half-marathon	2.2
10K to marathon	4.7
Half- to marathon	2.1
Marathon to 50K	1.3

I recommend taking one easy day of running (including rest days) for each mile to kilometer of the race. This table expresses that figure in weeks per racing distance, with a one-week recovery minimum:

Race distance	Recovery time
8K and below	1 week
10K to 12K	1 to 2 weeks
15K to half-marathon	2 to 3 weeks
25K to 20 miles	3 to 5 weeks
Marathon	4 to 6 weeks
50K	5 to 7 weeks

18. MILING

This chapter and the next several serve as guides to predicting times and pacing races, starting with the mile and its metric companion, the 1500 meter. Predictions are based on a recent 800-meter result times 2.1. Pacing is based on even splits plus or minus five seconds per mile.

Predicting		**Pacing**	
If you plan to run the mile (or 1500) in	**You need to race at least this time for 800 meters**	**If your mile (or 1500) time goal is**	**You need to run the first half-mile (or 800) in this time range**
5:00 (4:39)	2:23	5:00 (4:39)	2:28 to 2:33
6:00 (5:35)	2:51	6:00 (5:35)	2:58 to 3:03
7:00 (6:31)	3:20	7:00 (6:31)	3:28 to 3:33
8:00 (7:27)	3:48	8:00 (7:27)	3:58 to 4:03
9:00 (8:23)	4:17	9:00 (8:23)	4:28 to 4:33
10:00 (9:18)	4:46	10:00 (9:18)	4:58 to 5:03

19. 5K-ING

Predictions for the 5K are based on a recent 3K result times 1.7. Pacing is based on even splits plus or minus five seconds per mile.

Predicting		Pacing	
If you plan to run the 5K in	You need to race at least this time for 3K (or 2 miles)	If your 5K time goal is	You need to run the first 1.5 miles (or 2.5K) in
14:00	8:14 (8:51)	14:00	6:39 to 6:54 (6:52 to 7:07)
16:00	9:25 (10:07)	16:00	7:37 to 7:52 (7:52 to 8:07)
18:00	10:35 (11:22)	18:00	8:35 to 8:50 (8:52 to 9:07)
20:00	11:46 (12:39)	20:00	9:33 to 9:48 (9:52 to 10:07)
22:00	12:57 (13:55)	22:00	10:31 to 10:46 (10:52 to 11:07)
24:00	14:07 (15:11)	24:00	11:30 to 11:45 (11:52 to 12:07)
26:00	15:18 (16:27)	26:00	12:29 to 12:44 (12:52 to 13:07)
28:00	16:28 (17:42)	28:00	13:28 to 13:43 (13:52 to 14:07)
30:00	17:39 (18:58)	30:00	14:26 to 14:41 (14:52 to 15:07)

20. 10K-ING

Predictions for the 10K are based on a recent 5K result times 2.1. Pacing is based on even splits plus or minus five seconds per mile.

Predicting		Pacing	
If you plan to run the 10K in	You need to race at least this time for 5K	If your 10K time goal is	You need to run the first 3 miles (or 5K) in
30:00	14:29	30:00	14:15 to 14:45 (14:45 to 15:15)
35:00	16:40	35:00	16:41 to 17:11 (17:15 to 17:45)
40:00	19:03	40:00	19:05 to 19:35 (19:45 to 20:15)
45:00	21:25	45:00	21:31 to 22:01 (22:15 to 22:45)
50:00	23:48	50:00	24:00 to 24:30 (24:45 to 25:15)
55:00	26:12	55:00	26:22 to 26:52 (27:15 to 27:45)
60:00	28:34	60:00	28:50 to 29:20 (29:45 to 30:15)
65:00	30:57	65:00	31:12 to 31:42 (32:15 to 32:45)

21. HALF-MARATHONING

Predictions for the half-marathon are based on a recent 10K result times 2.2. Pacing is based on even splits plus or minus five seconds per mile.

Predicting		Pacing	
If you plan to run the half-marathon in	**You need to race at least this time for 10K**	**If your half-marathon time goal is**	**You need to run the first 6 miles (or halfway) in**
1:10	31:49	1:10	31:37 to 32:35 (34:30 to 35:30)
1:20	36:22	1:20	36:07 to 37:06 (39:30 to 40:30)
1:30	40:54	1:30	40:48 to 41:46 (44:30 to 45:30)
1:40	45:27	1:40	45:19 to 46:17 (49:30 to 50:30)
1:50	50:00	1:50	50:00 to 50:58 (54:30 to 55:30)
2:00	54:33	2:00	54:31 to 55:29 (59:30 to 60:30)
2:10	59:06	2:10	59:12 to 60:10 (64:30 to 65:30)
2:20	63:38	2:20	63:42 to 64:40 (69:30 to 70:30)
2:30	68:11	2:30	68:13 to 69:12 (74:30 to 75:30)

22. MARATHONING

Predictions for the marathon are based on a recent half-marathon result times 2.1. Pacing is based on even splits plus or minus five seconds per mile.

Predicting		Pacing	
If you plan to run the marathon in	**You need to race at least this time for half-marathon**	**If your marathon time goal is**	**You need to run the first half in**
2:30	1:11:25	2:30	1:14:00 to 1:16:00
2:45	1:18:34	2:45	1:21:30 to 1:23:30
3:00	1:25:43	3:00	1:29:00 to 1:31:00
3:15	1:32:51	3:15	1:36:30 to 1:38:30
3:30	1:40:00	3:30	1:44:00 to 1:46:00
3:45	1:47:09	3:45	1:51:30 to 1:53:30
4:00	1:54:17	4:00	1:59:00 to 2:01:00
4:15	2:01:25	4:15	2:06:30 to 2:08:30
4:30	2:08:34	4:30	2:14:00 to 2:16:00
4:45	2:15:43	4:45	2:21:30 to 2:23:30
5:00	2:22:51	5:00	2:29:00 to 2:31:00
5:15	2:30:00	5:15	2:36:30 to 2:38:30
5:30	2:37:09	5:30	2:44:00 to 2:46:00

23. ULTRARUNNING

Predictions for the 50K are based on a recent marathon result times 1.3. Pacing is based on even splits plus or minus five seconds per mile.

Predicting		Pacing	
If you plan to run the 50K in	You need to race at least this time for marathon	If your 50K time goal is	You need to run the first 25K in
3:00	2:18	3:00	1:28 to 1:32
3:30	2:42	3:30	1:43 to 1:47
4:00	3:04	4:00	1:58 to 2:02
4:30	3:28	4:30	2:13 to 2:17
5:00	3:51	5:00	2:28 to 2:32
5:30	4:14	5:30	2:43 to 2:47
6:00	4:37	6:00	2:58 to 3:02
6:30	5:00	6:30	3:13 to 3:17
7:00	5:23	7:00	3:28 to 3:32
7:30	5:46	7:30	3:43 to 3:47

24. FUN-RACING

Races are whatever you want to make of them: competitions against other runners, time trials against your personal records, harder-than-training efforts, normal training runs but with company, or social events. All races can be made fun, but some are more enjoyable than others.

Most popular with my students are the relays. Here two runners team up and alternately run short intervals for two to four miles (depending on the class).

Many of these students enjoy the relays so much that they later enter a local marathon relay (five runners per team). Some even graduate to one of the largest relays in the world, the 195-mile Hood to Coast (with twelve-member teams).

I know the attraction. Two of my most fun events were a twenty-four-hour relay on the track with nine teammates, and a seventy-two-mile relay around Lake Tahoe with six fellow runners.

25. EASING

"Easing" doesn't have to mean running less. My biggest easing came in 1966, when my pace slowed by multiple minutes per mile. At the same time, however, the distances more than doubled.

This happened again later. I eased out of a routine that had grown too strict—runs of exactly thirty minutes every weekend. The result was more running per day with less rigidity.

26. SIMPLIFYING

A recent simplification of mine was to drop walk breaks as a regular practice. I love these breaks and would reinsert them immediately if training for a marathon.

The walks became counterproductive on everyday runs. They sometimes masked pains I would have heeded otherwise, thereby slowing the healing. While running steadily, I pay notice to the pains more and react to them by stopping early and taking a single walk break—back to the starting point.

27. WRITING

The flip-side of writing is reading, and runners will never lack for material. Publications abound, as do websites.

The national running magazines and their web addresses:
American Track & Field (www.american-trackandfield.com)
Marathon & Beyond (www.marathonandbeyond.com)
National Masters News (www.nationalmastersnews.com)
Running Times (www.runningtimes.com)
Runner's World (www.runnersworld.com)
Track & Field News (www.trackandfieldnews.com)
Trail Runner (www.trailrunnermag.com)
Ultrarunning (www.ultrarunning.com)

You can find more than you ever needed to know about running on the web. Search for it by name, and you'll likely find it.

Most of the books ever written about running are available somewhere. Start the hunt at Barnes & Noble (www.bn.com), which has a vast network of book sources.

28. TALKING

The woman runner mentioned in the "Meet and Greet" segment, the one who scowled at me with mistrust, must have read the original column. Later I got a small smile and nod from her.

29. DEFENDING

America's runners continue to spread out. More of them are taking longer to finish marathons than ever before, which is healthy for the nation as well as the mass sport. At the same time, the top U.S. runners are speeding up again after years of stagnation. Only two marathoners ran fast enough to qualify for the 2000 Olympics. In 2004, the country sent a full team of six to the Athens Games.

30. TRAVELING

I still love being at places where runners gather, but increasingly loathe getting there. Flying long distances long ago lost all glamour for me. Running does help ease the stress. A run soon after landing helps greatly to lighten and shorten the jet-lag.

31. WATCHING

Those who stand and watch also participate. If you've gone to a marathon to support the runners you knew, to wait for their faces to appear in the crowd, then you've been involved too.

Each year I watch former students of mine, from running classes at the University of Oregon, graduate into marathons. They took their early steps with me, then passed their final and most vital exam by continuing to run on their own. Marathoning was their idea and the training of their design, not mine.

At their marathon start I feel more nervous for them than I'd felt before all of my own marathons combined. At their finish I shed more tears for them than for all of my races.

We who stand and watch also serve. We cheer the runners who do what we once did, giving them support that we once received. No one knows them better than one who has passed this way before.

32. AGING

Updating the piece titled "Aging Agendas" to the time of this book's conclusion in mid-2004: my then-critically ill friend, Dr. Joe Goodman, recovered and died in 2004 at age 92. Paul Reese, at 87, continued to plot treks across states, now at a walk. Jim O'Neil, now 79, and Ruth Anderson, 74, extended their perfect records through the latest World Masters Championships, run in 2003. *Runner's World* founder Bob Anderson, 56, finished fourth in the most recent Fifty-Plus 8K race.

33. LASTING

My running streaking is long retired, never to be revived. But a writing streak lives on. I've put a new page into my diary every day since 1971. Once a streaker, always one.

34. COPING

A call from Barnes & Noble, giving the go-ahead on the project that would grow into this book, came in September 2003. I was visiting my ailing mother in Des Moines, Iowa, at the time. As the book neared its finish line, Virginia King Henderson died at age 86.

35. ENJOYING

"No Mile Wasted," which ends the final chapter, was my last column in *Runner's World.* It brought the writing there full-circle. My first feature article for the magazine, written in 1969, had introduced long slow distance running. The last piece defended LSD.

Index

About the Author

Joe Henderson began his magazine career in 1967 with *Track & Field News*. He was editor of *Runner's World* from 1970 to 1977, and continued as a columnist for the magazine until 2004. That year he began writing a column for *Marathon & Beyond*. He also edits the *Running Commentary* newsletter (www.joehenderson.com). Henderson has written more than two dozen books about running.

Born in 1943, Henderson grew up in Iowa, where he began running races at age fourteen and won several state high school titles. He competed in track and cross-country at Drake University in Des Moines, and later graduated to longer distances. He has raced more than 700 times, at distances of less than 100 meters to more than 100 kilometers.

He speaks to running groups regularly, and has taught classes in both writing and running at the University of Oregon. He is a three-time winner of the R.R.C.A. Journalism Excellence Award, a member of the R.R.C.A. Hall of Fame, and a recipient of the Emil Zatopek Award from the Fifty-Plus Fitness Association.

Henderson is married to writer Barbara Shaw, and lives in Eugene, Oregon.

Also by the Author

Books

Long, Slow Distance (1969)
Road Racers and Their Training (1970)
Thoughts on the Run (1970)
Run Gently, Run Long (1974)
The Long Run Solution (1976)
Jog, Run, Race (1977)
Run Farther, Run Faster (1979)
The Running Revolution (1980)
Running, A to Z (1983)
Running Your Best Race (1984)
Running for Fitness, for Sport and for Life (1984)
Joe Henderson's Running Handbook (1985)
Total Fitness (1988)
Think Fast (1991)
Masters Running and Racing (with Bill Rodgers and Priscilla
   Welch, 1991)
Fitness Running (with Richard Brown, 1994)
Did I Win? (1994)
Better Runs (1995)
Road Racers and Their Training: Second Edition (1995)
Marathon Training (1997)
Coaching Cross-Country Successfully (with Joe Newton, 1997)
Best Runs (1999)
Running 101 (2000)
The Running Encyclopedia (with Richard Benyo, 2001)
Fitness Running: Second Edition (with Richard Brown, 2003)
Marathon Training: Second Edition (2004)

Videos/DVD's

Running and Racing with Joe Henderson (2003)

Photo Credits

©Corbis: pages 6, 10, 18-19, 21, 22, 114-115, 117, 212-213, 216

Digital Vision: pages 25, 31, 37, 45, 53, 61, 69, 77, 85, 95, 105, 121, 129, 137, 143, 151, 159, 167, 173, 179, 185, 191, 197, 205, 219, 225, 231, 239, 247, 255, 261, 269, 277, 283, 289

©Index Stock Imagery: page 118

PhotoDisc: pages 14, 215, 298